PENGUIN BOOKS

The Penguin Span

Jill Norman enjoys exploring language, speaks several
languages and has travelled widely. Jill also created the
Penguin Cookery Library in the 1960s and 1970s, bringing
many first-class authors to the list. She has written several
award-winning books on food and cookery, and is a leading
authority on the use of herbs and spices. She is the literary
trustee of the Elizabeth David estate, and was Mrs David's
publisher for many years.

THE PENGUIN
SPANISH
PHRASEBOOK

Fourth Edition

Jill Norman
María Victoria Alvarez
Pepa Román de Olins
Amparo Lallana

PENGUIN BOOKS

PENGUIN BOOKS

Published by the Penguin Group
Penguin Books Ltd, 80 Strand, London WC2R ORL, England
Penguin Group (USA) Inc., 375 Hudson Street, New York, New York 10014, USA
Penguin Group (Canada), 90 Eglinton Avenue East, Suite 700, Toronto, Ontario, Canada M4P 2Y3
(a division of Pearson Penguin Canada Inc.)
Penguin Ireland, 25 St Stephen's Green, Dublin 2, Ireland (a division of Penguin Books Ltd)
Penguin Group (Australia), 707 Collins Street, Melbourne, Victoria 3008, Australia
(a division of Pearson Australia Group Pty Ltd)
Penguin Books India Pvt Ltd, 11 Community Centre, Panchsheel Park, New Delhi – 110 017, India
Penguin Group (NZ), 67 Apollo Drive, Rosedale, Auckland 0632, New Zealand
(a division of Pearson New Zealand Ltd)
Penguin Books (South Africa) (Pty) Ltd, Block D, Rosebank Office Park, 181 Jan Smuts Avenue,
Parktown North, Gauteng 2193, South Africa

Penguin Books Ltd, Registered Offices: 80 Strand, London WC2R ORL, England

www.penguin.com

First edition 1968
Second edition 1978
Third edition 1988
This revised and updated edition published 2013

014

Copyright © Jill Norman and María Victoria Alvarez, 1968, 1978
Third edition material © Jill Norman and Pepa Román de Olins, 1988
Revised and updated material © Jill Norman and Amparo Lallana, 2013

Set in 9/12pt TheSans and TheSerif
Typeset by Jouve (UK), Milton Keynes
Printed in England by Clays Ltd, Elcograf S.p.A.

ISBN: 978-0-141-03907-7

www.greenpenguin.co.uk

CONTENTS

INTRODUCTION

This series of phrasebooks includes words and phrases essential to travellers of all kinds: the business traveller; the holidaymaker, whether travelling alone, with a group or the family; and the owner of a house, an apartment or a time-share. For easy use the phrases are arranged in sections which deal with specific situations and needs.

The book is intended to help travellers who never had the opportunity to learn Spanish, as well as serving as an invaluable refresher course for those whose Spanish has gone rusty.

Pronunciation is given for each phrase and for all words in the extensive vocabulary. See pp xi-xiii for the pronunciation guide which should be read carefully before starting to use the book.

Some of the Spanish phrases are marked with an **asterisk*** – these give an indication of the kind of reply you might get to your questions, and of questions you may be asked in turn.

For those who would like to know a little more about the Spanish language, the main points of its grammar are covered at the end of the book (pp. 251–60).

PRONUNCIATION

The pronunciation guide is intended for people with no knowledge of Spanish. As far as possible the system is based on English pronunciation. This means that complete accuracy may sometimes be lost for the sake of simplicity, but the reader should be able to understand Spanish pronunciation, and be understood after reading this section carefully. Each phrase and each word in the vocabulary is given with a pronunciation guide.

Vowels

All Spanish vowel sounds are pure, they are not slurred as in English. Final **e** is always pronounced.

Pronounce:

a as **a** in father	casa – house (ka-sa)	symbol **a**
e as **e** in bed	negro – black (ne-gro)	symbol **e**
and as **ai** in air	poder – to be able (po-dair)	symbol **ai, ay**
i as **i** in machine	fin – end (feen)	symbol **ee**
o as **o** in porter	todo – all (to-do)	symbol **o**
u as **oo** in boot	mucho – much (moo-cho)	symbol **oo**

Compound vowels

In the groups ia, ie, io the **i** sound resembles **y** in yes	alguien – anyone (alg-yen)	symbol **y**, **ee**
In the groups ue, ui, uo the **u** sound resembles **w** as in wet	bueno – good (bwe-no)	symbol **w**, **oo**

Consonants

Many are similar to English consonants but note the following:

c before e or i is pronounced **th** as in thin	cerrar – to shut (ther-rar)	symbol **th**
c before a, o, u or a consonant is pronounced **k**	coche – car (ko-che)	symbol **k**
final **d** is not always pronounced	usted – you (oo-ste)	
g before e or i is pronounced like English **h** (hot) or Scottish **ch** (loch)	gente – people (hen-te)	symbol **h**
g before a, o, u or a consonant is pronounced **g** as in got	gafas – glasses (ga-fas)	symbol **g**
h is always silent		

j is like English **h** (hot) or Scottish **ch** (loch)	mujer – woman (moo-hair)	symbol **h**
ll is like **lli** in million	llamar – to call (llya-mar)	symbol **lly**
ñ is like **ni** in onion	mañana – morning (ma-nya-na)	symbol **ny**
q(u) is pronounced as **k**	queso – cheese (ke-so)	symbol **k**
r is trilled, **rr** trilled even more strongly		
v is pronounced as **b**	vaso – glass (ba-so)	symbol **b**
z is pronounced **th** as in thin	manzana – apple (man-tha-na)	symbol **th**

This is the pronunciation used in Spain. In Spanish-speaking America there are one or two differences, notably **c** + **e** or **i** and **z** are pronounced **s** not **th**.

Stress

Words ending in a vowel, **n** or **s** are stressed on the last syllable but one	**ca**sa, **ga**fas, **ven**den
Words ending in a consonant other than **n** or **s** are stressed on the last syllable	ha**blar**, espa**ñol**
Exceptions to these rules are indicated by a written accent.	ca**fé**, auto**bús**, esta**ción**

In the pronunciation guide, words with irregular stress have the stressed syllable printed in **bold** type.

The Spanish Alphabet

a	a	a
b	be	beh
c	ce	theh
d	de	deh
e	e	eh
f	efe	eh-feh
g	ge	heh
h	hache	ah-cheh
i	i	ee
j	jota	ho-ta
k	ka	ka
l	ele	eh-leh
m	eme	eh-meh
n	ene	eh-neh
ñ	eñe	eh-nyeh
o	o	o
p	pe	peh
q	cu	koo
r	ere	eh-reh
s	ese	eh-seh
t	te	teh
u	u	oo

v	uve	oo-beh
w	uve doble	oo-beh doh-bleh
x	equis	eh-kees
y	i griega	ee grie-ga
z	zeta	the-tah

ESSENTIALS

First Things

Key Phrases

Yes	**Sí**	See
No	**No**	No
OK	**Vale**	Ba-le
Please	**Por favor**	Por fa-bor
Thank you	**Gracias**	Grath-yass
You're welcome	**De nada**	De na-da
Excuse me	**Perdone**	Pair-do-ne
I am sorry	**Lo siento**	Lo see-en-to

Greetings

Key Phrases

Good morning/ Good day	**Buenos días**	Bwe-nos **dee**-as
Good afternoon	**Buenas tardes**	Bwe-nas tar-des
Good evening/ Good night	**Buenas noches**	Bwe-nas no-ches

Good-bye	**Adiós**	A-dee-**os**
Hello	**¡Hola!/¿Qué hay?/ ¿Qué tal?**	O-la/Kay eye/Kay tal
How are you?	**¿Cómo está (usted)?**	Ko-mo es-**ta** (oos-te)
Very well, thank you	**Muy bien, gracias**	Mwee bee-en grath-yass

See you soon	**Hasta luego**	As-ta lwe-go
Have a good journey	**¡Buen viaje!**	Bwen bee-a-he
Good luck/All the best	**¡Buena suerte!/ ¡Que le vaya bien!**	Bwe-na soo-er-te/ Ke le ba-ya bee-en

Polite Phrases

Key Phrases

Excuse me (to pass)	**Me permite, por favor**	May pair-mee-te por fa-bor
That's all right	**Está bien**	Es-**ta** bee-en
Is everything all right?	***¿Todo bien?**	To-do bee-en
Good/That's fine	**Bien/Está muy bien**	Bee-en/Es-**ta** mwee bee-en

Not at all/Don't mention it	**De nada**	De na-da
Don't worry	**No se preocupe**	No se pre-o-koo-pe
It doesn't matter	**No importa**	No eem-por-ta
I beg your pardon?	**¿Qué?/¿Cómo dice?**	Kay/Ko-mo dee-the

Am I disturbing you?	¿(Le) molesto?	(Le) mo-les-to
I'm sorry to have troubled you	Siento haberle molestado	See-en-to a-bair-le mo-les-ta-do
With pleasure	Con mucho gusto	Kon moo-cho goos-to

Language Problems

Key Phrases

Do you speak English?	¿Habla inglés?	Ab-la een-gles
Does anyone here speak English?	¿Habla inglés alguien aquí?	Ab-la een-gles alg-yen a-kee
I don't speak Spanish	No hablo español	No ab-lo es-pan-yol
Do you understand (me)?	¿(Me) entiende?	(May) en-tee-en-de
Please speak slowly	Hable despacio, por favor	Ab-le des-pa-thyo por fa-bor
Please write it down	Por favor escríbamelo	Por fa-bor es-kree-ba-me-lo

I'm English/American	Soy inglés/americano (inglesa/americana)	Soy een-gles/a-mer-ee-ka-no (een-gle-sa/a-mer-ee-ka-na)
I speak a little Spanish	Hablo un poco español	Ab-lo oon po-ko es-pan-yol
I understand	Entiendo	En-tee-en-do
I don't understand	No entiendo	No en-tee-en-do
Would you say that again, please?	Repita eso, por favor	Re-pee-ta eso por fa-bor

What is it called in Spanish?	**¿Cómo se llama en español?**	Ko-mo se llya-ma en es-pan-yol
How do you say that in Spanish?	**¿Cómo se dice en español?**	Ko-mo se dee-the en es-pan-yol
What does that mean?	**¿Qué significa eso?**	Kay seeg-nee-fee-ka e-so
Can you translate this for me?	**¿Puede traducirme esto?**	Pwe-de tra-doo-theer-me es-to
Please show me the word in the book	**Por favor enséñeme la palabra en el libro**	Por fa-bor en-se-nye-me la pa-la-bra en el lee-bro

Questions

Key Phrases

Where is/are . . . ?	**¿Dónde está/están . . . ?**	Don-de es-ta/es-tan
When?	**¿Cuándo?**	Kwan-do
Who?	**¿Quién?**	Kee-en
Why?	**¿Por qué?**	Por kay
What?	**¿Qué?**	Kay
How?	**¿Cómo?**	Ko-mo
How much/many?	**¿Cuánto/Cuántos?**	Kwan-to/Kwan-tos
How much is/are . . . ?	**¿Cuánto es/son . . . ?**	Kwan-to es/son

How long?	**¿Cómo es de largo?**	Ko-mo es de lar-go
How far?	**¿Qué distancia hay?**	Kay dees-tan-thya eye
What's that?	**¿Qué es eso?**	Kay es e-so
What do you want?	**¿Qué desea?**	Kay de-se-a

What must I do?	¿Qué debo hacer?	Kay de-bo a-thair
Have you ...?	¿Tiene ...?	Tee-e-ne
Is/Are there ...?	¿Hay ...?	Eye
Have you seen ...?	¿Ha visto ...?	A bees-to
Where is there a ...?	¿Dónde hay un/una ...?	Don-de eye oon/oon-a
Where can I find ...?	¿Dónde puedo encontrar ...?	Don-de pwe-do en-kon-trar
What is the matter?	¿Qué le pasa?	Kay le pa-sa
Is anything the matter (with you)?	¿(Le) ocurre algo?	(Le) o-koo-rre al-go
Can you help me?	¿Puede ayudarme?	Pwe-de a-yoo-dar-me
Can I help you?	*¿Puedo ayudarle?	Pwe-do a-yoo-dar-le
Can you tell me/give me/show me?	¿Puede decirme/darme/enseñarme?	Pwe-de de-theer-me/dar-me/en-se-nyar-me

Useful Statements

Key Phrases		
It is ...	Es ...	Es
It isn't ...	No es ...	No es
I would like ...	Me gustaría ...	May goos-ta-**ree**-a
I need ...	Necesito ...	Ne-the-see-to
There is/are ...	Hay ...	Eye
It's urgent	Es urgente	Es oor-hen-te

I have …	**Tengo …**	Ten-go
I don't have …	**No tengo …**	No ten-go
I want …	**Quiero …**	Kee-e-ro
I like it	**Me gusta**	May goos-ta
OK/That's fine	**Vale/Está bien**	Ba-le/Es-**ta** bee-en
I'm lost	**Estoy perdido**	Es-toy pair-dee-do
We're looking for …	**Estamos buscando …**	Es-ta-mos boos-kan-do
Here it is	**Aquí está**	A-**kee** es-ta
There they are	**Allí están**	A-**llyee** es-**tan**
It's important	**Es importante**	Es eem-por-tan-te
You are mistaken	**Está (usted) equivocado**	Es-**ta** (oos-te) e-kee-bo-ka-do
I'm not sure	**No estoy seguro**	No es-toy se-goo-ro
I know	**Ya sé**	Ya se
I don't know	**No sé**	No se
I didn't know (that)	**No (lo) sabía**	No (lo) sa-**bee**-a
I think so	**Creo que sí**	Kre-o ke see
I'm hungry/thirsty	**Tengo hambre/sed**	Ten-go am-bre/sed
I'm tired	**Estoy cansado**	Es-toy kan-sa-do
I'm in a hurry	**Tengo prisa**	Ten-go pree-sa
I'm ready	**Estoy listo**	Es-toy lees-to
Leave me alone	**Por favor déjeme**	Por fa-bor **de**-he-me
Just a moment	**Un momento**	Oon mo-men-to
This way, please	**Por aquí sígame**	Por a-**kee** **see**-ga-me

Take a seat	**Siéntese**	See-**en**-te-se
Come in!	**¡Adelante!**	A-de-lan-te
It's cheap/expensive	**Es barato/caro**	Es ba-ra-to/ka-ro
It's too much	**Es demasiado**	Es de-ma-see-a-do
That's all	**Es todo**	Es to-do
You're right	**Tiene razón**	Tee-e-ne ra-**thon**
You're wrong	**No tiene razón**	No tee-e-ne ra-**thon**
Thank you for your help	**Muchas gracias por su ayuda**	Moo-chas grath-yass por soo a-yoo-da
It's beautiful	**Es bonito/precioso**	Es bo-nee-to/ pre-thee-o-so

SIGNS AND PUBLIC NOTICES[1]

Abierto de … a …	Open from … to …
Agotado	Sold out
Agua potable	Drinking water
Ascensor	Lift/elevator
Aseos	Toilets
Banco	Bank
Caballeros	Gentlemen
Caja	Cash desk
(CAP) Centro de Atención Primaria	Surgery
Cerrado	Closed
Circulen por la derecha	Keep right
Comisaría	Police station
Correos	Post office
Empujar	Push
Entrada	Entrance
Entrada gratuita/libre	Free admission
Guía	Guide

1. See also SIGNS TO LOOK FOR AT AIRPORTS AND STATIONS (p. 16) and ROAD SIGNS (p. 49).

(Hotel) Completo	No vacancies
Información	Information
Intérprete	Interpreter
Lavabos	Lavatory
Libre	Vacant/free/unoccupied
Liquidación	Sale
Llamar	Knock/ring
Multa	Fine (penalty)
No hay entradas/localidades	Sold out/house full (at the cinema, etc.)
(No) Hay habitaciones	(No) Vacancies/rooms to let
No pasar	No entry
No pisar el césped/la hierba	Keep off the grass
No tocar	Do not touch
Ocupado	Engaged/occupied
Particular/privado	Private
Peatones	Pedestrians
Peligro	Danger
Precaución	Caution
Prohibido ... bajo multa de ... € (euros)	Do not ... /It is forbidden to ... Penalty ... (€) euros
Prohibido ... /Se prohibe ...	Do not ... /It is forbidden to ...
Prohibido el paso	No entry
Rebajas/saldo	Sale

Reservado	Reserved
Reservado el derecho de admisión	Reserved right of admission
Salida	Exit
Salida de emergencia	Emergency exit
Se alquila	To let/for hire
Se alquilan habitaciones/apartamentos	Rooms/flats to let
Se prohibe fumar	No smoking
Se ruega no ...	Kindly refrain from ...
Se vende	For sale
Señoras	Ladies
Servicios	Lavatory/toilets
Solo socios	Members only
Tirar	Pull

Acronyms

Avda.	**avenida**	avenue
C/	**calle**	street
c/c	**cuenta corriente**	current account
cía	**compañía**	company
dcha.	**derecha**	right
EE UU	**Estados Unidos**	USA
ej.	**por ejemplo**	for example

h	**hora**	hour
izq., izda.	**izquierda**	left
N°, núm	**número**	number
Ntra. Sra.	**Nuestra Señora**	Our Lady
P.V.P.	**precio venta al público**	price
pág.	**página**	page
R.E.N.F.E.	**Red nacional de ferrocarriles españoles**	Spanish railways
S., Sta.	**san, santa**	saint
S.A.	**sociedad anónima**	ltd, inc. plc
Sr.	**señor**	Mr
Sra.	**señora**	Mrs
Srta.	**señorita**	Miss
Ud., Vd. /Uds., Vds.	**usted/ustedes**	you (formal)

GETTING AROUND

Arrival

Key Phrases

I've lost my passport, I must have dropped it on the plane	**He perdido el pasaporte. Se me habrá caído en el avión**	Ai pair-dee-do el pa-sa-por-te. Se me a-**bra** ka-ee-do en el a-**byon**
My luggage has not arrived	**Mi equipaje no ha llegado**	Mee e-kee-pa-he no a llye-ga-do
My luggage is damaged	**Mi equipaje está dañado**	Mee e-kee-pa-he es-**ta** da-nya-do
Is there an ATM/ currency exchange?	**¿Hay un cajero/ cambio de moneda?**	Eye oon ka-he-ro/ kam-byo de mo-ne-da
Is there a train/ underground/ bus into the town?	**¿Hay tren/metro/ autobús a la ciudad?**	Eye tren/me-tro/ ow-toh-**boos** a la thee-oo-dad
How can I get to ...?	**¿Cómo puedo ir a ...?**	Ko-mo pwe-do eer a

Passports

Passport control	***Control de pasaportes**	Kon-**trol** de pa-sa-por-tes
Your passport, please	***El pasaporte, por favor**	El pa-sa-por-te por fa-bor

We are together	**Viajamos juntos**	Bya-ha-mos hoon-tos
I am travelling with a group/that group	**Viajo en un grupo/ ese grupo**	Bya-ho en oon group-o/ e-se group-o
I'm travelling alone	**Viajo solo/a**	Bya-ho so-lo/a
I'm travelling with my wife/a friend	**Viajo con mi esposa/ un amigo**	Bya-ho kon mee es-po-sa/oon a-mee-go
I'm here on business/ on holiday	**Vengo de negocios/ de vacaciones**	Ben-go de ne-go-thyos/ de ba-ka-thyo-nes
This is my address in Madrid	**Mi dirección en Madrid es ésta**	Mee dee-rek-**thyon** en Ma-drid es es-ta
I am staying at the . . . hotel	**Me alojo en el hotel . . .**	May a-lo-ho en el o-tel
How long are you staying here?	*¿**Cuánto tiempo va a estar usted aquí?**	Kwan-to tee-em-po ba a es-tar oos-te a-**kee**

Customs

Customs	*Aduana	A-dwan-a
Goods to declare	*Artículos que declarar	Ar-**tee**-koo-loos ke de-kla-rar
Nothing to declare	*Nada que declarar	Na-da ke de-kla-rar
Which is your luggage?	*¿Cuál es su equipaje?	Kwal es soo e-kee-pa-he
Do you have more luggage?	*¿Tiene más equipaje?	Tee-e-ne mas e-kee-pa-he
This is (all) my luggage	Esto es (todo) mi equipaje	Es-to es (to-do) mee e-kee-pa-he

Have you anything to declare?	*¿Algo que declarar?	Al-go ke de-kla-rar
I have only my personal things in it	Sólo llevo mis cosas personales	So-lo llye-bo mees ko-sas pair-son-al-es
Open your bag, please	*Abra la maleta, por favor	Ab-ra la ma-le-ta por fa-bor
Can I shut my case now?	¿Puedo cerrar la maleta ya?	Pwe-do the-rar la ma-le-ta ya
May I go through?	¿Puedo pasar ya?/¿Puedo irme?	Pwe-do pa-sar ya/ Pwe-do eer-me

Luggage

luggage	el equipaje	e-kee-pa-he
luggage lockers	la consigna automática	kon-seeg-na ow-to-ma-tee-ka
backpack	la mochila	mo-chee-la
suitcase	la maleta	ma-le-ta
Only one/two piece(s) of luggage per person	Solo un/dos bulto (s) por persona	So-lo oon/dos bool-to (s) por per-so-na
My luggage has not arrived	Mi equipaje no ha llegado	Mee e-kee-pa-he no a llye-ga-do
My luggage is damaged	Mi equipaje está dañado	Mee e-kee-pa-he es-ta da-nya-do
One suitcase is missing	Falta una maleta/un bulto	Falta oon-a ma-le-ta/ oon bool-to
I've lost a suitcase/ bag/rucksack	He perdido una maleta/un bulto/ una mochila	Ai per-dee-do oo-na ma-le-ta/oon bool-to/ oo-na mo-chee-la

Are there any luggage trollies?	¿Hay carritos para el equipaje?	Eye kar-ree-tos pa-ra el e-kee-pa-he
Where is the left luggage office?	¿Dónde está la consigna?	Don-de es-ta la kon-seeg-na
That's not mine	Eso no es mío	Eso no es mee-o

Moving on

Where is the information desk?	¿Dónde está (la oficina de) información?	Don-de es-ta (la o-fee-thee-na de) een-for-ma-thyon
Is there a train/ underground/bus into the town?	¿Hay tren/metro/ autobús a la ciudad?	Eye tren/me-tro/ow-toh-boos a la thee-oo-dad
How can I get to ...?	¿Cómo puedo ir a ...?	Ko-mo pwe-do eer a
Does this bus go to the town centre?	¿Este autobús va al centro?	Es-te ow-toh-boos va al then-tro
money	dinero	dee-ne-ro
£	libras	lee-bras
€	euros	ai-oo-ros
Where can I change money?	¿Dónde puedo cambiar dinero?	Don-de pw e-do kam-bee-ar dee-ne-ro
Is there an ATM/ currency exchange?	¿Hay un cajero/ cambio de moneda?	Eye oon ka-he-ro/kam-byo de mo-ne-da
How much do I owe?	¿Cuánto le debo?	Kwan-to le de-bo
How much is it?	¿Cuánto es/cuesta?	Kwan-to es/kwes-ta
Can I pay by card?	¿Puedo pagar con tarjeta?	Pwe-do pa-gar kon tar-he-ta

Signs at Airports and Stations

Arrivals	Llegadas
ATM	Cajero automático
Baggage reclaim	Recogida de equipaje
Booking office	Despacho de billetes/taquilla
Buses	Autobuses
Car rental	Alquiler de coches
Connections	Transbordos
Departures	Salidas
Exchange	Cambio
Gentlemen	Servicios/caballeros/señores
Hotel reservations	Reservas hotel
Information	Información
Ladies	Servicios/señoras
Left luggage	Consigna
Lost property	Oficina de objetos perdidos
Luggage lockers	Consigna automática
Main lines	Largo recorrido/larga distancia
Newsstand	Kiosco
No smoking	Se prohibe fumar
Refreshments	Cafetería/bar/restaurante

Reservations	Reservas
Suburban lines	(Trenes de) cercanías
Taxi rank	Parada de taxis
Tickets	Billetes
Toilets	Aseos
Tourist office	Oficina de turismo
Transit desk	Mostrador de tránsito
Underground	Metro
Waiting room	Sala de espera

By Air

Key Phrases

What is the baggage allowance?	¿Cuánto equipaje se puede llevar?	Kwan-to e-kee-pa-he se pwe-de llye-bar
I'd like to change my reservation to . . .	Quiero cambiar mi reserva para . . .	Kee-e-ro kam-bee-ar mee re-sair-ba pa-ra
Can I check in online?	¿Se puede facturar en internet?	Se pwe-de fak-too-rar en in-ter-net
I have only hand luggage	Solo llevo equipaje de mano	So-lo llye-bo e-kee-pa-he de ma-no
The flight has been cancelled	*El vuelo ha sido cancelado	El bwe-lo a see-do kan-the-la-do

Where's the airline office?	¿Dónde está la oficina de líneas aéreas?	Don-de es-**ta** la o-fee-thee-na de **lee**-ne-as **eye**-re-as
Where is the . . . counter?	¿Dónde está el mostrador de . . .?	Don-de es-**ta** el mos-tra-dor de
I'd like to book two seats on the plane to . . .	Quiero reservar dos billetes para el avión de . . .	Kee-e-ro re-sair-bar dos bee-llye-tes pa-ra al a-**byon** de
Is that the cheapest price?	¿Es ése el más barato?	Es e-sai el mas ba-ra-to
First class	Primera clase	Pree-me-ra kla-se
Business class	Clase business	Kla-se bees-nees
Economy	Clase turista	Kla-se too-ris-ta
How long is the flight?	¿Cuánto dura el vuelo?	Kwan-to doo-ra el bwe-lo
I'd like an aisle/ window seat	Quería asiento de pasillo/de ventanilla	Ke-**ree**-a as-ee-ain-to de pa-see-llyo/de ven-ta-nee-llya
Can I order a vegetarian/special meal?	¿Puedo encargar el menú vegetariano/ especial?	Pwe-do en-kar-gar el me-**noo** ve-he-ta-rya-no/ es-pe-thee-al
Is there a flight to . . .?	¿Hay algún vuelo a . . .?	Eye al-**goon** bwe-lo a
A direct flight	Un vuelo directo	Oon bwe-lo di-rek-to
A flight stopping over at . . .	Un vuelo con escala en . . .	Oon bwe-lo kon es-ka-la en
When does the plane leave?	¿A qué hora sale el avión?	A kay o-ra sa-le el a-**byon**

When does it arrive?	**¿A qué hora llega?**	A kay o-ra llye-ga
When's the next plane?	**¿A qué hora es el próximo avión?**	A kay o-ra es el **pro**-see-mo a-**byon**
Is there a bus/train to the airport/town/centre?	**¿Hay autobús/tren al aeropuerto/a la ciudad/al centro?**	Eye ow-toh-**boos**/tren al eye-ro-pwer-to/a la thee-oo-dad/al then-tro
I want to cancel my reservation to ...	**Quiero anular mi reserva para ...**	Kee-e-ro a-noo-lar mee re-sair-ba pa-ra
I have an open ticket	**Tengo un billete abierto**	Ten-go oon bee-llye-te a-bee-air-to
Can I change my ticket?	**¿Puedo cambiar mi billete?**	Pwe-do kam-bee-ar mee bee-llye-te
Will it cost more?	**¿Me costará más?**	May kos-ta-**ra** mas
Which airport/terminal does the flight leave from?	**¿De qué aeropuerto/terminal sale el avión?**	De ke eye-ro-pwer-to/tair-mi-nal sa-le el a-**byon**
Must I change terminal?	**¿Hay que cambiar de terminal?**	Eye ke kam-bee-ar de tair-mi-nal
Where are the check-in desks for (Iberia)?	**¿Dónde está (el mostrador de) facturación de (Iberia)?**	Don-de es-**ta** (el mos-tra-dor de) fak-too-ra-**thyon** de (ee-be-rya)
What is the flight number?	**¿Cuál es el número de vuelo?**	Kwal es el **noo**-me-ro de bwe-lo
When must I check in?	**¿A qué hora hay que facturar?**	A ke o-ra eye ke fak-too-rar
I've booked a wheelchair to take me to the plane	**He reservado una silla de ruedas que me lleve hasta el avión**	Eye re-sair-ba-do oo-na see-llya de rwe-das ke me llye-be as-ta el a-**byon**

Do I have to pay for excess baggage?	¿Tengo que pagar exceso de equipaje?	Ten-go ke pa-gar es-the-so de e-kee-pa-he
The plane leaves from gate ...	El avión sale por la puerta de embarque número ...	El a-**byon** sa-le por la pwer-ta de em-bar-ke **noo**-me-ro
I've lost my boarding card	He perdido la tarjeta de embarque	Ai pair-dee-do la tar-he-ta de em-bar-ke
Flight ... to ... has been delayed until ...	*El vuelo ... con destino ... ha retrasado su salida hasta las ...	El bwe-lo ... kon des-tee-no ... a re-tra-sa-do soo sa-lee-da as-ta las
The flight has closed	*El vuelo está cerrado	El bwe-lo es-**ta** ther-rra-do
air steward	*personal de cabina/azafata/o	per-so-nal de ka-bee-na/a-tha-fa-tah/toh
boarding gate	*puerta de embarque	pwer-ta de em-bar-ke

By Boat or Ferry

Key Phrases

Is there a boat from here to ...?	¿Hay barco de aquí a ...?	Eye bar-ko de a-**kee** a
When does the next boat leave?	¿Cuándo sale el próximo barco?	Kwan-do sa-le el **pro**-see-mo bar-ko
I'd like a one way/return ticket	Quiero un billete de ida/de ida y vuelta	Kee-e-ro oon bee-llye-te de ee-da/de ee-da ee bwel-ta

Where is the port?	¿Dónde está el puerto?	Don-de es-**ta** el pwer-to
Where does the ferry leave from?	¿De dónde sale el ferry?	De don-de sa-le el fer-ree
How long does the boat take?	¿Cuánto tiempo tarda?	Kwan-to tee-em-po tar-da
How often does the boat leave?	¿Cada cuánto tiempo sale el barco?	Ka-da kwan-to tee-em-po sa-le el bar-ko
Does the boat call at ...?	¿Toca (el barco) puerto/ Hace escala en ...?	To-ka (el bar-ko) pwer-to/A-the es-ka-la en
How much is it for children under 5/ over 65s?	¿Cuánto cuesta el billete para menores de 5/mayores de 65?	Kwan-to kwes-ta el bee-llye-te pa-ra me-no-res de think-o/ma-jo-res de se-sent-a ee think-o
How much is it for	¿Cuánto cuesta para	Kwan-to kwes-ta pa-ra
a bicycle?	una bicicleta?	oo-na bee-thee-klay-ta
a motor cycle?	una motocicleta?	oo-na mo-to-thee-klay-ta
a caravan?	una caravana?	oo-na ka-ra-van-a
Can I book	¿Puedo reservar	Pwe-do re-sair-bar
a single berth cabin?	un camarote individual?	oon ka-ma-ro-te een-dee-bee-doo-al
a first class cabin?	un camarote de primera?	oon ka-ma-ro-te de pree-mair-a
a second class cabin?	un camarote de segunda?	oon ka-ma-ro-te de se-goon-da
a luxury cabin?	un camarote de lujo?	oon ka-ma-ro-te de loo-ho

How many berths are there in this cabin?	¿Cuántas literas hay en esta cabina?	Kwan-tas lee-tair-as eye en es-ta ka-bee-na
How do we get on to the deck?	¿Cómo podemos subir a cubierta?	Ko-mo po-de-mos soo-beer a koo-bee-air-ta
When must we go on board?	¿A qué hora hay que estar a bordo?	A kay o-ra eye ke es-tar a bor-do
When do we dock?	¿A qué hora se desembarca?	A kay o-ra se de-sem-bar-ka
How long do we stay in port?	¿Cuánto tiempo estamos en el puerto?	Kwan-to tee-em-po es-ta-mos en el pwer-to
Where are the toilets?	¿Dónde están los aseos?	Don-de es-tan los a-se-os
I feel seasick	Me siento mal/ Estoy mareado	May see-en-to mal/ Es-toy ma-re-a-do
(car) ferry	ferry (de coches)	fer-ree (de ko-ches)
lifeboat	la lancha salvavidas	lan-cha sal-ba-bee-das
lifejacket	el chaleco salvavidas	cha-lai-ko sal-ba-bee-das

By Bus or Coach[1]

Key Phrases

Where can I buy a bus ticket?	**¿Dónde puedo comprar el billete de autobús?**	Don-de pwe-do kom-prar el bee-llye-te de ow-toh-**boos**
Do I pay the driver?	**¿Tengo que pagar al conductor?**	Ten-go kay pa-gar al kon-dook-tor
When's the next bus?	**¿Cuándo sale el próximo autobús?**	Kwan-do sa-le el **pro-**see-mo ow-toh-**boos**
Where can I get a bus to ...?	**¿Dónde puedo tomar el autobús para ...?**	Don-de pwe-do tom-ar el ow-toh-**boos** pa-ra
Where do I get off?	**¿Dónde tengo que bajarme?**	Don-de ten-go kay ba-har-me

booking reference	**(número) localizador**	(**noo-**me-ro) lo-kal-ee-tha-dor
bus stop	**parada de autobuses**	pa-ra-da de ow-toh-boos-es
request stop	**parada discrecional**	pa-ra-da dees-kre-thyo-nal

1. Alsa, Enatcar, Continental Auto are three coach companies operating nationwide. There will be other local coach companies in various provinces. There are very reliable coach services between most cities and towns. Virtually every village can be reached by coach.

Bus tickets can be purchased online for most major companies. Once the booking is made and the fee paid, customers choose to receive confirmaton via mobile phone. On boarding the bus, all they need to produce is their booking reference.

Is there a daily/weekly ticket?	¿Hay billetes para todo el día/para una semana?	Eye bee-llye-tes pa-ra to-do el **dee**-a/pa-ra oo-na sai-ma-nah
I bought the ticket online	Compré el billete por internet	Kom-**preh** el bee-llye-te por in-ter-**net**
Where's the bus/coach station?	¿Dónde está la estación de autobuses/coches de línea?	Don-de es-**ta** la es-ta-**thyon** de ow-toh-boos-es/ko-ches de **lee**-nea?
I'd like to reserve a seat at the front of the coach	Quería reservar un billete en las primeras filas	Ke-ree-a re-sair-bar oon bee-llye-te en las pree-me-ras phee-las
Which is my seat number?	¿Que plaza/(número de) asiento tengo?	Kay pla-tha/(**noo**-mer-o de) a-see-en-to ten-go
Which is my seat?	¿Cuál es mi asiento?	Kwal es mee a-see-en-to
When does the coach leave?	¿A qué hora sale el autocar?	A kay o-ra sa-le el ow-toh-kar
Which bay does the bus leave from?	¿De qué andén sale el autobús?	De kay an-**dain** sa-le el ow-toh-**boos**
When does the coach get to ...?	¿A qué hora llega el autocar a ...?	A kay o-ra llye-ga el ow-toh-kar a
Does it stop at all?	¿Hace alguna parada?	A-the al-goo-na pa-ra-da
What stops does it make?	¿En qué sitios para?	En kay see-tyos pa-ra

How long is the journey?	¿Cuánto se tarda?	Kwan-to se tar-da
How much is the fare/ a bus pass/bus travel card?	¿Cuánto cuesta (el billete)/un bonobús?	Kwan-to kwes-ta (el bee-llye-te)/ oon bo-no-**boos**
Does this bus go to	¿Va este autobús	Ba es-te ow-toh-**boos**
the beach?	a la playa?	a la pla-ya
the station?	a la estación?	a la es-ta-**thyon**
the town centre?	al centro?	al then-tro
How often do the buses run?	¿Cada cuánto tiempo hay autobús?	Ka-da kwan-to tee-em-po eye ow-to-**boos**
Does this bus go near ...?	¿Pasa este autobús cerca de ...?	Pa-sa es-te ow-toh-**boos** thair-ka de
Which bus goes to ...?	¿Qué autobús va a ...?	Kay ow-toh-**boos** va a
I want to go to ...	Quiero ir a ...	Kee-e-ro eer a
The bus to ... stops over there	*El autobús de ... para allí	El ow-toh-**boos** de ... pa-ra a-**llye**
You must take a number ...	*Tome el ...	To-me el
You get off at the next stop	*Bájese en la próxima parada	Bah-es-se en la **pro**-see-ma pa-ra-da
The buses run every ten minutes/every hour	*Hay autobuses cada diez minutos/cada hora	Eye ow-toh-boos-es ka-da dy-eth mee-noo-tos/ ka-da o-ra

By Taxi[1]

Key Phrases

Please get me a taxi	**Por favor, (llámeme) un taxi**	Por fa-bor (llya-me-me) oon ta-xi
Where can I find a taxi?	**¿Dónde puedo encontrar un taxi?**	Don-de pwe-do en-kon-trar oon ta-xi
Please wait for me here	**Espere aquí, por favor**	Es-pe-re a-**kee** por fa-bor
Stop here	**Pare aquí**	Pa-re a-**kee**

taxi rank	**parada de taxis**	pa-ra-da de ta-xis
meter	**taxímetro**	ta-xee-me-troh
fixed starting rate	**bajada de bandera**	ba-ha-dah de band-air-a
What is the fixed starting rate?	**¿Cuánto es la bajada de bandera?**	Kwan-to es la ba-ha-dah de band-air-a
I'd like to book a taxi for tomorrow at . . . (time)	**Quería reservar un taxi para mañana a las . . .**	Ke-**ree**-a re-sair-bar un ta-xi pa-ra ma-nya-na a las
Are you free?	**¿Está libre?**	Es-**ta** lee-bre
Please turn on the meter	**Ponga en marcha el taxímetro, por favor**	Pong-a en mar-cha el ta-xee-me-troh por fa-bor

1. A taxi ride begins with a fixed starting rate after which the meter starts running. Supplements are charged for luggage, picking up or dropping at stations, airports, etc. The tariff is usually displayed inside the taxi. If not, ask for it.

Please take me to the Madrid hotel	Al hotel Madrid, por favor	Al o-tel ma-drid por fa-bor
Please take me to the station	A la estación, por favor	A la es-ta-**thyon** por fa-bor
Please take me to this address/to the city centre	A esta dirección/al centro, por favor	A es-ta dee-rek-**thyon**/al then-tro/por fa-bor
Please hurry; I'm late	Dése prisa, por favor; llego tarde	**De**-se pree-sa por fa-bor; llye-go tar-de
Is it far?	¿Está lejos?	Es-**ta** le-hos
How far is it to...?	¿Cuánto hay a...?	Kwan-to eye a
Turn right/left at the next corner	En la próxima esquina tuerza a la derecha/izquierda	En la **pro**-see-ma es-kee-na twer-tha a la de-re-cha/ eeth-kee-air-da
Straight on	Todo recto	To-do rek-to
How much do you charge by the hour/ for the day?	¿Cuánto cobra por hora/todo el día?	Kwan-to ko-bra por o-ra/to-do el **dee**-a
How much will you charge to take me to...?	¿Cuánto costaría ir a...?	Kwan-to kos-ta-**ree**-a eer a
How much is it?	¿Cuánto es?	Kwan-to es
That's too much	Es demasiado	Es de-ma-see-a-do
I'd like a receipt, please	Hágame un recibo (del viaje), por favor	**Ah**-ga-me oon reth-ee-bo (del bee-a-he) por fa-bor

By Train[1]

Key Phrases

Where's the railway station?	¿Dónde está la estación de ferrocarril/de tren?	Don-de es-**ta** la es-ta-**thyon** de fer-ro-kar-ril/de tren
What is the cheapest fare?	¿Cuál es el billete más barato?	Kwal es el bee-llye-te mas ba-ra-to
Is there a day return?	¿Hay billete de ida y vuelta en el día?	Eye bee-llye-te de ee-da ee bwel-ta en el **dee**-a
Where do I change?	¿Dónde hay que hacer transbordo?	Don-de eye ke a-thair trans-bor-do
What station is this?	¿Qué estación es ésta?	Ke es-ta-**thyon** es es-ta

Where is the ticket office?	¿Dónde está la taquilla/la oficina de billetes?	Don-de es-**ta** la ta-kee-llya/la o-fee-thee-na de bee-llye-tes
Have you a timetable for trains to ...?	¿Tiene(n) un horario de trenes a ...?	Tee-e-ne(n) oon or-a-ryo/de tre-nes a
A ticket to ...[2]	Un billete para ...	Oon bee-llye-te pa-ra

1. For help in understanding these and similar questions see TIME AND DATES (p. 233), NUMBERS (p. 243) and DIRECTIONS (p. 52).
2. La Renfe, the Spanish railway system, has an office in the centre of most large towns. Tickets can be purchased from ticket offices at railway stations as well. Train tickets cost the same whether purchased in advance or on the day but booking in advance is recommended, especially for long distances or night travelling. Train tickets can nowadays be purchased online from www.renfe.es. A reference number (*localizador*) is provided to pick up tickets from the ticket office at the station prior to boarding the train.

A single/one way to …	Un billete de ida a …	Oon bee-llye-te de ee-da a
A return to …	Un billete de ida y vuelta a …	Oon bee-llye-te de ee-da ee bwel-ta a
How much is it first class to …?	¿Cuánto cuesta un billete de primera a …?	Kwan-to kwes-ta oon bee-llye-te de pree-mair-a a
How long is this ticket valid?	¿Cuánto tiempo dura este billete?	Kwan-to tee-em-po doo-ra es-te bee-llye-te
When are you coming back?	*¿Cuándo vuelve?	Kwan-do bwel-be
How much is it for a child under 5/over 65s?	¿Cuánto cuesta el billete para menores de 5/mayores de 65?	Kwan-to kwes-ta el bee-llye-te pa-ra me-no-res de think-o/ma-jo-res de se-sent-a ee think-o
How old is the child?	*¿Qué edad tiene el niño?	Kay e-dad tee-e-ne el nee-nyo
Do I need to reserve a seat?	¿Tengo que hacer una reserva?	Ten-go kay a-ther oo-na re-sair-ba
I want a sleeper/ a window seat	Quiero una litera/ un asiento de ventanilla	Kee-e-ro oon-a lee-tair-a/ oon a-see-en-to de ben-ta-nee-llya
When is the next train to …?	¿Cuándo sale el próximo tren para …?	Kwan-do sa-le el pro-see-mo tren pa-ra
What sort of train is it?[3]	¿Qué clase de tren es?	Kay kla-se de tren es

3. Most long distance trains (Talgo, Alvia, etc.) running in Spain consist of first and second class carriages. The AVE (high speed train) connects Madrid with some major cities; *trenes de cercanías* are commuter trains, usually stopping frequently and operating in greater urban areas. The *tren-hotel* for night travelling includes single and double car-sleepers.

| Is there an earlier/ later train? | ¿Hay un tren antes/ más tarde? | Eye oon tren an-tes/mas tar-de |
| Is there a restaurant/ café/bar on the train? | ¿Lleva restaurante/ cafetería/bar el tren? | Llye-ba res-tow-ran-te/ ka-fe-te-**ree**-a/bar el tren |

Changing

Is there a through train to ...?	¿Hay tren directo a ...?	Eye tren dee-rek-to a
Do I have to change?	¿Hay que hacer transbordo?	Eye ke a-thair trans-bor-do
Where do I change?	¿Dónde hay que hacer transbordo?	Don-de eye ke a-thair trans-bor-do
Change at ... and take the local train	*Cambiar en ... y coger el cercanías	Kam-bee-ar en ... ee ko-hair el therk-a-**nee**-as

Departure

When does the train leave?	¿A qué hora sale el tren?	A kay o-ra sa-le el tren
Which platform does the train to ... leave from?	¿De qué andén sale el tren para ...?	De kay an-**den** sa-le el tren pa-ra
Is this the train for ...?	¿Es éste el tren para ...?	Es es-te el tren pa-ra
There will be a delay of ...	*Habrá un retraso de ...	A-**bra** oon re-tra-so de ...

On the train

dining car	**coche-restaurante**	ko-che res-tow-ran-te
ticket inspector	**interventor**	een-ter-ben-tor
We have reserved seats	**Tenemos reservas**	Ten-e-mos re-sair-bas
Is this seat free?	**¿Está este asiento libre?**	Es-**ta** es-te a-see-en-to lee-bre
This seat is taken	**Este asiento está ocupado**	Es-te a-see-en-to es-**ta** o-koo-pa-do
When is the buffet car open?	**¿Cuándo abre el restaurante?**	Kwan-do a-bre el res-tow-ran-te
Where is the sleeping car?	**¿Dónde está el coche-cama?**	Don-de es-**ta** el ko-che ka-ma
Which is my sleeper?	**¿Cuál es mi litera?**	Kwal es mee lee-tair-a
Could you let me know when we reach my stop?	**¿Puede avisarme cuando sea mi parada?**	Pwe-de a-bee-sar-me kwan-do sai-a mee pa-ra-da
Could you wake me at ... (time)?	**¿Puede despertarme a las ...?**	Pwe-de des-pair-tar-me a las
The heating is very high/low	**La calefacción está muy alta/baja**	La ka-le-fa-**thyon** es-**ta** mwee al-ta/ba-ha
I can't open/close the window	**No puedo abrir/ cerrar la ventana**	No pwe-do a-breer/ ther-rar la ben-ta-na
What station is this?	**¿Qué estación es ésta?**	Ke es-ta-**thyon** es es-ta
How long do we stop here?	**¿Cuánto paramos aquí?**	Kwan-to pa-ra-mos a-**kee**

By Underground

Key Phrases

Where is the nearest underground station?	¿Dónde está la estación de metro más cercana?	Don-de es-ta la es-ta-thyon de me-tro mas thair-ka-na
Does this train go to…?	¿Este tren va a…?	Es-te tren ba a
Have you a map of the underground?	¿Tiene un mapa del metro?	Tee-e-ne oon ma-pa del me-tro

Is there a daily/weekly/ten-trip ticket?	¿Hay un bono de viaje diario/semanal/de diez viajes?	Eye oon bo-no de bee-a-he dee-a-ryo/se-ma-nal/de dyeth bee-a-hes
Can I use it on the bus and the underground?	¿Puedo utilizarlo en el autobús y metro también?	Pwe-do oo-tee-lee-thar-lo en el ow-toh-boos ee me-tro tam-byen
Is there a supplementary charge?	¿Hay que pagar algún suplemento?	Eye ke pa-gar al-goon soo-ple-men-to
Which line goes to…?	¿Qué línea va a…?	Kay lee-nea ba a
Where do I change for…?	¿Dónde tengo que cambiar para…?	Don-de ten-go ke kam-bee-ar pa-ra
Is the next station…?	¿Es la próxima estación…?	Es la pro-see-ma es-ta-thyon
What station is this?	¿Qué estación es ésta?	Kay es-ta-thyon es es-ta

By Car[1]

Key Phrases

Where is the nearest garage?	**¿Dónde está el garaje más próximo?**	Don-de es-**ta** el ga-ra-he mas **pro**-see-mo
Have you a road map?	**¿Tiene un mapa de carreteras?**	Tee-e-ne oon ma-pa de kar-re-te-ras
Where is there a car park?	**¿Dónde hay un aparcamiento?**	Don-de eye oon a-par-ka-mee-en-to
May I see your licence/logbook, please?	**¿Su permiso/la documentación del coche, por favor?*	Soo pair-mees-o/la do-koo-men-ta-**thyon** del ko-che por fa-bor

How far is the next petrol station?	**¿A qué distancia está la próxima gasolinera?**	A kay dees-tan-thya es-**ta** la **pro**-see-ma ga-so-lee-nair-a
Can I park here?	**¿Puedo aparcar aquí?**	Pwe-do a-par-kar a-**kee**
How long can I park here?	**¿Cuánto tiempo puedo aparcar aquí?**	Kwan-to tee-em-po pwe-do a-par-kar a-**kee**
Have you any change for the meter?	**¿Tiene cambio para el parquímetro?**	Tee-e-ne kam-byo pa-ra el par-**kee**-me-tro
Is this your car?	**¿Es éste su coche?*	Es es-te soo ko-che
You were speeding	**Iba usted por encima del límite de velocidad*	Ee-ba oos-tay por en-thee-ma del **lee**-mee-te de be-lo-thee-dad

1. See also DIRECTIONS (p. 52) and ROAD SIGNS (p. 49).

garage	el taller de reparaciones	ta-llyair de re-pa-ra-thyo-nes
pedestrian crossing	**paso de peatones**	pass-o de pea-to-nes
speed limit	**límite de velocidad**	**lee**-mee-te de be-lo-thee-dad
traffic lights	**semáforo**	sem-**a**-pho-roh

Car Rental

Where can I hire a car?	**¿Dónde puedo alquilar un coche?**	Don-de pwe-do al-kee-lar oon ko-che
I want to hire a small/large car	**Quiero alquilar un coche pequeño/grande**	Kee-e-ro al-kee-lar oon ko-che pe-ke-nyo/gran-de
I want to hire	**Quiero alquilar un coche**	Kee-e-ro al-kee-lar oon ko-che
an automatic	**automático**	ow-to-**ma**-tee-ko
a car with air conditioning	**con aire acondicionado**	kon eye-re a-kon-dee-thee-o-na-do
a car with a sun roof	**con techo solar**	kon te-cho so-lar
a convertible	**descapotable**	des-ka-po-ta-ble
a four-wheel-drive	**todo-terreno**	to-do-te-rre-no
a manual	**de cambio manual**	de kam-byo man-wal
Does it have a GPS system?	**¿Tiene navegador?**	Tee-e-ne na-be-ga-**dor**
Does it have a mobile phone/iPod port?	**¿Tiene una entrada para (teléfono) móvil/iPod?**	Tee-e-ne oo-na en-tra-da pa-ra (te-**le**-fo-no) **mo**-beel/eye-pod?

We've reserved a camper van	**Hemos reservado una autocaravana**	He-mos re-sair-ba-do oona ow-toh-ka-ra-ba-na
How much is the deposit?	**¿Cuánto es el depósito?**	Kwan-to es el de-**po**-see-to
Can I rent a baby/child seat?	**¿Puedo alquilar una silla de niño?**	Pwe-do al-kee-lar oo-na see-llya de nee-nyo
What kind of fuel does it take?	**¿Qué combustible lleva?**	Kay kom-boo-stee-blay llye-ba
Is there a weekend/midweek rate?	**¿Hay una tarifa de fin de semana/de entre semana?**	Eye oo-na ta-ree-fa de feen de se-ma-na/de en-tre se-ma-na
How much is it by the hour/the day/the week?	**¿Cuánto cuesta por hora/por día/por semana?**	Kwan-to kwes-ta por o-ra/por **dee**-a/por se-ma-na
Does that include unlimited mileage?	**¿Incluye kilometraje sin límite?**	Een-kloo-ye kee-lo-me-tra-he seen **lee**-mee-te
The charge per kilometre is ...	*El precio por kilómetro es ...**	El pre-thyo por kee-**lo**-met-ro es
Can I return it to your office in ...?	**¿Puedo devolverlo en la oficina de ...?**	Pwe-do de-bol-ber-lo en la o-fee-thee-na de
Do you want full insurance?	*¿Quiere seguro a todo riesgo?**	Kee-e-re se-goo-ro a to-do ree-es-go
You must return the car with a full tank	*Tiene que devolverlo con el depósito lleno**	Tee-e-ne ke de-bol-ber-lo kon el de-**po**-see-to llye-no
You have to pay the first ... euros	*Lleva franquicia de ... euros**	Llye-ba fran-ke-thy-a de ... e-oo-ros
I will pay by credit card	**Pagaré con tarjeta de crédito**	Pa-ga-**re** kon tar-he-ta de **kre**-dee-to
May I see your driving licence and passport, please?	*¿Su pasaporte y permiso de conducir?**	Soo pa-sa-por-te ee per-mee-so de kon-doo-theer

Could you show me how to work	¿Puede enseñarme a usar	Pwe-de en-sen-yar-me a oos-ar
the horn?	el claxon?	el klak-son
the lights?	las luces?	las loo-thes
the windscreen wipers?	el limpiaparabrisas?	el leem-pee-a-pa-ra-bree-sas
this?	ésto?	es-to
The car is scratched/dented here	El coche está rayado/abollado aquí	El ko-che es-**ta** ra-ya-do/a-bo-llya-do a-**kee**

At a Garage or Petrol Station

...litres of standard petrol/diesel/unleaded	...litros de gasolina normal/diesel/sin plomo	...lee-tros de ga-so-lee-na nor-mal/dee-e-sel/seen plo-mo
Fill it up, please	Llénelo, por favor	**Llye**-ne-lo por fa-bor
How much is petrol a litre?	¿A cuánto el litro?	A kwan-to el lee-tro
Please clean the windscreen	Límpieme el parabrisas, por favor	**Leem**-pee-e-me el pa-ra-bree-sas por fa-bor
Please check	Por favor compruebe	Por fa-bor com-proo-ay-bay
the battery	la batería	la ba-tair-**ree**-a
the brakes	los frenos	los fre-nos
the oil	el aceite	el a-thay-te
the tyre pressure, including the spare	la presión de los neumáticos, incluido el de recambio	la pre-**syon** de los ne-oo-**ma**-tee-kos een-kloo-ee-do el de re-kam-byo

The oil needs changing	El aceite necesita cambiarse	El a-thay-te ne-the-see-ta kam-bee-ar-se
Please wash the car	Láveme el coche, por favor	La-be-me el ko-che por fa-bor
I want my car serviced	Quería hacerle una revisión al coche	Ke-**ree**-a a-ther-le oo-na re-bee-see-**on** al ko-che
Can I leave the car here?	¿Puedo dejar aquí el coche?	Pwe-do de-har a-**kee** el ko-che
What time does the garage close?	¿A qué hora se cierra el garaje?	A ke o-ra se thee-er-ra el ga-ra-he
Where are the toilets?	¿Dónde están los servicios?	Don-de es-**tan** los sair-bee-thyos
Please pay at the cash desk	*Por favor, pague en caja	Por fa-bor pah-ge en ka-ha

Problems and repairs

I've run out of petrol	Me he quedad sin gasolina	May ay ke-da-do seen ga-so-lee-na
I've lost my car keys	He perdido las llaves del coche	Ay pair-dee-do las llya-bes del ko-che
I've locked the keys in the car	Me he dejado las llaves dentro del coche	May ay de-ha do las llya-bes den-tro del ko-che
The door doesn't open	La puerta no abre	La pwer-ta no a-bre
My car won't start	No arranca el coche	No a-rran-ka el ko-che
Can you give me a lift to a telephone/a garage?	¿Me puede llevar hasta un teléfono/un taller?	May pwe-de llye-bar as-ta oon te-**le**-fo-no/oon ta-llair

May I use your phone?	¿Puedo usar su teléfono?	Pwe-do oos-ar soo te-**le**-fo-no
Do you have a breakdown service?	¿Hay servicio de ayuda en carretera?	Eye sair-bee-thyo de a-yoo-da en kar-re-te-ra
Is there a mechanic?	¿Hay un mecánico?	Eye oon me-**ka**-nee-ko
My car's broken down; can you send someone to tow it?	He tenido una avería en el coche; ¿puede mandarme una grúa?	Ay ten-ee-do oo-na a-ber-**ee**-a en el ko-che; pwe-de man-dar-me oo-na **groo**-a
Can you send someone to look at it?	¿Puede enviar a alguien que me lo mire?	Pwe-de en-bee-ar a alg-yen ke may lo mee-re
It is an automatic	Es automático	Es ow-to-**ma**-tee-ko
Where are you?	*¿Dónde está usted?	Don-de es-**ta** oos-te
Where is your car?	*¿Dónde está su coche?	Don-de es-**ta** soo ko-che
I'm on the road from … to …, near kilometre post …	Estoy en la carretera de … a …, a la altura del kilómetro …	Es-toy en la kar-re-te-ra de … a … a la al-too-ra del kee-**lo**-metro
How long will you be?	¿Cuánto tiempo tardará?	Kwan-to tee-em-po tar-da-**ra**
The battery is flat, it needs charging	La batería está descargada, necesita cargarse	La ba-tai-**ree**-a es-**ta** des-kar-ga-da ne-the-see-ta kar-gar-se
It's not running properly	No va bien	No ba bee-en
Please change the wheel	Cambie la rueda, por favor	Kam-bye la rwe-da por fa-bor
This tyre is flat/ punctured	Este neumático está desinflado/pinchado	Es-te ne-oo-**ma**-tee-ko es-**ta** de-seen-fla-do/ peen-cha-do
The exhaust is broken	El tubo de escape está roto	El too-bo de es-ka-pe es-**ta** ro-to

The windscreen wipers do not work	El limpiaparabrisas no funciona	El leem-pee-a-pa-ra-bree-sas no foon-thyo-na
The valve is leaking	La válvula pierde	La bal-boo-la pee-er-de
The radiator is leaking	Gotea el radiador	Go-te-a el ra-dee-a-dor
The engine is overheating	El motor se calienta	El mo-tor se ka-lee-en-ta
The engine is firing badly	El motor funciona mal	El mo-tor foon-thyo-na mal
Can you change this faulty plug?	¿Puede cambiarme esta bujía estropeada?	Pwe-de kam-bee-ar-me es-ta boo-hee-a es-tro-pe-a-da
There's a petrol/oil leak	Pierde gasolina/aceite	Pee-er-de gas-o-lee-na/a-thay-te
There's a smell of petrol/rubber	Hay olor a gasolina/goma	Eye o-lor a gas-o-lee-na/go-ma
There's a rattle	Hace ruido	A-thay roo-ee-do
Something is wrong with	Hay algo que no va bien en	Eye al-go ke no ba bee-en en
the brakes	los frenos	los fre-nos
the clutch	el embrague	el em-bra-ge
the engine	el motor	el mo-tor
the gearbox	la caja de cambios	la ka-ha de kam-byos
the lights	las luces	las loo-thes
the steering	la dirección	la dee-rek-thyon
I've got electrical/mechanical trouble	Se me ha estropeado el coche: debe ser algo eléctrico/mecánico	Se me a es-tro-pe-a-do el ko-che: de-be ser al-go el-ek-tree-ko/me-ka-nee-ko

The carburettor needs adjusting	**El carburador precisa un reglaje**	El kar-boo-ra-dor pre-thee-sa oon re-gla-he
Can you repair it?	**¿Pueden arreglarlo?**	Pwe-den ar-re-glar-lo
How long will it take to repair?	**¿Cuánto tiempo necesita para arreglarlo?**	Kwan-to tee-em-po ne-the-see-ta pa-ra ar-re-glar-lo
What will it cost?	**¿Cuánto costará?**	Kwan-to kos-ta-ra
When will the car be ready?	**¿Cuándo estará el coche arreglado?**	Kwan-do es-ta-ra el ko-che ar-re-gla-do
I need it	**Lo necesito**	Lo ne-the-see-to
as soon as possible	**lo antes posible**	lo an-tes po-see-ble
in three hours	**dentro de tres horas**	den-tro de tres o-ras
in the morning	**mañana por la mañana**	ma-nya-na por la ma-nya-na
It will take two days	***Tardaremos dos días en arreglarlo**	Tar-dar-emos dos **dee**-as en ar-re-glar-lo
We can repair it temporarily	***Se puede arreglar provisionalmente**	Se pwe-de ar-re-glar pro-bee-syo-nal-men-te
We haven't the right spares	***No tenemos los recambios necesarios**	No ten-e-mos los re-cam-byos ne-the-sa-ryos
We have to send for the spares	***Tenemos que pedir los recambios**	Ten-e-mos ke pe-deer los re-cam-byos
You will need a new ...	***Necesita un (una) ... nuevo (nueva)**	Ne-the-see-ta oon (oon-a)/nwe-bo (nwe-ba)
Could I have an itemized bill, please?	**¿Puede darme una factura detallada, por favor?**	Pwe-de dar-me oon-a fak-too-ra de-ta-llya-da por fa-bor

Parts of a car and other useful words

accelerate (to)	**acelerar**	a-the-le-rar
accelerator	**el acelerador**	a-the-le-ra-dor
aerial	**la antena**	an-te-na
airpump	**la bomba de aire**	bom-ba de eye-ray
alarm/anti-theft device	**la alarma/ el antirrobo**	a-lar-mah/ an-tee-rro-boh
anti-freeze	**el anticongelante**	an-tee-con-he-lan-te
automatic transmission	**la transmisión automática**	trans-mee-**syon** ow-to-**ma**-tee-ka
axle	**el eje**	e-he
battery	**la batería**	ba-tai-**ree**-a
bonnet	**el capó**	ka-**po**
boot/trunk	**el maletero**	ma-le-ter-o
brake	**el freno**	fre-no
brake lights	**las luces del freno**	loo-thes del fre-no
brake lining	**los cojinetes del freno**	ko-hee-ne-tes del fre-no
brake pad	**la guarnición del freno**	gwar-nee-**thyon** del fre-no
breakdown	**la avería**	a-ber-**ee**-a
bulb	**la luz/la bombilla**	looth/bom-bee-llya
bumper	**los parachoques**	pa-ra-cho-kes
carburettor	**el carburador**	kar-boo-ra-dor

CD player	el CD/el reproductor de CDs	thai-dai/re-pro-dook-tor de thai-dais
choke	el aire	eye-ray
clutch	el embrague	em-bra-ge
cooling system	el sistema de refrigeración	sees-te-ma de re-free-he-ra-**thyon**
crank-shaft	el cigüeñal	thee-gwe-nyal
cylinder	el cilindro	thee-leen-dro
differential gear	el diferencial	dee-fer-en-thyal
dip stick	el indicador de nivel de aceite	een-dee-ka-dor de nee-bel de a-thay-te
distilled water	el agua destilada	a-gwa des-tee-la-da
distributor	el distribuidor	dee-stree-boo-ee-dor
door	la puerta	pwer-ta
doorhandle	la manilla	ma-nee-llya
drive (to)	conducir	kon-doo-theer
drive shaft	el árbol de transmisión	ar-bol de trans-mee-**syon**
driver	el conductor	kon-dook-tor
dynamo	la dinamo	dee-na-mo
engine	el motor	mo-tor
exhaust	el (tubo de) escape	(too-bo de) es-ka-pe
fan	el ventilador	ben-tee-la-dor
fanbelt	la correa del ventilador	kor-re-a del ben-tee-la-dor

(oil) filter	**el filtro (de aceite)**	feel-tro (da a-thay-te)
flat tyre	**la rueda pinchada**	rwe-da peen-cha-da
foglamp	**el antiniebla**	an-tee-nee-eb-la
fusebox	**la caja de fusibles**	ka-ha de foo-see-bles
gasket	**la empaquetadura**	em-pa-ke-ta-doo-ra
gearbox	**la caja de cambios**	ka-ha de kam-byos
gear-lever	**la palanca de cambios**	pa-lan-ka de kam-byos
gears	**las velocidades**	be-lo-thee-da-des
grease (to)	**engrasar**	en-gra-sar
handbrake	**el freno de mano**	fre-no de ma-no
headlights	**las luces delanteras**	loo-thes de-lan-tair-as
heater	**la calefacción**	ka-le-fak-**thyon**
horn	**la bocina/el claxon**	bo-thee-na/klak-son
hose	**el manguito**	man-gee-to
ignition key	**la llave del contacto**	llya-be del kon-tak-to
indicator	**el indicador**	een-dee-ka-dor
jack	**el gato**	ga-to
key	**la llave**	llya-be
mirror	**el espejo**	es-pe-ho
number plate	**la (placa de) matrícula**	(pla-ka de) ma-**tree**-koo-la
nut	**la tuerca**	twer-ka
oil	**el aceite**	a-thay-te

parking lights	**las luces de aparcar**	loo-thes de a-par-kar
pedal	**el pedal**	pe-dal
petrol	**la gasolina**	ga-so-lee-na
petrol can	**la lata de gasolina**	la-ta de ga-so-lee-na
piston	**el émbolo**	**em**-bo-lo
plug	**la bujía**	boo-**hee**-a
points	**las conexiones**	ko-ne-see-o-nes
(oil/water) pump	**la bomba (de aceite/agua)**	bom-ba (de a-thay-te/ a-gwa)
puncture	**el pinchazo**	peen-cha-tho
radiator	**el radiador**	ra-dee-a-dor
rear lights	**las luces traseras**	loo-thes tra-sair-as
rear view mirror	**el espejo retrovisor**	es-pe-ho re-tro- bee-sor
reverse	**la marcha atrás**	mar-cha a-**tras**
reversing lights	**las luces de marcha atrás**	loo-thes de mar-cha a-**tras**
(sliding) roof	**el techo (descapotable)**	te-cho (des-ka-po-ta-blay)
screwdriver	**el destornillador**	des-tor-nee-llya-dor
seat	**el asiento**	a-see-en-to
seat belt	**el cinturón de seguridad**	thin-too-**ron** de se-goo-ree-dad
shock absorber	**el amortiguador**	a-mor-tee-gwa-dor

silencer	el silenciador	see-len-thee-a-dor
spanner	la llave inglesa	llya-be een-gle-sa
spare wheel	la rueda de repuesto	rwe-da de re-pwes-to
spares	los recambios	re-cam-byos
speedometer	el cuentakilómetros	kwen-ta-kee-**lo**-me-tros
spring	el resorte/el muelle	re-sor-te/mwe-llye
stall (to)	atascarse	a-tas-kar-se
steering	la dirección	dee-rek-**thyon**
steering wheel	el volante	bo-lan-te
sunroof	el techo solar	te-cho so-lar
suspension	la suspensión	soos-pen-**syon**
tank	el depósito	de-**po**-see-to
tappets	los alza-válvulas	al-tha-**bal**-boo-las
transmission	la transmisión	trans-mee-**syon**
tyre	el neumático	ne-oo-**ma**-tee-ko
valve	la válvula	**bal**-boo-la
warning light	las luces de avería/ los intermitentes	loo-thes de a-be-**ree**-a/ een-ter-mee-ten-tes
wheel (back/front)	la rueda de atrás/de adelante	rwe-da de a-**tras**/ de a-de-lan-te
window	la ventanilla	ben-tan-ee-llya
windscreen	el parabrisas	pa-ra-bree-sas
windscreen wipers	el limpiaparabrisas	leem-pee-a-pa-ra-bree-sas

By Bike or Moped[1]

Key Phrases

Where can I hire	¿Dónde puedo alquilar	Don-de pwe-do al-kee-lar
a bicycle?	una bicicleta?	oo-na bee-thee-klay-ta?
a moped?	un ciclomotor/ una vespa?	oon thick-lo-mo-tor/ oo-na bes-pa
a motorbike?	una motocicleta?	oo-na mo-to-thee-klay-ta
a mountain bike?	una bici de montaña?	oo-na bee-thee de mon-ta-nya
Is it obligatory to wear a helmet?	¿Es obligatorio llevar casco?	Es o-blee-ga-to-ryo llye-bar kas-ko
Do you repair bicycles?	¿Reparan bicicletas aquí?	Re-pa-ran bee-thee-klay-tas a-**kee**

What does it cost per day/per week?	¿Cuánto cuesta al día/a la semana?	Kwan-to kwes-ta al **dee**-a a/la se-ma-na
I'd like a lock, please	Quiero un candado, por favor	Kee-e-ro oon kan-da-do por fa-bor
The saddle is too high/too low	El sillín está muy alto/bajo	El see-**llyeen** es-**ta** mwee al-to/ba-ho
Where is the cycle shop?	¿Dónde hay una tienda de bicicletas?	Don-de eye oon-a tee-en-da de bee-thee-klay-tas
The brake isn't working	El freno no funciona	El fre-no no foon-thyo-na

1. See also DIRECTIONS (p. 52) and ROAD SIGNS (p. 49).

Could you tighten/ loosen the brake cable?	**¿Puede tensar/ aflojar el cable del freno?**	Pwe-de ten-sar/a-flo-har el ka-ble del fre-no
A spoke is broken	**Un radio está roto**	Oon ra-dyo es-**ta** ro-to
The tyre is punctured	**La rueda está pinchada**	La rwe-da es-**ta** peen-cha-da
The gears need adjusting	**Los cambios necesitan ajustar**	Los kam-byos ne-the-see-tan a-hoos-tar
Could you straighten the wheel?	**¿Puede enderezarme el neumático?**	Pwe-de en-dair-re-thar-me el ne-oo-**ma**-tee-ko
The handlebars are loose	**El manillar está suelto**	El ma-nee-llyar es-**ta** swel-to
Could you lend me a spanner?	**¿Me puede prestar una llave inglesa?**	May pwe-de pres-tar oon-a llya-be een-gle-sa
Can I take my bike on the boat/train?	**¿Puedo llevar la bici en el barco/el tren?**	Pwe-do llye-bar la bee-thee en el bar-ko/ el tren

Parts of a bicycle and other useful words

axle	**el eje**	e-he
basket	**la cesta**	thest-a
bell	**el timbre**	teem-bre
brake (front/rear)	**el freno delantero/ trasero**	fre-no de-lan-te-ro/ tra-se-ro
brake cable	**el cable de freno**	ka-ble de fre-no
brake lever	**la palanca de freno**	pa-lan-ka de fre-no
bulb	**la bombilla**	bom-bee-llya

chain	la cadena	ka-de-na
chain guard	el cubrecadena	koo-bre-ka-de-na
child's seat	la silla de niño	si-llya de nee-nyo
dynamo	la dinamo	dee-na-mo
fork	la horquilla	or-ki-llya
frame	el cuadro	kwa-dro
gear cable	el cable de marchas	ka-ble de mar-chas
gear lever	el cambio de marcha	kam-byo de mar-cha
gears	las velocidades/las marchas	be-lo-thee-da-des/ mar-chas
handlebars	el manillar	ma-nee-llyar
helmet	el casco	kas-ko
high visibility jacket	la chaqueta reflectante	cha-ke-ta re-flek-tan-te
inner tube	la llanta	llyan-ta
light (front/rear)	la luz delantera/ trasera	looth de-lan-te-ra/ tra-se-ra
mudguard	el guardabarros	gwar-da-ba-rros
panniers	la bolsa/mochila de bicicleta	bol-sa/mo-chee-la de bee-thee-klay-ta
pedal	el pedal	pe-dal
pump	la bomba de hinchar	bom-ba de een-char
puncture repair kit	los parches para pinchazos	par-ches pa-ra peen-cha-thos
reflector	el reflector	re-flek-tor

rim	**la llanta**	llyan-ta
saddle	**el sillín**	see-**llyeen**
saddlebag	**la alforja**	al-for-ha
spoke	**el radio**	ra-dyo
suspension	**la suspensión**	soos-pen-**syon**
tyre	**el neumático**	ne-oo-**ma**-tee-ko
valve	**la válvula**	**bal**-boo-la
wheel	**la rueda**	rwe-da

Road Signs

Aduana	Customs
Alto	Stop
Aparcamiento	Car park
Atención/Cuidado/Precaución	Caution
Autopista	Motorway
Calle estrecha	Narrow road
Carretera cortada	No through road
Carretera obstruida/cerrada	Road blocked/closed
Carril autobús	Bus lane
Ceda el paso	Give way
Circulen por la derecha/por la izquierda	Keep right/left
Curvas (peligrosas)	(Dangerous) bends
Desnivel	Steep hill

Despacio	Slow
Desprendimiento de rocas	Falling rocks
Desviación	Diversion
Dirección prohibida	No entry
Dirección única/obligatoria	One way (street/system)
Encender las luces delanteras	Switch on headlights
Estación de servicio	Petrol station
Estacionamiento limitado	Restricted parking
Estacionamiento prohibido	No parking
Firme irregular	Uneven surface
Gasolinera	Petrol station
Hielo	Ice
Inundaciones	Flooding
Mantenga la distancia	Keep the adequate distance
Niebla	Fog
Nieve	Snow
Obras	Roadworks
Paso a nivel	Railway (level) crossing
Peaje	Toll
Peatones	Pedestrians
Peligro	Danger
Prohibido adelantar	No overtaking
Prohibido aparcar	No parking
Prohibido aparcar. Llamo grúa	Cars parked here will be towed away

Prohibido el paso	No entry
Reduzca la velocidad	Reduce speed
Salido de camiones	Lorry exit
Solo para peatones	Pedestrians only
Taller de reparaciones	Garage
Zona azul	Limited parking zone
Zona de descanso	Rest area
Zona libre de aparcamiento	Free parking zone

DIRECTIONS

Key Phrases

Where is ...?	¿Dónde está ...?	Don-de es-**ta**
How do I get to ...?	¿Por dónde se va a ...?	Por don-de se ba a
How many kilometres?	¿Cuántos kilómetros?	Kwan-tos kee-**lo**-me-tros
Please show me on the map	Indíquemelo en el mapa, por favor	Een-**dee**-ke-me-lo en el ma-pa por fa-bor
You are going the wrong way	*Está usted yendo en dirección equivocada	Es-**ta** oos-tay yen-do en dee-rek-**thyon** e-ki-bo-ka-da

Could you tell me the way to	¿Podría usted decirme cómo se va	Pod-**ree**-a oos-tay de-theer-me ko-mo se ba
the post office?	a (la oficina de) correos?	a (la o-fee-thee-na de) ko-rre-os
the station?	a la estación?	a la es-ta-**thyon**
the town centre?	al centro?	al then-tro
Is there is an ATM/ an Internet café/a chemist's near here?	¿Hay un cajero/un café internet/una farmacia por aquí?	Eye oon ka-he-ro/oon ka-**fe** een-ter-net/oo-na far-ma-thya por a-**kee**
It's that way	*Es por ahí	Es por eye-**ee**
It isn't far	*No está lejos	No es-**ta** le-hos
It's on the square/ opposite ... hotel/at the end of the street	*Está en la plaza/ frente al ... hotel/ al final de la calle	Es-**ta** en la pla-tha/ fren-te al ... o-tel/ al fee-nal de la ka-llye

There is one in the pedestrian street	*Hay una en la calle peatonal	Eye oo-na en-la ka-llye pe-a-to-nal
How far is it to ...?	¿A qué distancia está ...?	A kay dees-tan-thya es-ta
How do we get on to the motorway to ...?	¿Por dónde se sale a la autopista de ...?	Por don-de se sa-le a la ow-to-pees-ta de
Which is the best road to ...?	¿Cuál es la mejor carretera para ...?	Kwal es la me-hor kar-re-te-ra pa-ra
Is there a scenic route to ...?	¿Hay una ruta pintoresca a ...?	Eye oon-a roo-ta peen-to-res-ka a
Is this the right road for ...?	¿Es ésta la carretera para ...?	Es es-ta la kar-re-te-ra pa-ra
Where does this road lead to?	¿A dónde va esta carretera?	A don-de ba es-ta kar-re-te-ra
Is it a good road?	¿Es buena la carretera?	Es bwe-na la kar-re-te-ra
Is there a motorway?	¿Hay autopista?	Eye ow-to-pees-ta
Is there a toll?	¿Hay peaje?	Eye pe-a-he
Is the tunnel/pass open?	¿Está abierto el túnel/puerto?	Es-ta a-bee-air-to el too-nel/pwer-to
Is the road to ... clear?	¿La carretera para ... está bien?	La kar-re-te-ra pa-ra ... es-ta bee-en
How far is the next village/petrol station?	¿A qué distancia está el próximo pueblo/la próxima gasolinera?	A kay dees-tan-thya es-ta el pro-see-mo pwe-blo/la pro-see-ma ga-so-lee-nair-a
Will we get to ... by evening?	¿Llegaremos a ... antes de anochecer?	Llye-gar-e-mos a ... an-tes de a-no-che-thair

How long will it take	¿Cuánto se tarda	Kwan-to se tar-da
by bicycle?	en bicicleta?	en bee-thee-klay-ta
by car?	en coche?	en ko-che
on foot?	a pie?	a pee-ay
Where are we now?	¿Dónde estamos ahora?	Don-de es-ta-mos a-o-ra
What is the name of this place?	¿Cuál es el nombre de este sitio?	Kwal es el nom-bre de es-te see-tyo
Follow signs for . . .	*Siga las señales a . . .	See-ga las se-nya-les a
Follow this road for five kilometres	*Siga esta carretera unos cinco kilómetros	See-ga es-ta kar-re-te-ra oon-os theen-ko kee-lo-me-tros
Keep straight on	*Siga adelante/ derecho	See-ga a-del-an-te/ de-re-cho
Turn right at the crossroads	*Tuerza a la derecha en el cruce	Twer-tha a la de-re-cha en el kroo-the
Take the second road on the left	*Tome la segunda carretera a la izquierda	To-me la se-goon-da kar-re-te-ra a la eeth-kyair-da
Turn right at the traffic lights	*Tuerza a la derecha en el semáforo	Twer-tha a la de-re-cha en el se-ma-for-o
Turn left after the bridge	*Tuerza a la izquierda después del puente	Twer-tha a la eeth-kyair-da des-pwes del pwen-te
The best road is the . . .	*La mejor carretera es la . . .	La me-hor kar-re-te-ra es la
Take the . . . and ask again	*Tome la . . . y pregunte de nuevo	To-me la . . . ee preg-oon-te de nwe-bo

Take junction 12/ the exit for ...	*Salga por la salida número 12/Tome la salida para ...	Sal-ga por la sa-lee-da noo-me-ro do-the/ To-me la sa-lee-da pa-ra
one-way system	dirección única	dee-rek-thyon oo-nee-ka
north	norte	nor-te
south	sur	soor
east	este	es-te
west	oeste	o-es-te

ACCOMMODATION[1]

Campsite	**el camping/ la acampada**	kam-ping/a-kam-pa-da
Cottage	**la casa rural**	ka-sa roo-ral
Country inn	**la fonda/la casa rural**	fon-da/ka-sa roo-ral
Guesthouse	**la pensión/el hostal**	pen-see-**on**/os-tal
Youth hostel	**el albergue juvenil**	al-ber-ge hoo-be-neel
Rooms to let/ Vacancies	**Se alquilan habitaciones**	Se al-kee-lan a-bee-ta-thyo-nes
No vacancies	**No hay habitaciones/ Completo**	No eye a-bee-ta-thyo-nes/ Kom-ple-to
No camping	**Prohibido acampar**	Pro-ee-be-do a-kam-par
Can you show me on the map where the hotel is?	**¿Puede indicarme en el mapa dónde está el hotel?**	Pwe-de een-dee-kar-me en el ma-pa don-de es-**ta** el o-tel
Is it in the centre?	**¿Está en el centro?**	Es-ta en el then-tro
Is it near a bus stop/ bus station/train station?	**¿Está cerca de la parada de autobús/ estación de autobuses/estación de tren?**	Es-ta ther-ka de la pa-ra-da de ow-to-**boos**/ es-ta-**thyon** de ow-to-boos-es-ta-**thyon** de tren
Is it on a train/metro line?	**¿Se puede ir en tren/ en metro?**	Se pwe-de eer en tren/ en me-tro

1. In addition to privately owned hotels and pensions, Spain also has state-run accommodation called *paradores*, *refugios* and *albergues de carretera*. You are not allowed to stay in an *albergue* for more than forty-eight hours.

Check In

Key Phrases

Do you have a room for the night/for two or three nights?	¿Tienen habitación para esta noche/para dos o tres noches?	Tee-e-nen a-bee-ta-**thyon** pa-ra es-ta no-che/pa-ra dos o tres no-ches
Does the hotel/the room have wi-fi?	¿Tienen wi-fi en el hotel/en las habitaciones?	Tee-e-nen wee-fee en el o-tel/en las a-bee-ta-thyo-nes
I've reserved a room; my name is ...	Tengo una habitación reservada a nombre de ...	Ten-go oo-na a-bee-ta-**thyon** re-sair-ba-da a nom-bre de
Is there a lift/elevator?	¿Hay ascensor?	Eye as-then-sor
How much is the room per night?	¿Cuánto cuesta la habitación por noche?	Kwan-to kwes-ta la a-bee-ta-**thyon** por no-che

Where is there a cheap hotel?	¿Dónde hay un hotel barato?	Don-de eye oon o-tel ba-ra-to
How many nights?	*¿Para cuántas noches?	Pa-ra kwan-tas no-ches
Have you a room with twin beds/a king-size bed?	¿Tiene habitación de dos camas/cama de matrimonio extragrande?	Tee-e-ne a-bee-ta-**thyon** de dos ka-mas/ka-ma de ma-tree-mo-nyo es-tra-gran-de
How long will you be staying?	*¿Cuánto tiempo se van a quedar?	Kwan-to tee-em-po se ban a ke-dar
Is it for one night only?	*¿Sólo una noche?	So-lo oon-a no-che

Can you recommend	¿Puede recomendarme	Pwe-de re-kom-en-dar-me
a moderately priced hotel?	un hotel no muy caro?	oon o-tel no mwee ka-ro
an inexpensive hotel?	un hotel barato?	oon o-tel ba-ra-to
another good hotel?	otro hotel bueno?	ot-ro o-tel bwe-no
Is the room airconditioned?	¿Hay aire acondicionado en la habitación?	Eye eye-ray a-kon-dee-thee-o-na-do en la a-bee-ta-**thyon**
Is there an Internet connection in the rooms?	¿Hay conexión internet en las habitaciones?	Eye ko-nek-**syon** een-ter-net en las a-bee-ta-thyo-nes
Yes, it's free/it costs €... per hour	*Sí, es gratis/ cuesta ... € por hora	See, es gra-tees/ kwes-ta ... ai-oo-ros por o-ra
Does the hotel have a business centre?	¿Tienen salón de conferencias?	Tee-e-nen sa-**lon** dai kon-fe-ren-thyas
Is there a fitness centre?	¿Hay gimnasio?	Eye him-na-syo
Does the hotel have a swimming pool/ private beach?	¿El hotel tiene piscina/playa particular?	El o-tel tee-e-ne pees-thee-na/pla-ya par-tee-koo-lar
I want a single room with a shower	Quiero una habitación individual con ducha	Kee-e-ro oo-na a-bee-ta-**thyon** een-dee-bee-doo-al kon doo-cha
We want	Queremos	Ke-rai-mos
a room with a double bed and a bathroom	una habitación con cama de matrimonio y baño	oo-na a-bee-ta-**thyon** kon ka-ma de mat-ree-mo-nyo ee ba-nyo

a family room	una habitación para familia con niños	oo-na a-bee-ta-**thyon** pa-ra fa-mee-lya kon nee-nyos
adjoining rooms	habitaciones contiguas	a-bee-ta-thyo-nes kon-tee-gwas
I want a room/ two rooms	Quiero una habitación/dos habitaciones	Kee-e-ro oo-na a-bee-ta-**thyon**/dos a-bee-ta-thyo-nes
for two or three days	para dos o tres días	pa-ra dos o tres **dee**-as
for a week	para una semana	pa-ra oon-a se-ma-na
until Friday	hasta el viernes	as-ta el byair-nes
What floor is the room on?	¿En qué piso está la habitación?	En kay pee-so es-**ta** la a-bee-ta-**thyon**
Is there a lift/elevator?	¿Hay ascensor?	Eye as-then-sor
Is there parking for customers?	¿Hay aparcamiento para clientes?	Eye a-par-ka-mee-en-to pa-ra klee-en-tes
Are there facilities for the disabled?	¿Está preparado el hotel para discapacitados?	Es-**ta** pre-pa-ra-do el o-tel pa-ra dees-ka-pa-theet-a-dos
Have you a room on the first floor?	¿Tiene habitación en el primer piso?	Tee-en-e a-bee-ta-**thyon** en el pree-mair pee-so
May I see the room?	¿Puedo ver la habitación?	Pwe-do ber la a-bee-ta-**thyon**
I'll take this room	Me quedo con esta habitación	Me ke-do kon es-ta a-bee-ta-**thyon**
We've only a twinbedded room	*Sólo tenemos habitación doble	So-lo te-ne-mos a-bee-ta-**thyon** do-ble

Have you a room looking on to the street/the sea?	¿Tiene habitación que dé a la calle/ al mar?	Tee-en-e a-bee-ta-**thyon** ke de a la ka-llye/al mar
I'd like a room with a balcony	Me gustaría una habitación con balcón	May goos-ta-**ree**-a oon-a a-bee-ta-**thyon** kon bal-**kon**
I don't like this room	No me gusta esta habitación	No me goo-sta es-ta a-bee-ta-**thyon**
Have you another one?	¿Tiene otra?	Tee-en-e ot-ra
I want a quiet room/a bigger room	Quiero una habitación tranquila/ más grande	Kee-er-o oon-a a-bee-ta-**thyon** tran-kee-la/mas gran-de
It's very noisy in this room	Hay mucho ruido en esta habitación	Eye moo-cho roo-ee-do en es-ta a-bee-ta-**thyon**
This is the only room vacant	*Esta es la única habitación que tenemos	Es-ta es la **oo**-nee-ka a-bee-ta-**thyon** ke te-ne-mos
We shall have another room tomorrow	*Tendremos otra habitación mañana	Ten-dre-mos ot-ra a-bee-ta-**thyon** ma-nya-na
The room is only available tonight	*La habitación sólo está disponible esta noche	La a-bee-ta-**thyon** so-lo es-**ta** dees-po-nee-ble es-ta no-che
How much is the room per night?	¿Cuánto cuesta la habitación por noche?	Kwan-to kwes-ta la a-bee-ta-**thyon** por no-che
Have you nothing cheaper?	¿No tienen habitaciones más baratas?	No tee-en-en a-bee-ta-thyo-nes mas ba-ra-tas

What do we pay for the child/children?	¿Cuánto se paga por el niño/los niños?	Kwan-to se pa-ga por el nee-nyo/los nee-nyos
Could you put a cot/an extra bed in the room?	¿Pueden poner una cuna/una cama adicional en la habitación?	Pwe-den po-nair oon-a koo-na/oon-a ka-ma ad-dee-thee-o-nal en la a-bee-ta-**thyon**
Is VAT included in that price?	¿El precio incluye el IVA?	El pre-thyo een-klu-ye el ee-ba?
Is breakfast included?	¿Está incluido el desayuno?	Es-ta een-kloo-ee-do el de-sa-yoo-no
How much is full board/half board?	¿Cuánto es la pensión completa/media pensión?	Kwan-to es la pen-**syon** kom-ple-ta/me-dya pen-**syon**
How much is the room without meals?	¿Cuánto es sólo la habitación?	Kwan-to es so-lo la a-bee-ta-**thyon**
What is the weekly rate?	¿Cuánto cuesta por semana?	Kwan-to kwes-ta por se-ma-na
It's too expensive	Es demasiado caro	Es de-ma-see-a-do ka-ro
Are you paying cash or card?	*Pagarán en metálico ó con tarjeta?	Pa-ga-**ran** en me-**ta**-lee-ko o kon tar-he-ta
Please fill in the registration form	*¿Pueden llenar la hoja de registro, por favor?	Pwe-den llye-nar la o-ha de re-hees-tro por fa-bor
Could I have your passport, please?	*El pasaporte, por favor	El pas-a-por-te por fa-bor
Name/surname	*Nombre/apellido	Nom-bre/a-pe-llyee-do
Address	*Dirección	Dee-rek-**syon**

Date and place of birth	*Fecha y lugar de nacimiento	Fe-cha ee loo-gar de na-cee-mee-en-to
Passport number	*Número/N° de pasaporte	Noo-mer-ro de pa-sa-por-te
Car registration number	*Matrícula de su coche	Ma-tree-koo-la de soo ko-che

Check Out

Key Phrases

Can you have my bill ready, please?	¿Me prepara la cuenta, por favor?	May pre-pa-ra la kwen-ta por fa-bor
There is a mistake on the bill	Hay un error en la factura	Eye oon er-ror en la fak-too-ra
Please store the luggage, we will be back at . . .	Por favor guárdeme el equipaje, volveremos a . . .	Por fa-bor gwar-de-me el e-kee-pa-he bol-bair-e-mos a

What time do we have to vacate the room?	¿A qué hora hay que dejar la habitación?	A kay o-ra eye kay de-har la a-bee-ta-thyon
I'm leaving tomorrow	Me voy mañana	Me boy ma-nya-na
I had just a . . . from the minibar	Sólo he tomado un . . . del minibar	So-lo ai to-ma-do oon . . . del mee-nee-bar
Do you accept credit cards?	¿Aceptan tarjetas de crédito?	A-thep-tan tar-he-tas de kre-dee-to
Sorry, we do not accept American Express. Do you have another card?	*Lo siento, no trabajamos con American Express. ¿Tiene otra tarjeta?	Lo see-en-to no tra-ba-ha-mos kon a-me-ree-kan eks-press. Tee-e-ne o-tra tar-he-ta

I shall be coming back on . . . Can I book a room for that date?	Volveré el . . . ¿Pueden reservarme habitación para ese día?	Bol-be-**re** el . . . Pwe-den re-sair-bar-me a-bee-ta-**thyon** pa-ra es-e **dee**-a
Could you have my luggage brought down?	¿Pueden bajarme el equipaje?	Pwe-den ba-har-me el e-kee-pa-he
Please order a taxi for me at 11 a.m.	Pídame un taxi para las once, por favor	**Pee**-da-me oon ta-xi pa-ra las on-the por fa-bor
Thank you for everything	Muchas gracias por todo	Moo-chas grath-yass por to-do

Problems and Complaints

The air conditioning/ the television doesn't work	El aire/la tele no funciona	El eye-ray/la te-le no foon-thyo-na
There are no towels in my room	No hay toallas en mi habitación	No eye to-a-llyas en mee a-bee-ta-**thyon**
There's no soap	No hay jabón	No eye ha-**bon**
There's no (hot) water	No hay agua (caliente)	No eye a-gwa (ka-lee-en-te)
There's no plug in my washbasin	El lavabo no tiene tapón	El la-ba-bo no tee-en-e ta-**pon**
The washbasin is blocked	El lavabo no corre	El la-ba-bo no kor-re
There's no toilet paper in the lavatory	No hay papel higiénico en el cuarto de baño	No eye pa-pel ee-hee-e-nee-ko en el kwar-to de ba-nyo

The lavatory won't flush	**La cadena del cuarto de baño no funciona**	La ka-de-na del kwar-to de ba-nyo no foon-thyo-na
The bidet leaks	**El bidé gotea**	El bee-**de** go-te-a
The light doesn't work	**La luz no funciona**	La looth no foon-thyo-na
The lamp is broken	**La lámpara está rota**	La **lam**-pa-ra es-**ta** ro-ta
The blind is stuck	**La persiana está atascada**	La pair-see-a-na es-**ta** a-tas-ka-da
The curtains won't close properly	**Las cortinas no cierran bien**	Las kor-tee-nas no thee-er-ran bee-en

Camping

Key Phrases

Is there a campsite nearby?	**¿Hay un camping cerca?**	Eye oon kam-ping thair-ka
May we camp	**¿Podemos acampar**	Po-de-mos a-kam-par
here?	**aquí?**	a-**kee**
in your field?	**en su campo?**	en soo kam-po
on the beach?	**en la playa?**	en la pla-ya
Where can I buy butane gas?	**¿Dónde puedo comprar una bombona de butano?**	Don-de pwe-do kom-prar oo-na bom-bo-na de boo-ta-no

Where should we put our tent/caravan?	¿Dónde podemos poner la tienda/el remolque?	Don-de po-de-mos po-nair la tee-en-da/ el re-mol-ke
Can I park the car next to the tent?	¿Puedo aparcar el coche al lado de la tienda?	Pwe-do a-par-kar el ko-che al la-do de la tee-en-da
Can we hire a tent on the site?	¿Podemos alquilar una tienda en el camping?	Po-de-mos al-kee-lar oon-a tee-en-da en el kam-ping
Is/Are there	¿Hay	Eye
drinking water?	agua potable?	a-gwa po-ta-ble
electricity?	electricidad?	e-lek-tree-thee-dad
a launderette?	lavandería?	la-ban-dair-**ree**-a
a playground?	columpios?	ko-loom-pee-os
a restaurant?	restaurante?	res-tow-ran-te
a shop?	tienda?	tee-en-da
showers?	duchas?	doo-chas
a swimming pool?	piscina?	pees-thee-na
toilets?	servicios?	sair-bee-thyos
What does it cost	¿Cuánto cuesta	Kwan-to kwes-ta
per car?	el coche?	el ko-che
per caravan?	la caravana/el remolque?	la ka-ra-ba-na/ el re-mol-ke
per motorbike?	una moto?	oo-na mo-to
per person?	por persona?	por pair-so-na

per tent?	**una tienda?**	oo-na tee-en-da
per night?	**por noche?**	por no-che
per week?	**por semana?**	por se-ma-na
Can I buy ice?	**¿Venden hielo?**	Ben-den ee-e-lo
Where do I put rubbish?	**¿Dónde se tiran las basuras?**	Don-de se tee-ran las ba-soo-ras
Where de we sort the rubbish (for recycling)?	**¿Dónde se reciclan las basuras?**	Don-de se re-theek-lan las ba-soo-ras
Where can I wash up/wash clothes?	**¿Dónde puedo fregar/lavar?**	Don-de pwe-do fre-gar/la-bar
Is there somewhere to dry clothes/equipment?	**¿Hay tendederos?**	Eye ten-de-dair-os
My butane gas has run out	**Me he quedado sin gas**	May ay ke-da-do seen gas
The toilet is blocked	**El baño está atascado**	El ba-nyo es-**ta** a-tas-ka-do
The shower doesn't work/is flooded	**La ducha no funciona/está inundada**	La doo-cha no foon-thyo-na/es-ta ee-noon-da-da
What is the voltage?	**¿Qué voltaje hay?**	Kay bol-ta-he eye
May we light a fire/a barbecue?	**¿Se puede hacer fuego/barbacoa?**	Se pwe-de a-thair foo-e-go/bar-ba-ko-a
Please prepare the bill, we are leaving today	**Por favor prepare la factura, nos vamos hoy**	Por fa-bor pre-pa-re la fak-too-ra nos ba-mos oy
How long do you want to stay?	***¿Cuánto tiempo se van a quedar?**	Kwan-to tee-em-po se ban a ke-dar

I'm afraid the campsite is full	*Lo siento el camping está lleno	Lo see-en-to el kam-ping es-ta llye-no
What time do we have to leave the site?	¿A qué hora hay que salir del camping?	A ke o-ra eye ke sa-leer del kam-ping

Hostels

Is there a youth hostel here?	¿Hay aquí algún albergue juvenil?	Eye a-**kee** al-**goon** al-bair-ge hoo-ben-eel
How long is the walk to the youth hostel?	¿Cuánto hay a pie hasta el albergue juvenil?	Kwan-to eye a pee-e as-ta el al-bair-ge hoo-be-neel
Have you a room/bed for the night?	¿Tiene habitación/cama para esta noche?	Tee-è-ne a-bee-ta-**thyon**/ka-ma pa-ra es-ta no-che
How many days can we stay?	¿Cuántos días podemos quedarnos?	Kwan-tos **dee**-as po-de-mos ke-dar-nos
Here is my membership card	Aquí está mi carnet de alberguista	A-**kee** es-ta mee kar-ne de al-bair-gees-ta
Do you serve meals?	¿Sirven comidas?	Seer-ben ko-mee-das
Can I use the kitchen?	¿Puedo usar la cocina?	Pwe-do oo-sar la ko-thee-na
Is there somewhere cheap to eat nearby?	¿Hay algún sitio barato para comer?	Eye al-**goon** see-tyo ba-ra-to pa-ra ko-mer
Can I rent a sheet for my sleeping bag?	¿Se puede alquilar una sábana para el saco de dormir?	Se pwe-de al-kee-lar oon-a **sa**-ba-na pa-ra el sa-ko de dor-meer
Does the hostel have wi-fi/an Internet connection?	¿Hay wi-fi/internet en el albergue?	Eye wee-fee/een-ter-net en el al-bair-ge

Hotels

In your room

chambermaid	**la camarera**	ka-ma-rai-ra
room service	**servicio de habitaciones**	sair-bee-thyo de a-bee-ta-thyo-nes
I'd like breakfast in my room	**Quisiera tomar el desayuno en la habitación**	Kee-see-e-ra to-mar el des-a-yoo-no en la a-bee-ta-**thyon**
I'd like more ice cubes	**Quiero más cubitos de hielo**	Kee-e-ro mas koo-bee-tos de ee-e-lo
Can I have more hangers, please?	**Quisiera más perchas, por favor**	Kee-see-e-ra mas per-chas por fa-bor
Is there a point for an electric razor?	**¿Hay enchufe para la maquinilla de afeitar?**	Eye en-choo-fe pa-ra la ma-kee-nee-llya de a-fay-tar
Where is the bathroom?	**¿Dónde está el baño?**	Don-de es-**ta** el ba-nyo
Is there a shower?	**¿Tiene ducha?**	Tee-e-ne doo-cha
May I have another blanket/pillow, please?	**Quisiera otra manta/ almohada, por favor**	Kee-see-air-ra o-tra man-ta/al-mo-a-da por fa-bor
The sheets on my bed haven't been changed	**No han cambiado las sábanas de mi cama**	No an kam-bee-a-do las **sa**-ba-nas de mee ka-ma
I can't open my window; please open it	**No puedo abrir la ventana; haga el favor de abrirla**	No pwe-do ab-reer la ben-tan-a; a-ga el fa-bor de ab-reer-la

It's too hot/cold	**Hace demasiado calor/frío**	A-the de-ma-see-a-do ka-lor/**free**-o
Can the heating be turned up/down?	**¿Pueden subir/ bajar un poco más la calefacción?**	Pwe-den soo-beer/ ba-har oon po-ko mas la ka-le-fak-**thyon**
Can the heating be turned on/off?	**¿Pueden abrir/cerrar la calefacción?**	Pwe-den a-breer/ the-rar la ka-le-fak-**thyon**
Come in	**Adelante/Pase**	A-de-lan-te/Pa-se
Put it on the table, please	**Póngalo en la mesa**	**Pon**-ga-lo en la me-sa
How long will the laundry take?	**¿Cuánto tarda la lavandería?**	Kwan-to tar-da la la-ban-dair-**ee**-a
Have you a needle and thread?	**¿Tiene aguja e hilo?**	Tee-e-ne a-goo-ha e ee-lo
I want these shoes cleaned	**¿Pueden limpiarme los zapatos?**	Pwe-den leem-pyar-me los tha-pa-tos
Could you get this dress/suit cleaned up a bit?	**¿Pueden limpiarme un poco este vestido/ traje?**	Pwe-den leem-pyar-me oon po-ko es-te bes-tee-do/tra-he
I want this suit pressed	**¿Pueden plancharme este traje?**	Pwe-den plan-char-me es-te tra-he
When will it be ready?	**¿Cuándo estará?**	Kwan-do es-ta-**ra**
It will be ready tomorrow	***Estará listo mañana**	Es-ta-**ra** lee-sto ma-nya-na

Other services

bellboy	**el botones**	bo-to-nes
hall porter	**el conserje**	kon-sair-he
maid	**la camarera**	ca-ma-rair-a
manager	**el gerente**	he-ren-te
night porter	**el portero de noche**	por-tair-o de no-che
porter	**el portero**	por-tair-o
telephonist	**la telefonista/ la operadora**	te-le-fo-nees-ta/ ow-pair-a-do-ra
A second key, please	**Otra llave, por favor**	O-tra llya-be por fa-bor
I've lost my key, sorry	**He perdido la llave, lo siento**	Ay pair-dee-do la llya-be lo see-e-nto
The key for room number . . . , please	**La llave de la . . . , por favor**	La llya-be de la . . . por fa-bor
Please wake me at 8.30	**Llámeme a las ocho y media**	**Llya**-me-me a las o-cho ee me-dya
Please post this	**Por favor ponga esto en el correo**	Por fa-bor pon-ga es-to en el kor-re-o
Are there any letters for me?	**¿Tengo (alguna) carta?**	Ten-go (al-goon-a) kar-ta
Are there any messages for me?	**¿Tengo algún recado?**	Ten-go al-**goon** re-kah-do
Is there fax?	**¿Hay fax?**	Eye fax
What code do I dial for an outside call?	**¿Qué número hay que marcar para llamar fuera?**	Kay **noo**-me-ro eye kay mar-kar pa-ra llya-mar fwe-ra

Can I dial direct to England/America?	¿Puedo marcar directamente a Inglaterra/Estados Unidos?	Pwe-do mar-kar dee-rek-ta-men-te a een-gla-ter-ra/es-ta-dos oo-ni-dos
I am expecting a call	Estoy esperando una llamada	Es-toy es-pe-ran-do oo-na llya-ma-da
If anyone phones, tell them I'll be back at 4.30	Si me llama por teléfono, digan que vuelvo a las cuatro y media	See may llya-ma por te-le-fo-no dee-gan kay bwel-bo a las kwat-ro ee me-dya
No one telephoned	*No le ha llamado nadie	No le a llya-ma-do na-dye
What is the international dialling code?	¿Cuál es el código de llamada internacional?	Kwal es el ko-dee-go de llya-ma-da een-ter-na-thee-o-nal
Can I send a fax?	¿Puedo enviar un fax?	Pwe-do en-bee-ar un fax
Are there computers for guests to use?	¿Hay ordenadores para uso de los clientes?	Eye or-de-na-do-res pa-ra oo-so de los clee-en-tes
Is there a charge for this?	¿Se paga ésto?	Se pa-ga es-to
Do I need a password?	¿Necesito una contraseña?	Ne-the-see-too oo-na kon-tra-se-nya
There's a lady/gentleman to see you	*Una señora/un señor pregunta por usted	Oon-a sen-yo-ra/oon sen-yor pre-goon-ta por oos-te
Please ask her/him to come up	Que suba a mi habitación, por favor	Kay soo-ba a mee a-bee-ta-thyon por fa-bor
I'm coming down (at once)	Bajo (en seguida)	Ba-ho (en se-gee-da)

Do you have	¿Tienen	Tee-en-en
envelopes?	sobres?	so-bres
stamps?	sellos?	se-llyos
writing paper?	papel de escribir?	pa-pel de es-kree-beer
Please send the chambermaid	La camarera, por favor	La ka-ma-rair-a por fa-bor
I need a guide/ interpreter	Necesito un guía/un intérprete	Ne-the-see-to oon gee-a/ oon een-tair-pre-te
Does the hotel have a babysitting service?	¿Tiene este hotel servicio de niñeras?	Tee-e-ne es-te o-tel sair-bee-thyo de nee-nye-ras
Can I leave this in your safe?	¿Puedo dejar esto en la caja fuerte?	Pwe-do de-har es-to en la ka-ha fwair-te
Where are the toilets?	¿Dónde están los servicios?	Don-de es-tan los sair-bee-thyos
Where is the cloakroom/the dining room?	¿Dónde está el guardarropa/el comedor?	Don-de es-ta el gwar-dar-ro-pa/el ko-me-dor
What time is	¿A qué hora es	A kay o-ra es
breakfast?	el desayuno?	el des-a-yoo-no
lunch?	la comida?	la kom-ee-da
dinner?	la cena?	la the-na
Is there a garage?	¿Hay aquí garaje?	Eye a-kee ga-ra-he
Where can I park the car?	¿Dónde puedo aparcar el coche?	Don-de pwe-do a-par-kar el ko-che
Is the hotel open all night?	¿Está el hotel abierto toda la noche?	Es-ta el o-tel a-bee-air-to to-da la no-che
What time does it close?	¿A qué hora cierra?	A kay o-ra thee-e-ra

APARTMENTS AND VILLAS

Key Phrases

Please show us around	**Por favor nos lo enseña por dentro**	Por fa-bor nos lo en-se-nya por den-tro
Please show me how this works	**Por favor enséñeme como funciona ésto**	Por fa-bor en-**se**-nye-me ko-mo foon-thyo-na es-to
Which days does the maid come?	**¿Qué días viene la asistenta?**	Kay **dee**-as bee-e-ne la a-sees-ten-ta
When is the rubbish collected?	**¿Cuándo recogen la basura?**	Kwan-do re-ko-hen la ba-soo-ra
Please give me another set of keys	**Por favor déjeme otro juego de llaves**	Por fa-bor **de**-he-me o-tro hwe-go de llya-bes

We've rented an apartment/a villa/a chalet	**Hemos alquilado un apartamento/una villa/un chalet**	E-mos al-kee-la-do oon a-par-ta-men-to/oon-a bee-llya/oon cha-le
Here is our reservation	**Aquí está nuestra reserva**	A-**kee** es-**ta** nwes-tra re-sair-ba
Does the cost include	**¿Está incluido en el precio**	Es-**ta** een-kloo-ee-do en el pre-thyo
electricity?	**la electricidad?**	la e-lek-tree-thee-dad
the gas cylinder?	**la bombona del gas?**	la bom-bo-na del gas
house cleaning?	**la limpieza?**	la leem-pee-e-tha
the maid?	**la asistenta?**	la a-sees-ten-ta

For how long does the maid come?	¿Cuánto tiempo viene la asistenta?	Kwan-to tee-em-po bee-e-ne la a-sees-ten-ta
Where is	¿Dónde está	Don-de es-ta
the electricity mains switch?	la llave de la luz?	la llya-be de la looth
the fusebox?	la caja de los fusibles?	la ka-ha de los foo-see-bles
the light switch?	el interruptor de la luz?	el een-tair-roop-tor de la looth
the power point?	el enchufe?	el en-choo-fe
the water mains stopcock?	la llave del agua?	la llya-be del a-gwa
How does the heating/hot water work?	¿Cómo funciona la calefacción/el agua caliente?	Ko-mo foon-thyo-na la ka-le-fak-**thyon**/el a-gwa ka-lee-en-te
Is there a spare gas cylinder?	¿Hay una bombona de gas de repuesto?	Eye oon-a bom-bo-na de gas de re-pwes-to
Do gas cylinders get delivered?	¿Traen la bombona de gas a casa?	Tra-en la bom-bo-na de gas a ka-sa
Is there a fly screen?	¿Hay mosquitera?	Eye mos-kee-tair-a
Is there a vacuum cleaner we can use?	¿Hay una aspiradora que podamos usar?	Eye oo-na as-pee-ra-do-ra ke po-da-mos oo-sar
Should we sort the rubbish for recycling?	¿Se reciclan las basuras?	Se re-theek-lan las ba-soo-ras
The rubbish hasn't been collected	No han recogido la basura	No an rai-ko-hee-do la ba-soo-ra

Where can we buy logs for the fire?	¿Dónde podemos comprar leña para la chimenea?	Don-de po-de-mos kom-prar le-nya pa-ra la chee-me-ne-a
Is there a barbecue?	¿Hay barbacoa?	Eye bar-ba-ko-a
Does someone come to clean the swimming pool?	¿Viene alguien a limpiar la piscina?	Bee-e-ne alg-yen a leem-pee-ar la pis-thee-na
Is there an inventory?	¿Hay un inventario?	Eye oon een-ben-ta-ryo
This was already broken when we arrived	Esto ya estaba roto cuando entramos en la casa	Es-to ya es-ta-ba ro-to kwan-do en-tra-mos en la ka-sa
We have replaced the broken ...	Hemos repuesto lo roto ...	E-mos re-pwes-to lo ro-to
Here is the bill	*Aquí está la factura	A-kee es-ta la fak-too-ra
Please return my deposit against breakages	Por favor devuélvame el depósito/la señal contra daños/roturas	Por fa-bor de-bwel-ba-may el de-po-see-to/ la se-nyal kon-tra da-nyos/ro-too-ras

Cleaning and DIY[1]

Where is a DIY centre/ hardware shop?	¿Dónde hay una tienda de bricolaje?	Don-de eye oo-na tee-en-da de bree-ko-la-he
Where can I get butane gas?	¿Dónde puedo comprar butano?	Don-de pwe-do kom-prar boo-ta-no
all-purpose cleaner	un limpiador general	leem-pee-a-dor ge-ne-ral
batteries	las pilas	pee-las

1. See also SHOPS AND SERVICES, (p. 173).

bleach	la lejía	le-**hee**-a
broom	la escoba	es-ko-ba
brush	el cepillo	the-pee-llyo
bucket	el cubo	koo-bo
cement	el cemento	the-men-to
charcoal	el carbón	kar-**bon**
clothes line	la cuerda para tendederos	kwer-da pa-ra ten-de-de-ros
clothes pegs	las pinzas de ropa	peen-thas de ro-pa
detergent	el detergente	de-ter-hen-te
dustbin	el cubo de basura	koo-bo de ba-soo-ra
dustpan	el recogedor	re-ko-he-dor
fire extinguisher	el extintor	es-teen-tor
hammer	el martillo	mar-tee-llyo
nails	los clavos/las puntas	kla-bos/poon-tas
paint	la pintura	peen-too-ra
paint brush	la brocha	bro-cha
plaster	la escayola	es-ka-yo-la
plastic	el plástico	**plas**-tee-ko
pliers	las tenazas	te-na-thas
rubbish sacks	las bolsas de basura	bol-sas de ba-soo-ra
saw	la sierra	see-e-rra
screwdriver	el destornillador	des-tor-nee-llya-dor
screws	los tornillos	tor-nee-llyos

spanner	**la llave inglesa**	llya-be een-gle-sa
stainless steel	**el acero inoxidable**	a-the-ro ee-no-see-da-ble
steel	**el acero**	a-the-ro
tiles	**las baldosas**	bal-do-sas
toilet/drain unblocking liquid	**el desatascador de baño/de cañería**	des-a-tas-ka-dor de ba-nyo/de ka-nye-ree-a
vacuum cleaner	**la aspiradora**	as-pee-ra-do-ra
washing powder	**el detergente**	de-tair-hen-te
washing-up liquid	**el detergente lavavajillas**	de-tair-hen-te la-ba-ba-hee-llyas
wire	**el alambre**	a-lam-bre
wood	**la madera**	ma-de-ra
wrench	**la llave inglesa**	llya-be een-gle-sa

Furniture and Fittings

armchair	**el sillón**	see-llyon
barbecue	**la barbacoa/la parrilla**	bar-ba-ko-a/par-ree-llya
bath	**la bañera**	ba-nye-ra
bed	**la cama**	ka-ma
blanket	**la manta**	man-ta
bolt (for door)	**el cerrojo**	ther-ro-ho
carpet	**la alfombra**	al-fom-bra
CD player	**el reproductor de CDs**	re-pro-dook-tor de thai-dais

central heating	**la calefacción central**	ka-le-fak-**thyon** then-tral
chair	**la silla**	see-llya
clock	**el reloj**	re-loh
cooker	**la cocina**	ko-thee-na
cupboard	**el armario**	ar-ma-ryo
curtains	**las cortinas**	kor-tee-nas
cushions	**los cojines**	ko-hee-nes
deckchair	**la tumbona/ la hamaca**	toom-bo-na/a-ma-ka
dishwasher	**el friegaplatos/ el lavaplatos**	free-e-ga-pla-tos/ la-ba-pla-tos
door	**la puerta**	pwer-ta
doorbell	**el timbre de la puerta**	teem-bre de la pwer-ta
doorknob	**el pomo de la puerta**	po-mo de la pwer-ta
dustbin	**el basurero**	ba-soo-re-ro
dustpan	**el recogedor**	re-ko-he-dor
DVD player	**el reproductor de DVDs**	re-pro-dook-tor de dai-oo-be-dais
hinge	**la bisagra**	bee-sa-gra
immersion heater	**el calentador de agua**	ka-len-ta-dor de a-gwa
iPod dock	**la estación de iPod**	es-ta-**thyon** de eye-pod
iron	**la plancha**	plan-cha
ironing board	**la tabla de planchar**	ta-bla de plan-char

key	la llave	llya-be
keyring	el llavero	llya-be-ro
lamp	la lámpara	lam-pa-ra
lampshade	la pantalla	pan-ta-llya
light bulb	la bombilla	bom-bee-llya
lock	el cerrojo	ther-ro-ho
mattress	el colchón	kol-chon
mirror	el espejo	es-pe-ho
padlock	el candado	kan-da-do
pillow	el almohadón/ la almohada	al-mo-a-don/ al-mo-a-da
pipe	la cañería	ka-nye-ree-a
plug (bath)	el tapón	ta-pon
plug (electric)	el enchufe	en-choo-fe
radio	la radio	ra-dee-o
refrigerator	el refrigerador/ la nevera	re-free-he-ra-dor/ ne-bair-a
sheet	la sábana	sa-ba-na
shelf	la estantería	es-tan-tair-ee-a
shower	la ducha	doo-cha
sink	el fregadero	fre-ga-de-ro
sofa	el sofá	so-fa
stool	el taburete	ta-boo-re-te
sun-lounger	la tumbona	toom-bo-na

table	la mesa	me-sa
tap	el grifo	gree-fo
television/TV	la televisión/la tele	te-le-bee-**syon**/te-le
toilet	el aseo/la taza del wáter	a-se-o/ta-tha del **ba**-tair
towel	la toalla	to-a-llya
washbasin	el lavabo	la-ba-bo
washing machine	la lavadora	la-ba-do-ra
window catch	el cierre de seguridad	thee-er-re de se-goo-ree-dad
window sill	la repisa de la ventana	re-pee-sa de la ben-ta-na

Kitchen Equipment

blender	la batidora	ba-tee-do-ra
bottle opener	el abrebotellas	a-bre-bo-te-llyas
bowl	el tazón	ta-**thon**
can opener	el abrelatas	a-bre-la-tas
candle	la vela	be-la
chopping board	la tabla de cocina	ta-bla de ko-thee-na
coffee pot	la cafetera	ka-fe-te-ra
colander	el escurridor	es-koo-ree-dor
coolbag	la nevera portátil	ne-be-ra por-**ta**-teel
corkscrew	el sacacorchos	sa-ka-kor-chos

cup	**la taza**	ta-tha
fork	**el tenedor**	te-ne-dor
frying pan	**la sartén**	sar-**ten**
glass/wine glass	**el vaso/la copa**	ba-so/ko-pa
grill	**el grill**	grill
ice tray	**la bandeja para el hielo/la hielera**	ban-de-ha pa-ra el ee-e-lo/ee-e-le-ra
jug	**la jarra**	har-ra
juicer	**el exprimidor**	es-pree-mee-dor
kettle (not common)	**la tetera para calentar agua**	te-te-ra pa-ra ka-len-tar a-gwa
knife	**el cuchillo**	koo-chee-llyo
lighter	**el mechero**	me-che-ro
matches	**las cerillas**	the-ree-llyas
microwave	**el microondas**	mee-kro-on-das
mixing bowl	**el bol**	bol
pan	**el cazo**	ka-tho
plate	**el plato**	pla-to
pot (with lid)	**la cazuela (con tapa)**	ka-thwe-la (kon ta-pa)
pressure cooker	**la olla exprés**	la ow-llya es-**press**
scissors	**las tijeras**	tee-her-as
sieve	**el colador**	ko-la-dor
spoon	**la cuchara**	koo-cha-ra
teapot	**la tetera**	te-te-ra

teatowel	**el paño de cocina**	pa-nyo de ko-thee-na
toaster	**la tostadora**	toss-ta-doh-ra
torch	**la linterna**	leen-tair-na

Parts of a House and Grounds

balcony	**el balcón**	bal-**kon**
banister/handrail	**la barandilla/ el pasamanos**	ba-ran-dee-llya/ pa-sa-ma-nos
bathroom	**el cuarto de baño**	kwar-to de ba-nyo
bedroom	**el dormitorio**	dor-mee-to-ryo
ceiling	**el techo**	te-cho
chimney	**la chimenea**	chee-me-ne-a
corridor	**el pasillo**	pa-see-llyo
door	**la puerta**	pwer-ta
fence	**la valla/la verja**	ba-llya/ber-ha
fireplace	**la chimenea**	chee-me-ne-a
floor	**el suelo**	swe-lo
garage	**el garaje**	ga-ra-he
garden	**el jardín**	har-**deen**
gate	**la verja del jardín**	ber-ha del har-**deen**
hall	**el vestíbulo/el hall**	bes-**tee**-boo-lo/hol
kitchen	**la cocina**	ko-thee-na
living room	**el salón/el cuarto de estar**	sa-lon/kwar-to de es-tar

patio	**el patio**	pa-tyo
roof	**el techo**	te-cho
shutters	**las persianas**	pair-see-a-nas
stairs	**las escaleras**	es-ka-lair-as
swimming pool	**la piscina**	pees-thee-na
terrace	**la terraza**	ter-ra-tha
wall	**la pared**	pa-red
window	**la ventana**	ben-ta-na

Problems

The drain/sink is blocked	**El desagüe/el fregadero está atascado**	El de-sa-gwe/el fre-ga-de-ro es-**ta** a-tas-ka-do
The pipe is blocked	**La cañería está atascada**	La ka-nye-**ree**-a es-**ta** a-tas-ka-da
The toilet doesn't flush	**La cadena del wáter no funciona**	La ka-de-na del **ba**-ter no foon-thyo-na
There's no water	**No hay agua**	No eye a-gwa
We can't turn the water off/shower on	**No podemos cerrar el agua/abrir la ducha**	No po-de-mos the-rrar el a-gwa/a-breer la doo-cha
There is a leak/a broken window	**Hay goteras/una ventana rota**	Eye go-te-ras/oon-a ben-ta-na ro-ta
The shutters won't close	**Las persianas no cierran**	Las pair-see-a-nas no thee-er-ran
The window won't open	**La ventana no se puede abrir**	La ben-ta-na no se pwe-de a-breer

The electricity has gone off	**No hay luz**	No eye looth
The heating/cooker/ immersion heater doesn't work	**La calefacción/la cocina/el calentador no funciona**	La ka-le-fak-**thyon**/ la ko-thee-na/el ka-len-ta-dor no foon-thyo-na
The lock is stuck	**La cerradura está atascada**	La ther-ra-doo-ra es-**ta** a-tas-ka-da
This is broken	**Esto está roto**	Es-to es-**ta** ro-to
This needs repairing	**Esto necesita arreglarse**	Es-to ne-the-see-ta ar-re-glar-se
The apartment/villa has been burgled	**Han robado en el apartamento/la villa**	An ro-ba-do en el a-par-ta-men-to/ la bee-llya

COMMUNICATIONS

Key Phrases

Is there an Internet café near here?	¿Hay un café internet por aquí?	Eye oon ka-**fe** in-ter-net por a-**kee**
Do I need a password?	¿Hace falta contraseña?	A-thai fal-ta kon-tra-se-nya
Can I print this page?	¿Puedo imprimir esta página?	Pwe-do eem-pree-meer es-ta **pa**-hee-na
What is your email address?	¿Cuál es su dirección de correo electrónico?	Kwal es soo dee-rek-**thyon** de kor-re-o e-lek-**tro**-nee-ko
I want to get a local SIM card for this phone	Quería una tarjeta SIM local para este móvil	Ke-**ree**-a oo-na tar-he-ta seem lo-kal pa-ra es-te **mo**-beel
Where's the main post office?	¿Dónde está la oficina principal de correos?	Don-de es-**ta** la o-fee-thee-na preen-thee-pal de kor-re-os

Email and Internet

@	la arroba	ar-ro-ba
adaptor	un adaptador	ad-ap-ta-dor
black and white print	una copia en blanco y negro	ko-pya en blank-o ee ne-gro

colour print	una copia en color	ko-pya en ko-lor
computer	un ordenador	or-dai-na-dor
email	un correo electrónico	kor-re-o (e-lek-**tro**-nee-ko)
email address	la dirección de correo electrónico	dee-rek-**thyon** de kor-re-o e-lek-**tro**-nee-ko
lead	un cable	ka-ble
memory stick	el lápiz de memoria/ el USB	la-peeth de me-mo-rya/ oo-e-se-be
mouse	el ratón	ra-**ton**
print (to)	imprimir	eem-pree-meer
printer	la impresora	eem-pre-so-ra
web page	la página web	**pa**-hee-na web
wi-fi	el wi-fi	wee-fee
Does this café have wi-fi?	¿Tiene wi-fi este café?	Tee-e-ne wee-fee es-te ca-fe
Is there a connection fee?	¿Cuánto cuesta conectarse?	Kwan-to kwes-ta kon-nek-tar-se
Can I access the Internet?	¿Puedo conectarme a internet?	Pwe-do ko-nek-tar-me a in-ter-net
Can I check email?	¿Puedo ver mi correo?	Pwe-do ber mee ko-rre-o
Can I use any computer?	¿Puedo usar cualquier ordenador?	Pwe-do oo-sar kwal-kee-er or-dai-na-dor
How much does it cost for half an hour/ an hour?	¿Cuánto cuesta media hora/una hora?	Kwan-to kwes-ta me-dya o-ra/oo-na o-ra
How do I turn on this computer?	¿Como se enciende este ordenador?	Ko-mo se en-thee-en-de es-te or-dai-na-dor

How do I log on/ log off?	¿Cómo me conecto/ desconecto?	Ko-mo may ko-nek-to/ des-ko-nek-to
The computer doesn't respond	El ordenador no hace nada	El or-dai-na-dor no a-thai na-da
The computer has frozen	El ordenador se ha congelado	El or-dai-na-dor se a kon-hai-la-do
This mouse doesn't work	Este ratón no funciona	Es-te ra-ton no foon-thyo-na
I can't open my email	No puedo abrir mi correo	No pwe-do a-breer mee kor-re-o
The computer cannot read my memory stick	El ordenador no lee mi lápiz de memoria	El or-dai-na-dor no lai-ai mee la-peeth de me-mo-rya
Can you change this to an English keyboard?	¿Podría cambiarme al teclado inglés?	Po-dree-a kam-bee-ar-me al te-kla-do een-gles
Where is the @ sign?	¿Dónde está la arroba?	Don-de es-ta la ar-ro-ba
Do you have a colour printer?	¿Tiene impresora a color?	Tee-e-ne eem-pre-so-ra a ko-lor
How much is it to print in black and white/colour?	¿Cuánto cuesta imprimir en blanco y negro/en color?	Kwan-to kwes-ta eem-pree-meer en blank-o ee ne-gro/en ko-lor
...cents per page	*A...céntimos (de euro) la página	A...then-tee-mos (de ai-oo-ro) la pa-hee-na
I need an adapter	Necesito un adaptador	Ne-thai-see-to oon ad-ap-ta-dor
My email address is...	Mi (dirección de) correo (electrónico) es...	Mee (dee-rek-thyon de) kor-re-o (e-lek-tro-nee-ko) es

Did you get my email?	¿Recibió usted mi correo?	Re-thee-**byo** oos-te mee kor-re-o
Email me, please	Envíeme un correo, por favor	En-**bee**-e-me oon kor-re-o por fa-bor
Do you have a website?	¿Tienen ustedes página web?	Tee-e-nen oos-te-des **pa**-hee-na web
It doesn't work	No funciona	No foon-thyo-na
I don't know what is wrong with this computer	No sé qué le pasa a este ordenador	No sai ke le pa-sa a es-te or-de-na-dor

Faxing and Copying

Do you have a fax?	¿Tienen fax?	Tee-e-nen fax
I want to send a fax	Quería enviar un fax	Ke-**ree**-a en-bee-ar oon fax
Can I send/receive a fax here?	¿Puedo enviar/ recibir un fax aquí?	Pwe-do en-bee-ar/re-thee-beer oon fax a-**kee**
How much does it cost per page?	¿Cuánto cuesta por página?	Kwan-to kwes-ta por **pa**-hee-na
What is your fax number?	¿Cuál es su número de fax?	Kwal es soo **noo**-me-ro de fax
Please resend this fax	Por favor, vuelva a enviar este fax	Por fa-bor bwel-ba a en-bee-ar es-te fax
Can I make photocopies here?	¿Puedo hacer fotocopias aquí?	Pwe-do ai-ther fo-to-ko-pyas-as a-**kee**
Can you scan this for me?	¿Pueden escanearme ésto?	Pwe-den es-ka-ne-ar-mai es-to

I want to send a (reply paid) telegram	**Quiero mandar un telegrama (con respuesta pagada)**	Kee-e-ro man-dar oon te-le-gram-a (kon res-pwes-ta pa-ga-da)
How much does it cost per word?	**¿Cuánto cuesta por palabra?**	Kwan-to kwes-ta por pa-la-bra

Post[1]

Where's the main post office?	**¿Dónde está la oficina principal de correos?**	Don-de es-ta la o-fee-thee-na preen-thee-pal de kor-re-os
Where's the nearest post office?	**¿Dónde está la oficina de correos más próxima?**	Don-de es-ta la o-fee-thee-na de kor-re-os mas pro-see-ma
What time does the post office open/ close?	**¿A qué hora abren/ cierran correos?**	A kay o-ra a-bren/ thee-er-an kor-re-os
Where's the post box?	**¿Dónde hay un buzón de correos?**	Don-de eye oon boo-thon de kor-re-os
Is there a stamp machine?	**¿Hay máquina que venda sellos?**	Eye ma-kee-na kay ben-da se-llyos
Which counter do I go to for	**¿Cuál es la ventanilla para**	Kwal es la ben-ta-nee-llya pa-ra
money orders?	**los giros?**	los heer-os
stamps?	**los sellos?**	los se-llyos
telegrams?	**los telegramas?**	los te-lai-gra-mas

1. You can buy stamps from a tobacconist's (*Estanco*) as well as from a post office.

How much is a postcard abroad/to England?	¿Qué sellos llevan las tarjetas postales para el extranjero/ para Inglaterra?	Kay se-llyos llye-ban las tar-he-tas pos-tal-es pa-ra el es-tran-he-ro/ pa-ra een-gla-te-rra
What's the airmail to the USA?	¿Qué sellos llevan las cartas por avión para los Estados Unidos?	Kay se-llyos llye-ban las kar-tas por a-bee-**on** pa-ra los es-ta-dos oon-ee-dos
How much is it to send a letter surface mail?	¿Qué sellos llevan las cartas por correo ordinario?	Kay se-llyos llye-ban las kar-tas por kor-re-o or-dee-na-ree-o
It's inland	Es para España	Es pa-ra es-pa-nya
Give me three . . . cents/euros stamps	Tres sellos de . . . céntimos/euros	Tres se-llyos de . . . **then-**tee-mos/ai-oo-ros
I want to send this letter express	Quiero mandar esta carta urgente	Kee-e-ro man-dar es-ta kar-ta oor-hen-te
I want to register this letter	Quiero mandar esta carta certificada	Kee-e-ro man-dar es-ta kar-ta thair-tee-fee-ka-da
I want to send a parcel	Quiero enviar un paquete	Kee-e-ro en-bee-ar oon pa-ke-te
Where is the poste restante section?	¿Dónde está lista de correos?	Don-de es-**ta** lees-ta de kor-re-os
Are there any letters for me?	¿Hay alguna carta a nombre de . . .?	Eye al-goo-na kar-ta a nom-bre de
What is your name?	*¿(Cuál es) su nombre, por favor?/¿Cómo se llama usted?	(Kwal es) soo nom-bre por fa-bor/Ko-mo se llya-ma oos-te
Have you any means of identification?	*¿Tiene algún documento que le identifique?	Tee-e-ne al-**goon** do-koo-men-to ke le ee-den-tee-fee-ke

Telephones, Mobiles and SMS[1]

Do you have a mobile (cell phone)?	¿Tiene (teléfono) móvil?	Tee-en-e (te-le-fo-no) mo-beel
What is your mobile (cell) number?	¿Cuál es su número de (teléfono) móvil?	Kwal es soo noo-me-ro de (te-le-fo-no) mo-beel
My mobile (cell phone) isn't working here	Mi (teléfono) móvil no funciona aquí	Mee (te-le-fo-no) mo-beel no foon-thyo-na a-kee
There is no signal here	No tengo cobertura aquí	No ten-go ko-bair-too-ra a-kee
I want to get a local SIM card for this phone	Quería una tarjeta SIM local para este móvil	Ke-ree-a oo-na tar-he-ta seem lo-kal pa-ra es-te mo-beel
Can you give me his mobile (cell) number?	¿Puede darme su número de (teléfono) móvil?	Pwe-de dair-me soo noo-me-ro de (te-le-fo-no) mo-beel
I'll send you a text/SMS	Se lo envío en un (mensaje de) texto	Se lo en-bee-o en oon (men-sa-he de) tes-to
Where's there a phone box?	¿Dónde hay un teléfono público?	Don-de eye oon te-le-fo-no poo-bleek-o
May I have change for the phone?	¿Me puede dar cambio para el teléfono?	May pwe-de dair kam-byo pa-ra el te-le-fo-no

1. Since the advent of mobile phones, public telephone boxes have been disappearing from cities. You can make both local calls as well as long-distance calls from any of them. Most will take coins and only some (in big cities, airports, etc.) may take credit cards. You can telephone from most bars, cafés and shopping centres. There is no link between Correos and Telefónica, they are separate services, and post offices do not contain telephones.

May I use your phone?	¿Puedo usar su teléfono?	Pwe-do oo-sar soo te-le-fo-no
Do you have a telephone directory for...?	¿Tienen una guía telefónica de...?	Tee-en-en oon-a gee-a te-le-fo-nee-ka de
I want to make a phone call	Quiero hacer una llamada telefónica	Kee-e-ro a-thair oon-a llya-ma-da te-le-fo-nee-ka
I'd like to reverse the charges	Quiero llamar a cobro revertido	Kee-e-ro llya-mar a ko-bro rai-vair-tee-do
Please put me through to number...	Por favor póngame con el número...	Por fa-bor pon-ga-me kon el noo-me-ro
What do I dial for an international call?	¿Qué hay que marcar para llamadas internacionales?	Kay eye kay mar-kar pa-ra llya-ma-das een-tair-na-thee-o-na-les
What is	¿Cuál es el código	Kwal es el ko-dee-go
the country code for the UK/ Australia?	para Reino Unido/ Australia?	pa-ra ray-no oo-ni-do/ a-oos-tra-lya
area code for...?	provincial de...?	pro-been-thyal de
Can I dial international direct?	¿Se puede marcar directamente para llamadas internacionales?	Se pwe-de mar-kar dee-rek-ta-men-te pa-ra llya-ma-das een-tair-na-thee-o-na-les
I was cut off. Can you reconnect me?	Se ha cortado. ¿Puede volverme a poner?	Se a kor-ta-do. Pwe-de bol-bair-me a po-nair
The line is engaged	*Está comunicando/ Comunica	Es-ta ko-moo-nee-kan-do/Ko-moo-nee-ka
There's no reply	*No contestan	No kont-es-tan

| You have the wrong number | *Tiene el número confundido | Tee-e-ne el noo-me-ro kon-foon-dee-do |
| That number is out of order/disconnected | *Ese número está estropeado/fuera de servicio | E-se noo-me-ro es-ta es-tro-pe-a-do/fwe ra de sair-bee-thyo |

On the phone

Hello	Sí/¿Dígame?	See/Dee-ga-me
May I speak to Señor Alvarez?	El Señor Alvarez, por favor	El Se-nyor Al-bar-eth por fa-bor
Please put me through to this extension/to Señor Gómez	Por favor, póngame con la extensión .../ con el Señor Gómez	Por fa-bor pon-ga-me kon la es-ten-syon/ kon el Se-nyor Go-meth
Who's speaking?	*¿De parte de quién?/ ¿Quién le llama?/ ¿Quién habla?	De par-te de kee-en/ Kee-en le llya-ma/ kee-en ha-bla
Hold the line	*No se retire	No se re-tee-re
We'll call you back	*Le llamaremos	Le llya-ma-rai-mos
He's not here	*No está en casa/aquí	No es-ta en ka-sa/a-kee
He's at ...	*Está en ...	Es-ta en
He/she can't come to the phone right now	*No se puede poner en este momento	No se pwe-de po-ner en es-te mo-men-to
When will he be back?	¿Cuándo volverá?	Kwan-do bol-bair-a
Will you take a message?	¿Puedo dejarle un recado?	Pwe-do de-har-le oon rai-ka-do
Tell him that ... phoned	Dígale que ha llamado ...	Dee-ga-le ke a llya-ma-do

I'll ring again later	Llamaré más tarde	Llya-ma-**re** mas tar-de
Please ask him to phone me	Dígale que me llame, por favor	Dee-ga-le ke me llya-me por fa-bor
What's your number?	*¿Cuál es su número?	Kwal es soo **noo**-me-ro
My number is ...	Mi número es ...	Mee **noo**-me-ro es
I can't hear you	No le oigo bien	No le o-ee-go bee-en
Please repeat that	¿Por favor, puede repetir?	Por fa-bor pwe-de re-pe-tir
Please speak slowly	¿Puede hablar más despacio, por favor?	Pwe-de ha-blar mas des-pa-thyo por fa-bor

DISABLED TRAVELLERS

Key Phrases

Is there a disabled parking area?	**¿Hay aparcamiento para discapacitados?**	Eye a-park-am-ee-en-to pa-ra dees-ka-pa-theet-a-dos
Are there facilities for the disabled?	**¿Está habilitado para discapacitados?**	Es-**ta** a-bee-lee-ta-do pa-ra dees-ka-pa-theet-a-dos
I'd like to reserve a wheelchair	**Quería reservar una silla de ruedas**	Ke-**ree**-a re-sair-bar oo-na see-llya de rwe-das
I need a bedroom on the ground floor/near the lift	**Necesito un dormitorio en el piso bajo/cerca del ascensor**	Ne-thai-see-to oon dor-mee-to-ryo en el pee-so ba-ho/thair-ka del as-thens-or
Do the buses take wheelchairs?	**¿Los autobuses admiten viajeros en silla de ruedas?**	Los ow-to-boo-ses ad-meet-ain bee-a-hai-ros en see-llya de rwe-das

Access

Can we borrow a wheelchair/mobility scooter?	**¿Puedo tomar prestada una silla de ruedas/un triciclo eléctrico?**	Pwe-do to-mar pres-ta-da oo-na see-llya de rwe-das/oon tree-thick-lo e-**lek**-tri-ko

I want to book a wheelchair from the check-in desk to the plane	Quería reservar una silla de ruedas desde el mostrador de facturación hasta el avión	Ke-**ree**-a re-sair-bar oo-na see-llya de rwe-das des-de el mos-tra-dor de fak-too-ra-**thyon** as-ta el a-**byon**
Is it possible to visit the old town in a wheelchair?	¿Se puede visitar el centro histórico en silla de ruedas?	Se pwe-de bee-si-tar el then-tro ees-**to**-ree-ko en see-llya de rwe-das
Is there wheelchair access to the exhibition/concert hall/theatre/museum?	¿Hay acceso para silla de ruedas en la exposición/la sala de conciertos/el teatro/el museo?	Eye a-thes-o pa-ra see-llya de rwe-das en la es-po-see-**thyon**/la sa-la de kon-thee-er-tos/el te-a-tro/el moo-se-o
Are the paths in the garden/park suitable for wheelchairs?	¿Hay caminos por los jardines/el parque para que pasen sillas de ruedas?	Eye ka-mee-nos por los har-dee-nes/el park-e pa-ra ke pa-sen see-llyas de rwe-das
Is there a wheelchair ramp?	¿Hay rampa para silla de ruedas?	Eye ramp-a pa-ra see-llya de rwe-das
Are there seats reserved for the disabled?	¿Hay asientos para discapacitados?	Eye a-see-en-tos pa-ra dees-ka-pa-theet-a-dos
Is there a table with place for a wheelchair?	¿Hay una mesa con espacio para silla de ruedas?	Eye oo-na me-sa kon es-pa-thyo pa-ra see-llya de rwe-das
Are mobility scooters allowed inside?	¿Se puede entrar con triciclo eléctrico?	Se pwe-de en-trar kon tree-thick-lo e-**lek**-tri-ko
Where is the lift?	¿Dónde está el ascensor?	Don-de es-**ta** el as-thens-or
Are there disabled toilets?	¿Hay aseos para discapacitados?	Eye a-sai-os pa-ra dees-ka-pa-theet-a-dos

Is there a reduction for the disabled?	¿Los discapacitados tienen descuento?	Los dees-ka-pa-theet-a-dos tee-e-nen des-kwen-to
Are guide dogs allowed?	¿Se puede entrar con un perro lazarillo?	Se pwe-de en-trar kon oon pair-ro la-tha-ree-llyo
I can't walk far	No puedo caminar mucha distancia	No pwe-do ka-mee-nar moo-cha dees-tan-thya
I can't climb stairs	No puedo subir escaleras	No pwe-do soo-beer es-ka-le-ras
I need a bedroom on the ground floor near the lift	Necesito un dormitorio en el piso bajo cerca del ascensor	Ne-thai-see-to oon kwart-o en el pee-so ba-ho thair-ka del as-thens-or
Is the bathroom equipped for the disabled?	¿Está habilitado el baño para discapacitados?	Es-ta a-bee-lee-ta-do el ba-nyo pa-ra dees-ka-pa-theet-a-dos

Assistance

Please hold the door open	Por favor sujéteme la puerta	Por fa-bor soo-he-te-me la pwer-ta
Can you help me, please?	¿Me ayuda, por favor?	May a-yoo-da por fa-bor
I am deaf; please speak louder	Soy sordo; hábleme más alto por favor	Soy sor-do; a-blai-mai mas al-to por fa-bor
Could you help me cross the road, please?	¿Me ayuda a cruzar la calle, por favor?	May a-yoo-da a kroo-thar la ka-llye por fa-bor

Travel

Do the buses take wheelchairs?	¿Los autobuses admiten viajeros en silla de ruedas?	Los ow-to-boo-ses ad-meet-ain bee-a-hai-ros en see-llya de rwe-das
Can I get onto the train/plane with a mobility scooter?	¿Puedo montar en el tren/avión con triciclo eléctrico?	Pwe-do mon-tar en el tren/a-**byon** kon tree-thick-lo e-**lek**-tri-ko
Could you order a taxi that will take a wheelchair please?	¿Me puede pedir un taxi que admita viajeros en silla de ruedas?	May pwe-de pe-deer oon ta-see ke ad-meet-a bee-a-hai-ros en see-llya de rwe-das

EATING OUT

Key Phrases

Can you suggest	¿Puede recomendarnos	Pwe-de re-kom-men-dar-nos
a cheap restaurant?	un restaurante económico/ barato?	oon res-tow-ran-te e-ko-**no**-mee-ko/ ba-ra-to
a good restaurant?	un buen restaurante?	oon bwen res-tow-ran-te
a vegetarian restaurant?	un restaurante vegetariano?	oon res-tow-ran-te be-he-ta-ree-a-no
I've reserved a table; my name is . . .	Tengo mesa reservada a nombre de . . .	Ten-go me-sa re-sair-ba-da a nom-bre de
May I see the menu, please?	El menú/la carta, por favor	El me-**noo**/la kar-ta, por fa-bor
May I see the wine list, please?	La carta de vinos, por favor	La kar-ta de bee-nos, por fa-bor
Is there a set menu?	Tienen menú del día?	Tee-e-nen me-**noo** del **dee**-a
What is your dish of the day?	¿Cuál es el plato del día?	Kwal es el pla-to del **dee**-a
That was a good meal, thank you	La comida estaba muy buena gracias	La ko-mee-da es-ta-ba mwee bwe-na grath-yass
The bill, please	La cuenta, por favor	La kwen-ta por fa-bor

I'd like to book a table for four at 2 p.m.	**Quisiera reservar mesa para cuatro para las dos**	Kee-see-e-ra re-sair-bar me-sa pa-ra kwa-tro pa-ra las dos
Have you reserved a table?	***¿Han reservado una mesa?**	An re-sair-ba-do oon-a me-sa
We did not make a reservation	**No, no hemos reservado**	No no em-os re-sair-ba-do
Have you a table for three?	**¿Hay una mesa para tres?**	Eye oon-a me-sa pa-ra tres
We'd like a table where there is room for a wheelchair	**Queríamos una mesa con sitio para una silla de ruedas**	Ke-**ree**-a-mos oo-na me-sa con see-tyo pa-ra oo-na see-llya de rwe-das
Do you have a high chair?	**¿Tienen una trona/ silla para niño?**	Tee-e-nen oo-na tro-na/ see-llya pa-ra nee-nyo
Is there a table	**¿Hay mesa**	Eye me-sa
in a corner?	**en un rincón?**	en oon reen-**kon**
on the terrace?	**en la terraza?**	en la ter-ra-tha
by the window?	**junto a la ventana?**	hoon-to a la ben-ta-na
We are in a (great) hurry	**Tenemos (mucha) prisa**	Te-ne-mos (moo-cha) pree-sa
This way, please	***Por aquí, por favor**	Por a-**kee**, por fa-bor
We shall have a table free in about half an hour	***Habrá mesa dentro de una media hora**	A-**bra** me-sa den-tro de me-dya o-ra
You will have to wait about . . . minutes	***Tendrán que esperar unos . . . minutos**	Ten-**dran** ke es-pe-rar oon-os . . . mee-noo-tos

We don't serve lunch until 1 p.m.[1]	*La comida no se sirve hasta la una	La ko-mee-da no se seer-be as-ta la oon-a
We don't serve dinner until 9 p.m.	*No se sirven cenas hasta las nueve	No se seer-ben then-as as-ta las nwe-be
Last orders at four o'clock	*La cocina se cierra a las cuatro	La ko-thee-na se thee-er-ra a las kwa-tro
Do you serve snacks?[2]	¿Sirven platos combinados/ bocadillos/pinchos?	Seer-ben pla-tos kom-bee-na-dos/bo-ka-dee-llyos/peen-chos
I am a vegetarian	Soy vegetariano	Soy ve-he-ta-rya-no
I am allergic to gluten/nuts/dairy products	Soy alérgico al gluten/a los frutos secos/a los lácteos	Soy a-**ler**-hee-ko al gloo-ten/a los froo-tos se-cos/a los lak-te-os
Does this dish contain/is it made with dairy products/ nuts/wheat?	¿Este plato lleva/está hecho con lácteos/ frutos secos/trigo?	Es-te plat-o llye-ba/es-**ta** e-cho kon **lak**-te-os/ froo-tos se-cos/gloo-ten
Sorry, the kitchen is closed	*Lo siento la cocina está cerrada	Lo see-en-to la ko-thee-na es-**ta** ther-ra-da

1. In Spain lunch is usually served from 1 p.m. to 4 p.m.; dinner from 8 p.m. to 11 p.m. Lunch is the main meal of the day and traditionally consists of two courses. Bars and cafés usually stay open until about 2 a.m.

2. A *plato combinado* is an 'everything on a plate' dish. It consists of a serving of various types of meat, vegetables, fish, eggs, etc., in different combinations. *Bocadillos* (baguette-like bread filled with cold meats, omelette, cheese, tuna, etc.) are more substantial than English sandwiches. *Pinchos* and *tapas* are quite substantial side dishes or hors d'œuvres which can make a meal in themselves. *Tapas* are usually eaten at the bar, served with a drink and shared.

Where is the lavatory?	¿Dónde están los servicios?	Don-de es-**tan** los sair-bee-thyos
It is downstairs/ upstairs	*Están abajo/arriba	Es-**tan** a-ba-ho/ar-ree-ba
It is at the end on the right/on the left	*Están al fondo a la derecha/a la izquierda	Es-**tan** al fon-do a la de-re-cha/a la eeth-kyair-da

Ordering

service (not) included	servicio (no) incluido	sair-bee-thyo (no) een-kloo-ee-do
waiter/waitress	camarero/camarera	ka-ma-rair-ro/ ka-ma-rair-ra
May I see the menu, please?	El menú/la carta, por favor	El me-**noo**/la kar-ta, por fa-bor
May I see the wine list, please?	La carta de vinos, por favor	La kar-ta de bee-nos por fa-bor
Is there a set menu?[1]	Tienen menú del día?	Tee-e-nen me-**noo** del **dee**-a
I'll have the 15 euro menu/today's special	Tomaré el menú de 15 euros/el especial de hoy	To-ma-**re** el me-**noo** de keen-thai ai-oo-ros/el es-pe-thyal de oy
I want something light	Quiero algo ligero/ algo para picar	Kee-er-o al-go lee-he-ro/ al-go pa-ra pee-kar

1. The *menú del día/cubierto* is the all-in price of a meal, usually including wine, bread and dessert. Service is always included, though it is customary to leave a small tip. There is no cover charge in Spanish restaurants.

Is there a children's menu?	¿Tienen menú infantil?	Tee-e-nen me-**noo** een-fan-teel
What is your dish of the day?	¿Cuál es el plato del día?	Kwal es el pla-to del **dee**-a
What do you recommend?	¿Qué me recomienda?	Kay may re-ko-mee-en-da
Can you tell me what this is?	¿Por favor, qué es ésto?	Por fa-bor kay es es-to
What is the speciality of the restaurant?	¿Cuál es la especialidad de la casa?	Kwal es la es-pe-thee-a-lee-dad de la ka-sa
What is the speciality of the region?	¿Cuál es el plato típico de la región?	Kwal es el pla-to **tee**-pee-ko de la ray-**hyon**
Do you have any local dishes/vegetarian dishes?	¿Tiene algún plato típico/vegetariano?	Tee-e-ne al-**goon** pla-to **tee**-pee-ko/be-he-ta-ree-a-no
What local dishes should we try?	¿Que platos típicos nos recomienda probar?	Kay plat-os **tee**-pee-kos nos re-co-mee-en-da pro-bar?
Would you like to try...?	*¿Quiere probar...?	Kee-e-re pro-bar
There's no more...	*No quedan...	No ke-dan
I'd like	Quiero	Kee-e-ro
as the first course	de primero	de pree-me-ro
as the main course	de segundo/plato principal	de se-goon-do/pla-to preen-thee-pal
for starters/to share	para picar	pa-ra pee-kar
as the side dish	para acompañar	pa-ra a-kom-pa-nyar

Is it hot or cold?	¿Es este plato caliente o frío?	Es es-te pla-to ka-lee-en-te o **free**-o
Without oil/sauce, please	Sin aceite/sin salsa, por favor	Seen a-thay-te/ seen sal-sa por fa-bor
Some more bread, please	Más pan, por favor	Mas pan por fa-bor
Salt and pepper/ napkins, please	Sal y pimienta/ servilletas, por favor	Sal ee pee-mee-en-ta/ sair-bee-llye-tas por fa-bor
Oil and vinegar, please	Aceite y vinagre, por favor	A-thay-te ee bee-na-gre por fa-bor
How would you like the meat cooked?	*¿Cómo le gusta la carne?	Ko-mo le goos-ta la kar-ne
Rare/medium/well done	Poco hecha/al punto/muy hecha	Po-ko e-cha/al poon-to/ mwee e-cha
Would you like all the dishes at the same time?	*¿Quiere que sirvamos todo al mismo tiempo?	Kee-e-re ke seer-ba-mos to-do al mees-mo tee-em-po
Would you like a dessert?	*¿Quiere algo de postre?	Kee-e-re al-go de pos-tre
Something to drink?	*¿Y para beber?	Ee pa-ra bai-bair
Is there a locally grown wine?	¿Hay algún vino de por aquí?	Eye al-**goon** bee-no de por a-**kee**
A bottle/half of the	Una/media botella de	Oo-na/me-dya bo-te-llya de
house red	tinto de la casa	teen-to de la ka-sa
house rosé	rosado de la casa	ro-sa-do de la ka-sa
house white	blanco de la casa	blan-ko de la ka-sa
house wine	vino de la casa	bee-no de la ka-sa

A jug of tap water	**Una jarra de agua del grifo**	Oo-na har-ra de a-gwa del gree-fo
A bottle of mineral water	**Una botella de agua mineral**	Oo-na bo-te-llya de a-gwa mee-nai-ral
Would you like anything else?	*¿Desean alguna cosa más?**	De-sai-an al-goo-na co-sa mas
Is everything all right?	*¿Está todo bien?**	Es-ta to-do bee-en

Paying

The bill, please	**La cuenta, por favor**	La kwen-ta por fa-bor
Please check the bill – I don't think it's correct	**Revise la cuenta, por favor; creo que no está bien**	Re-bee-se la kwen-ta por fa-bor; kre-o ke no es-ta bee-en
What is this amount for?	**¿De qué es esta cantidad?**	De kay es es-ta kan-tee-dad
I didn't have soup	**No he tomado sopa**	No ay tom-a-do so-pa
I had chicken, not lamb	**Tomé pollo y no cordero**	To-me po-llyo ee no kor-dair-o
May we have separate bills?	**¿Puede darnos la cuenta por separado?**	Pwe-de dair-nos la kwen-ta por se-pa-ra-do
Is service included?	**¿El servicio está incluido?**	El sair-bee-thyo es-ta een-kloo-ee-do
Can I pay with a credit card?	**¿Puedo pagar con tarjeta de crédito?**	Pwe-do pa-gar kon tar-he-ta de kre-dee-to
Keep the change	**Quédese el cambio**	Ke-de-se el kam-byo

Compliments

We enjoyed it, thank you	**Gracias, nos ha gustado mucho**	Grath-yass nos a goos-ta-do moo-cho
That was a good meal, thank you	**La comida estaba muy buena gracias**	La ko-mee-da es-ta-ba mwee bwe-na grath-yass
The food was delicious	**Estaba todo delicioso/buenísimo**	Es-ta-ba to-do de-lee-thee-o-so/bwen-**nee**-see-mo
We particularly liked ...	**Nos ha encantado sobre todo ...**	Nos a en-kan-ta-do so-bre to-do

Complaints

We have been waiting a long time for our drinks	**Llevamos mucho tiempo esperando las bebidas**	Llye-ba-mos moo-cho tee-em-po es-pe-ran-do las bai-bee-das
Why is the food taking so long?	**¿Por qué tardan tanto en servir la comida?**	Por kay tar-dan tan-to en sair-beer la com-ee-da
This isn't what I ordered, I want ...	**Esto no es lo que he pedido, yo quería ...**	Es-to no es lo kay ay ped-ee-do yo ke-**ree**-a
This is	**Esto está**	Es-to es-**ta**
bad	**malo (no está bueno)**	ma-lo (no es-**ta** bwe-no)
overcooked	**demasiado hecho**	de-ma-see-a-do e-cho
salty	**salado**	sa-la-do
stale	**pasado**	pa-sa-do

too cold	**demasiado frío**	de-ma-see-a-do **free**-o
tough	**duro**	doo-ro
undercooked	**poco hecho**	po-ko e-cho
This isn't fresh	**Esto no es fresco**	Es-to no es fres-ko
This plate/knife/ glass is not clean	**Este plato/cuchillo/ vaso no está limpio**	Es-te pla-to/koo-chee-llyo/ba-so no es-**ta** leem-pyo
This spoon is not clean	**Esta cuchara no está limpia**	Es-ta koo-cha-ra no es-**ta** leem-pya
I'd like to see the owner	**Quiero ver al dueño**	Kee-e-ro bair al dwe-nyo
Can you bring me a new one, please	**Tráigame otro, por favor**	Tra-ee-ga-mai o-tro por fa-bor

Breakfast and Tea

breakfast (to have)	**desayunar**	des-a-you-nar
breakfast	**el desayuno**	des-a-you-no
tea (afternoon meal)	**la merienda**	me-ree-en-da
an American coffee	**un café americano**	ka-**fe** a-mai-ree-ka-no
a black coffee	**un café solo**	ka-**fe** so-lo
a black coffee with a little milk	**un cortado**	kor-ta-do
decaffeinated coffee	**el descafeinado de máquina**	des-ka-fay-na-do de ma-**kee**-na
iced coffee	**el café con hielo**	ka-**fe** con ee-e-lo

a large white coffee	un café con leche grande	ka-fe kon le-che gran-de
chamomile tea	la manzanilla	man-than-ee-llya
China tea	el té chino	tay chee-no
a herbal tea	una infusión	een-foo-syon
iced tea[1]	el té con hielo	tay kon ee-e-lo
Indian tea	el té indio	tay een-dee-o
mint tea	la menta poleo	main-ta po-le-o
regular tea (nothing added)	el té solo	tay so-lo
tea with (cold) milk/lemon	un té con leche (fría)/limón	tay kon le-che (free-a)/lee-mon
I would like a herb tea	Quiero una infusión de hierbas	Kee-e-ro oon-a een-foo-syon de ee-er-bas
Which herb teas do you have?	¿Qué infusiones tienen?	Kay en-foo-syo-nes tee-e-nen
May we have some sugar, please?	Azúcar, por favor	A-thoo-kar por fa-bor
Do you have sweeteners?	¿Tiene sacarina?	Tee-e-ne sa-ka-ree-na
bread and butter	pan y mantequilla	pan ee man-te-kee-llya
toast	las tostadas	tos-ta-das
toast with olive oil	las tostadas con aceite	tos-ta-das kon a-thay-te
toast with jam	las tostadas con mermelada	tos-ta-das kon mair-me-la-da

1. Except in specialized outlets, there is little culture of tea drinking and tea varieties are not so easy to come by.

More butter, please	**Más mantequilla, por favor**	Mas man-te-kee-llya por fa-bor
Have you some jam?	**¿Tienen mermelada?**	Tee-e-nen mair-me-la-da
a soft-boiled egg	**un huevo pasado por agua**	oon we-bo pa-sa-do por a-gwa
a hard-boiled egg	**un huevo cocido**	oon we-bo ko-thee-do
a fried egg	**un huevo frito**	oon we-bo free-to
scrambled eggs	**los huevos revueltos**	we-bos re-bwel-tos
What fruit juices do you have?	**¿Qué zumos de frutas tienen?**	Kay thoo-mos de froo-tas tee-e-nen
orange/grapefruit/ tomato juice	**el zumo de naranja/ pomelo/tomate**	thoo-mo de na-ran-ha/ po-me-lo/to-mat-e
Help yourself at the buffet	***Sírvase usted mismo**	**Seer**-ba-se oos-tay mees-mo
cake	**el pastel/la tarta**	pas-tel/tar-ta
cereal	**los cereales**	thay-ray-a-les
doughnut-type pastries	**los churros**	choor-ros
fresh fruit	**la fruta**	froo-ta
honey	**la miel**	mee-el
chocolate milk	**el cacao con leche**	ka-ka-o kon lai-che
hot chocolate (thick)	**el chocolate**	cho-ko-la-te
hot chocolate with doughnut-type pastries	**el chocolate con churros**	cho-ko-la-te kon choor-ros
hot/cold milk	**leche caliente/fría**	le-che kal-yen-te/**free**-a
pastries	**bollería**	bo-llye-**ree**-a

yogourt	el yogur	yo-goor
Do you have ice creams or sorbets?	**¿Tienen helados o sorbetes?**	Tee-e-nen e-la-dos o sor-bay-tes
What flavours would you like?	*¿Qué sabores quiere?	Kay sa-bo-res kee-e-re
We have chocolate/vanilla/strawberry/pistachio/lemon	*Tenemos de chocolate/vainilla/fresa/pistacho/limón	Te-ne-mos de cho-ko-la-te/va-ee-nee-llya/fray-sa/pees-ta-cho/lee-**mon**

Dulces (Sweets)[1]

almendrado	macaroon
buñuelos	fritters
mantecado	enriched ice cream
mazapán	marzipan
merengue	meringue
turrón	kind of nougat
yemas	candied egg yolks

Drinks[2]

bar	el bar	bar
café	el café/la cafetería	ka-**fe**/ka-fe-tai-**ree**-a
What will you have to drink?	*¿Qué quieren beber?	Kay kee-er-en be-bair

1. These sweets are usually served with coffee on special occasions.
2. For the names of beverages, see p. 110–113, 135.

A bottle of the local wine	**Una botella de vino de la tierra**	Oon-a bo-te-llya de bee-no de la tee-er-ra
The wine list, please	**La carta de vinos, por favor**	La kar-ta de bee-nos por fa-bor
carafe/glass	**la jarra/el vaso**	har-ra/ba-so
bottle/half bottle	**la botella/la media botella**	bo-te-llya/me-dya bo-te-llya
good quality wine	**el vino de marca**	bee-no de mar-ka
vintage wine	**el vino de reserva**	bee-no de re-sair-ba
sherry	**el vino de jerez**	bee-no de he-**rez**
light, delicate	**fino**	fee-no
rich, dry	**amontillado**	a-mon-tee-llya-do
very rich	**oloroso**	o-lor-o-so
A glass of red/white/rosé wine	**Un vino tinto/blanco/rosado**	Oon bee-no teen-to/blank-o/ro-sa-do
A small glass of wine	**Un chato**	Oon chat-o
Three glasses of beer, please	**Tres cervezas, por favor**	Tres thair-be-thas por fa-bor
Do you have draught beer?	**¿Tienen cerveza de barril?**	Tee-en-en thair-be-tha de bar-reel
Two more beers	**Dos cervezas más**	Dos thair-be-thas mas
A small draught beer	**Una caña**	Oo-na ka-nya
Do you serve cocktails?	**¿Tienen cocktails?**	Tee-e-nen kok-te-les
Do you have a cocktail list?	**¿Tienen carta de cocktails?**	Tee-e-nen kar-ta de kok-te-les

soft drinks	**los refrescos**	re-fres-kos
What smoothies do you have?	**¿Qué batidos naturales tienen?**	Kay ba-tee-dos na-too-ra-les tee-e-nen
I'd like	**Quiero un**	Kee-e-ro oon
an apple juice	**zumo de manzana**	thoo-mo de man-tha-na
a fruit juice	**zumo de frutas**	thoo-mo de froo-tas
an iced lemon drink	**granizado de limón**	gra-nee-tha-dode lee-**mon**
a milk shake	**batido de leche**	ba-tee-do de le-che
an orange juice	**zumo de naranja**	thoo-mo de na-ran-ha
a soft drink with ice/without ice	**refresco con hielo/ sin hielo**	re-fres-ko kon ee-e-lo/ seen ee-e-lo
I'd like another glass of water, please	**Otro vaso de agua, por favor**	O-tro ba-so de a-gwa por fa-bor
mineral water (still/fizzy)	**el agua mineral (sin gas/con gas)**	a-gwa meen-e-ral (seen gas/kon gas)
neat/on the rocks	**solo/con hielo**	so-lo/kon ee-e-lo
with soda water	**con soda**	kon so-da
ice (cubes)	**(los cubitos de) hielo**	(koo-bee-tos de) ee-e-lo
Cheers!	**¡Salud!**	Sa-lood
The same again	**Lo mismo**	Lo mees-mo

Quick Meals and Snacks

What is there to eat?	**¿Qué tienen para picar?**	Kay tee-e-nen pa-ra peek-ar
What can you suggest that won't take long?	**¿Qué tienen de comer que tarde poco?**	Kay tee-e-nen de ko-mair kay tar-de po-ko
I only want a snack/something quick	**Sólo quiero picar algo/quiero algo rápido**	So-lo kee-e-ro peek-ar al-go/kee-e-ro al-go ra-pee-do
Is it to eat here or to take away?	***¿Para tomar aquí o para llevar?**	Pa-ra to-mar a-kee o pa-ra llye-bar
It's to take away	**Es para llevar**	Es pa-ra llye-bar
Go bar hopping	**Ir de tapas**	Eer de ta-pas
What sandwiches do you have?	**¿De qué tienen bocadillos?**	De kay tee-e-nen bo-ka-dee-llyos
A ... sandwich	**Un bocadillo de**	Oon bo-ka-dee-llyo de
cheese	**queso**	ke-so
cooked ham	**jamón de york**	ham-on de york
cured ham	**jamón serrano/ibérico**	ham-on sair-ra-no/ee-be-ree-ko
pâté	**paté**	pa-tai
salami	**salchichón**	sal-chee-chon
tuna	**atún**	at-oon
A toasted ham and cheese sandwich	**Un sandwich tostado de jamón y queso**	Oon sandwich tos-ta-do de ham-on ee ke-so

I'd like a sandwich with/without butter	Un sandwich con/sin mantequilla	Oon sandwich kon/seen man-te-kee-llya
I'm sorry, we've run out	*Lo siento, no nos queda	Lo see-en-to no nos ke-da
What are those things over there?	¿Qué es eso de ahí?	Kay es es-o de eye-ee
What are they made of?	¿De qué está hecho?	De kay es-ta e-cho
What is in them?	¿Qué tiene dentro?	Kay tee-e-ne den-tro
I'll have one of those, please	Uno de esos, por favor	Oo-no de e-sos por fa-bor
A portion of . . .	Una ración de . . .	Oo-na ra-thyon de
A small portion of . . .	Una tapa de . . .	Oo-na ta-pa de
biscuits	las galletas	ga-llye-tas
bread	el pan	pan
cheese	el queso	ke-so
chips	una (ración) de patatas fritas	oo-na (ra-thyon) de pa-ta-tas free-tas
chocolate bar	la chocolatina	cho-ko-la-tee-na
cold cuts	las fiambres	fee-am-bres
cold meats	los embutidos	em-boo-tee-dos
eggs	los huevos	we-bos
ice cream	el helado	e-la-do
light meals	los platos ligeros/los pinchos	pla-tos lee-he-ros/peen-chos

meatballs	**las albóndigas**	al-**bon**-dee-gas
omelette (plain)	**la tortilla francesa**	tor-tee-llya fran-thai-sa
cheese omelette	**la tortilla de queso**	tor-tee-llya de ke-so
Spanish omelette	**la tortilla de patata**	tor-tee-llya de pa-ta-ta
pancake	**el crepe**	krep
pasties (filled with meat or fish)	**las empanadillas**	em-pa-na-dee-llyas
pastries	**las empanadas**	em-pa-na-das
peanuts	**los cacahuetes**	ka-ka-wet-es
roll	**el panecillo/el bollo**	pa-ne-thee-llyo/bo-llyo
waffle	**el gofre**	goh-fre
warm baguette sandwich	**el bocadillo caliente**	bo-ka-dee-llyo ka-lee-en-te

Restaurant Vocabulary

artificial sweetener	**la sacarina**	sa-ka-ree-na
ashtray	**el cenicero**	then-ee-thair-o
beer	**la cerveza**	thair-be-tha
bill	**la cuenta**	kwen-ta
bread	**el pan**	pan
butter	**la mantequilla**	man-te-kee-llya
cloakroom	**el guardarropa**	gwar-dar-ro-pa
coffee	**el café**	ka-fe

course/dish	**el plato**	pla-to
cup	**la taza**	ta-tha
dessert	**el postre**	pos-tray
dish of the day	**el plato del día**	pla-to del **dee**-a
fork	**el tenedor**	te-ne-dor
glass	**el vaso**	ba-so
hungry (to be)	**tener hambre**	te-nair am-bre
jug of tap water	**la jarra de agua**	har-ra de a-gwa
knife	**el cuchillo**	koo-chee-llyo
lemon	**el limón**	lee-**mon**
matches	**las cerillas**	the-ree-llyas
mayonnaise	**la mayonesa**	ma-yo-ne-sa
menu	**el menú/la carta**	me-**noo**/kar-ta
mustard	**la mostaza**	mos-ta-tha
napkin	**la servilleta**	sair-bee-llye-ta
oil	**el aceite**	a-thay-te
pepper (spice)	**la pimienta**	pee-mee-en-ta
plate	**el plato**	pla-to
restaurant	**el restaurante**	res-tow-ran-te
salt	**la sal**	sal
sauce	**la salsa**	sal-sa
service	**el servicio**	sair-bee-thyo
set menu	**el menú del día**	me-**noo** del **dee**-a

spoon	**la cuchara**	koo-cha-ra
sugar	**el azúcar**	a-**thoo**-kar
table	**la mesa**	me-sa
tablecloth	**el mantel**	man-tel
thirsty (to be)	**tener sed**	te-nair sed
tip	**la propina**	pro-pee-na
toothpick	**el palillo**	pal-ee-llyo
tomato ketchup	**el ketchup**	ket-choop
tray	**la bandeja**	ban-de-ha
vegetarian	**vegetariano**	be-he-ta-ree-a-no
vinegar	**el vinagre**	bee-na-gray
waiter	**el camarero**	ka-ma-rair-o
waitress	**la camarera**	ka-ma-rair-a
water	**el agua**	a-gwa
wine	**el vino**	bee-no

THE MENU

Entremeses y Tapas[1]
Starters and Tapas

aceitunas / olives

alcachofas / artichokes

anchoas / anchovies

arenques / herring

boquerones/chanquetes / fresh anchovies

caracoles / snails

champiñones al ajillo / mushrooms in garlic sauce

chorizo / spicy red sausage

croquetas (de jamón, pollo, bacalao) / (ham, chicken, salt cod) croquettes

ensalada / green salad

ensaladilla rusa / potato salad

entremeses variados / mixed hors d'œuvres

espárragos / asparagus

1. *Tapas* are small servings of what may usually be upgraded to a bigger portion (*ración*) and/or to a full main course. *Tapas* can be ordered in most Spanish bars to accompany drinks and are displayed at the bar. Look at what is available and make your choice. In restaurants, it is also common to share *tapas* for starters.

fiambres / cold cuts

gambas / prawns

gambas a la plancha / grilled prawns

gambas al ajillo / garlic prawns

huevos rellenos / stuffed eggs

jamón de york / boiled ham

jamón serrano/ibérico / cured ham

mejillones rellenos (tigres) / stuffed, breaded and deep-fried mussels

melón / melon

mojama / dried cured fish

morcilla / black pudding

ostras / oysters

pan / bread

patatas bravas / potato wedges in spicy sauce

percebes / goose barnacles

pimientos de piquillo / red piquillo peppers

pincho moruno / spicy meat chunks on a skewer

pulpo a la gallega / octopus in olive oil and paprika sauce

quisquillas / shrimps

salchichón / salami

sardinas / sardines

tortilla de patata / Spanish omelette

Sopas / Soup

caldo/consomé / consommé

caldo de gallina / chicken consommé

cocido madrileño / meat and vegetable soup/stew

consomé al jerez / consommé with sherry

gazpacho / cold soup of tomatoes, cucumber, olive oil, garlic, etc.

sopa de ajo / garlic soup with bread, egg and meat

sopa de fideos / noodle soup

sopa de gallina / chicken soup

sopa de mariscos / shellfish soup

sopa de pescado / fish soup

sopa de verduras / vegetable soup

Pescados y Mariscos / Fish and Shellfish[1]

almejas / clams

anguilas / baby eels

atún/bonito / fresh tuna

bacalao / (dried) cod

bacalao a la vizcaína / cod stewed with olive oil, peppers, onion and tomatoes

1. These may be ordered as either a tapa or a main dish.

bacalao al pil-pil / cod stewed in a thick, rich sauce

besugo / sea bream

calamares / squid

calamares a la romana / squid fried in batter

calamares en su tinta / squid cooked in its own ink

cangrejo (de mar) / crab

cangrejo (de río) / crayfish

centolla/centollo / spider crab

chipirones / baby squid

chopitos / battered baby squid

cigalas / crayfish

gambas / prawns

langosta / lobster

langostinos / king prawns

lenguado / sole

mariscos / seafood

mejillones / mussels

merluza / hake

mero / grouper

ostras / oysters

pescadito frito / mixed fried fish

pez espada / swordfish

pulpo / octopus

quisquillas / shrimps

rape / monkfish

raya / skate

rodaballo / turbot

salmón / salmon

salmonete / red mullet

sardinas a la plancha / sardines 'grilled' on the hot plate

sardinas en escabeche / pickled sardines

sepia / cuttlefish

vieiras / scallops

zarzuela de pescados/de mariscos / fish/seafood in a sauce of tomatoes, onions, garlic, bay leaves, olive oil and wine

Carne / Meat

albóndigas / meatballs

bacón / bacon

bistec / beef steak

butifarra / Catalan pork sausage

cabrito / kid

callos / tripe

cerdo / pork

chorizo / sausage made from spiced, cured pig meat

chuleta / chop, cutlet

chuletillas / baby lamb chops

chuletón / T-bone steak

cochinillo / suckling pig

cola de buey / oxtail

cordero / lamb

embutidos / cold meats, cold cuts

entrecot / entrecôte steak

escalope / escalope

estofado / stew

fabada / black pudding, chorizo and bean stew

filete / fillet steak

hígado / liver

jamón / ham

lacón con grelos / shoulder of pork with turnip tops

lechazo / baby lamb

lengua / tongue

lomo / loin of pork

mollejas / sweetbreads

morcilla / black pudding

pote gallego / hotpot

riñones (al jerez) / kidneys (with sherry)

salchichas / sausages

sesos (fritos) / brains (fried)

solomillo de cerdo / pork fillet

solomillo de ternera / fillet steak

ternera / veal

tostón / suckling pig

vaca / beef

Aves y Caza / Poultry and Game

carne de venado / venison

codornices / quail

conejo / rabbit

faisán / pheasant

ganso / goose

jabalí / boar

liebre / hare

pato / duck

pavo / turkey

pechuga de pollo / chicken breast

perdiz / partridge

pichones / pigeons

pollo / chicken

Arroz / Rice

arroz a la cubana / rice, fried egg, banana and tomato sauce (Cuban style)

arroz caldoso / soupy paella

arroz catalana / rice with pork, spicy sausages and fish

arroz con azafrán / saffron rice

arroz negro / rice with seafood in squid ink sauce

fideuá / short thin noodles with seafood (paella style)

paella marinera / saffron rice with seafood

paella valenciana / saffron rice with chicken, green beans and seafood

pollo con arroz / rice with chicken

Legumbres y Verduras / Vegetables and Salads

ajo / garlic

alcachofa / artichoke

alubias / beans

apio / celery

berenjena / aubergine, eggplant

cebolla / onion

champiñón / cultivated mushroom

coles de bruselas / Brussels sprouts

coliflor / cauliflower

escarola / endive

espárragos / asparagus

espinacas / spinach

garbanzos / chickpeas

guisantes / peas

habas / broad beans

judías verdes / green beans

lechuga / lettuce

lentejas / lentils

nabo / turnip

patata / potato

pepino / cucumber

perejil / parsley

pimiento (rojo/verde) / pepper (red/green)

puerro / leek

rábano / radish

remolacha / beetroot

repollo / cabbage

seta / mushroom

tomate / tomato

zanahoria / carrot

Huevos / Eggs

cocidos/duros / hard-boiled

escalfados / poached

fritos / fried

huevos a la flamenca / eggs baked with onion, tomato and ham

pasados por agua / soft-boiled

revueltos / scrambled

tortilla de champiñones / mushroom omelette

tortilla de espárragos / asparagus omelette

tortilla de habas / broad bean omelette

tortilla de patata / Spanish omelette

tortilla francesa / plain omelette

Quesos / Cheese

burgos / soft creamy cheese from Burgos

cabrales / strong cheese made from ewe's milk

mahón / fairly bland hard cheese from Menorca

manchego / hard cheese made from ewe's milk in La Mancha

tabla de quesos / cheese board

Postres / Desserts

arroz con leche / rice pudding

cuajada / sweet milk curd

flan / crème caramel

fresas con nata / strawberries and cream

fruta del tiempo / fresh fruit

helado/sorbete / ice cream/sorbet

   de café / coffee

   de chocolate / chocolate

   de fresa / strawberry

   de la casa / home-made

   de vainilla / vanilla

macedonia / fruit salad

melocotón en almibar / peaches in syrup

natillas / Spanish custard

nueces con miel / walnuts in honey sauce

nueces con nata / walnuts and cream

tarta de frutas (de manzana, de plátano, de pera, de almendra, etc.) /
fruit tart/fruit cake (apple, banana, pear, almond, etc.)

tarta de queso / cheese tart/cheesecake

tarta helada / ice-cream cake

Frutas y Frutos Secos /
Fruits and Nuts

albaricoque / apricot

almendra / almond

avellana / hazelnut

cereza / cherry

chirimoya / custard apple

ciruela / plum

dátiles / dates

fresa / strawberry

higo / fig

lima / lime

limón / lemon

manzana / apple

melocotón / peach

membrillo / quince

naranja / orange

níspero / loquat

nueces / walnuts

pasas / raisins

pera / pear

piña / pineapple

plátano / banana

pomelo / grapefruit

sandía / watermelon

toronja / grapefruit

uvas / grapes

Some Cooking Methods and Sauces

a la brasa, a la barbacoa / barbecued

a la cazuela / stewed

a la marinera / with seafood sauce

a la parrilla, a la plancha / grilled on the hot plate

a la romana / fried in batter

a la vasca / with parsley, garlic and peas

adobado, en adobo / marinated in paprika

ahumado / smoked

al ajillo / cooked in oil and garlic

al horno / cooked in the oven, baked, roasted

al vapor / steamed

asado / roast, baked

caliente / hot

carne / meat

    poco hecha / rare

    en su punto / medium

    muy hecha / well-done

casero / home-made

cocido / boiled

con perejil / with parsley

con tomates y pimientos verdes / with tomatoes and green peppers

crudo / raw

empanado / breaded, in breadcrumbs

en aceite / in oil

en escabeche / marinated in oil and vinegar

en salsa verde / with parsley and garlic sauce

escalfado / poached

frío / cold

frito / fried

gratinado / finished under the grill

guisado, estofado / braised, stewed

macerado / marinated

mantequilla / butter

mostaza / mustard

rebozado / fried in batter

relleno / stuffed

salsa alioli / oil and garlic sauce

salsa mahonesa / mayonnaise

salsa romesco / sauce made of tomatoes, garlic and hot peppers

salsa vinagreta / vinaigrette

Bebidas / Drinks

agua / water

agua mineral con gas / sparkling mineral water

agua mineral sin gas / still mineral water

anís / anisette

batido de leche / milk shake

café / coffee

cava / sparkling wine

cerveza / beer

   de barril / draught

   de botella/en botellín / bottled

   de lata / in a can

   negra / dark

chocolate a la taza / hot chocolate

coñac / brandy

gaseosa / fizzy drink, lemonade

ginebra / gin

horchata / cold drink made from *chufa* root (tiger nut)

infusiones / herbal teas

leche / milk

limonada / lemonade

manzanilla / chamomile

menta-poleo / mint tea

mosto / sweet grape juice

naranjada / orangeade

refrescos / fizzy drinks, soft drinks

ron / rum

sangría / red wine mixed with lemonade (or champagne), served with ice cubes and slices of lemon and orange

sidra / cider

té / tea

tila / lime (blossom) tea

vino / wine

blanco / white

dulce / sweet

espumoso / sparkling

rosado / rosé

seco / dry

tinto / red

zumos de frutas / fruit juices

de manzana / apple juice

de melocotón / peach juice

de naranja / orange juice

de piña / pineapple juice

de pomelo / grapefruit juice

de tomate / tomato juice

de uva / grape juice

EMERGENCIES[1]

Key Phrases		
112	is the general phone number for all emergencies (police, ambulance, fire brigade, etc.). The operator will connect callers to the right services and/or deal with the emergency.	
091	is the phone number for the national police.	
092	is the phone number for the local police.	
Help!	**¡Socorro!/¡Auxilio!**	So-kor-roh/Aw-see-lyo
Help me!	**¡Ayúdenme!**	A-**yoo**-den-may
Danger!	**¡Peligro!**	Pe-lee-gro
Where's the police station?	**¿Dónde está la comisaría?**	Don-de es-**ta** la ko-mee-sa-**ree**-a
Call a doctor	**Llame a un médico**	Llya-me a oon **me**-dee-ko
Call an ambulance	**Llame una ambulancia**	Llya-me oon-a am-boo-lan-thya
Where is the nearest hospital/A&E?	**¿Dónde está el hospital más cercano?/¿Dónde está Urgencias?**	Don-de es-**ta** el os-pee-tal mas thair-ka-no/ Don-de es-**ta** oor-hen-thyas
My son/daughter is lost	**Se me ha perdido mi hijo/hija**	Se may a pair-dee-do mee ee-ho/ee-ha

1. For car breakdown see p. 39. For problems with a house rental see p. 86.

Call the police	Llame a la policía	Llya-me a la po-lee-**thee**-a
Where is the British consulate?	¿Dónde está el consulado inglés?	Don-de es-**ta** el kon-soo-la-do een-**gles**
Please let the consulate know	Pónganse en contacto con el consulado	**Pon**-gan-se en kon-tak-to kon el kon-soo-la-do
I want to speak to someone from the embassy	Quisiera hablar con la embajada	Kee-see-ay-ra a-blar kon la em-ba-ha-da
I want a lawyer who speaks English	Necesito un abogado que hable inglés	Ne-the-see-to un ab-o-ga-do ke a-bleh een-**gles**
It's urgent	Es urgente	Es oor-hen-te
It's an emergency	Es una emergencia	Es oo-na e-mer-hen-thya
Can you help me?	¿Puede ayudarme?	Pwe-de a-yoo-dar-me
Can anybody help me?	¿Alguien puede ayudarme?	Alg-yen pwe-de a-yoo-dar-me

Accidents[1]

A&E	Urgencias	Oor-hen-thyas
emergency exit	salida de emergencia	sa-lee-da de e-mer-hen-thya
fire brigade	los bomberos	bomb-ai-ros
fire extinguisher	el extintor	es-teen-tor
lifeguard	el salvavidas	sal-ba-bee-das
paramedics	los enfermeros/ los paramédicos	en-phair-mai-ros/ pa-ra-**med**-ee-kos
police	la policía	po-lee-**thee**-a

1. See also DOCTOR p. 149.

Call a doctor	**Llame a un médico**	Llya-me a oon **me**-dee-ko
Call an ambulance	**Llame una ambulancia**	Llya-me oon-a am-boo-lan-thya
Where is the nearest hospital/A&E?	**¿Dónde está el hospital más cercano?/¿Dónde está Urgencias?**	Don-de es-**ta** el os-pee-tal mas thair-ka-no/Don-de es-**ta** oor-hen-thyas
There has been an accident	**Ha habido un accidente**	A ab-ee-do oon ak-thee-den-te
We've had an accident	**Hemos tenido un accidente**	E-mos te-nee-do oon ak-thee-den-te
Is anyone hurt?	*¿Hay algún herido?	Eye al-**goon** e-ree-do
Do you need help?	*¿Necesitan ayuda?	Ne-the-see-tan a-yoo-da
Help him first	**Atiéndale a él primero**	A-tee-**end**-al-ay a el pre-may-ro
He's badly hurt	**Está gravemente herido/muy mal**	Es-**ta** gra-be-men-te e-ree-do/mwee mal
He has fainted	**Se ha desmayado**	Se a des-ma-ya-do
He's losing blood	**Está perdiendo sangre**	Es-**ta** pair-dee-en-do san-gre
Her arm is broken	**Tiene el brazo roto**	Tee-e-neel bra-tho ro-to
Please get some water/a blanket/some bandages	**(Traiga) agua/una manta/vendas, por favor**	(Tra-ee-ga) a-gwa/oon-a man-ta/ben-das por fa-bor
I've broken my glasses	**Se me han roto las gafas**	Se me an ro-to las ga-fas

I can't see	**No veo nada**	No bai-o na-da
A child has fallen in the water	**Se ha caído al agua un niño**	Se a ka-**ee**-do al a-gwa oon nee-nyo
A woman is drowning	**Se está ahogando una mujer**	Se es-**ta** a-o-gan-do oon-a moo-hair
There's a fire	**Hay fuego/un incendio**	Eye fwe-go/ oon een-then-dyo
I had an accident	**He tenido un accidente**	Ay ten-ee-do oon ak-thee-den-te
The other car hit my car	**El otro coche chocó con el mío**	El o-tro ko-che cho-**co** kon el **mee**-o
It was my fault/his fault	**Ha sido culpa mía/suya**	A see-do kul-pa **mee**-a/ soo-ya
I didn't understand the sign	**No entendía la señal**	No en-ten-**dee**-a la se-nyal
May I see your	***Quiero ver su (s)**	Kee-e-ro bair soo (s)
car rental documentation	**contrato del alquiler del coche**	kon-tra-to de al-kee-lair del ko-che
driving licence	**carnet de conducir**	kar-net de kon-doo-theer
insurance certificate	**póliza de seguros**	**po**-lee-tha de se-goo-ros
vehicle registration papers	**papeles del coche**	pa-pe-les del ko-che
What is the name and address of the owner?	***¿Nombre y dirección del propietario del coche?**	Nom-bre ee dee-rek-**thyon** del pro-pye-ta-ryo del ko-che
Are you willing to act as a witness?	**¿Está usted dispuesto a servir de testigo?**	Es-**ta** oos-te dees-pwes-to a ser-beer de tes-tee-go

Can I have your name and address, please?	*Su nombre y dirección, por favor	Soo nom-bre ee dee-rek-thyon por fa-bor
You must make a statement	*Tiene usted que declarar	Tee-e-ne oos-te kay de-kla-rar
I want a copy of the police report	Necesito una copia del informe de la policía	Ne-thai-see-to oo-na ko-pya del in-form-e de la po-lee-thee-a
You were speeding	*Iba usted por encima de la velocidad permitida	Ee-ba oos-te por en-thee-ma de la be-lo-thee-dad pair-mee-tee-da
How much is the fine?	¿Cuánto es la multa?	Kwan-to es la mool-ta

Lost Property

My luggage is missing	Mi equipaje ha desaparecido/Mis maletas no están	Mee e-kee-pa-he a dais-a-pa-re-thee-do/ Mees ma-le-tas no es-tan
Has my luggage been found yet?	¿Ya han encontrado mi equipaje?	Ya an en-kon-tra-do mee e-kee-pa-he
My luggage has been damaged/broken into	Me han estropeado la maleta/Me han abierto la maleta para robar	May an es-tro-pe-a-do la ma-le-ta/May an a-bee-air-to la ma-le-ta pa-ra ro-bar
I have lost	He perdido	Ay pair-dee-do
my luggage	el equipaje/ las maletas	el e-kee-pa-he/las ma-le-tas
my passport	el pasaporte	el pa-sa-por-te

my wallet	**la cartera**	la kar-te-ra
my credit card(s)	**la(s) tarjeta(s) de crédito**	la(s) tar-he-ta(s) de **kre**-dee-to
my (video) camera	**la cámara (de video)**	la **ka**-ma-ra (de vee-de-o)
my laptop/my tablet	**el (ordenador) portátil/la tableta**	el (or-dai-na-dor) por-ta-teel/la ta-ble-ta
my mobile phone	**el móvil**	el **mo**-beel
my keys	**las llaves**	las llya-bes
I've locked myself out (of the car/the flat)	**Me he dejado las llaves dentro (del coche/del apartamento)**	May ay de-ha-do las llya-bes den-tro (del ko-che/del a-part-a-ment-o)
Where is the lost property office?	**¿Dónde está la oficina de objetos perdidos?**	Don-de es-**ta** la o-fee-thee-na dob-he-tos pair-dee-dos
I found this in the street	**He encontrado esto en la calle**	Ay en-kon-tra-do es-to en la ka-llye

Missing Persons

My son/daughter is lost	**Se me ha perdido mi hijo/hija**	Se may a pair-dee-do mee ee-ho/ee-ha
He is ... years old, and wearing a blue shirt and shorts	**Tiene ... años y lleva camiseta azul y pantalones cortos**	Tee-e-ne ... a-nyos y llye-ba ka-mee-se-ta a-thool ee pan-ta-lo-nes kor-tos
This is his photo	**Esta es su foto**	Es-ta es soo fo-to

Could you help me find him?	**Por favor, ayúdeme a encontrarlo**	Por fa-bor a-**yoo**-de-may a en-kon-trar-lo
Have you seen a small girl with brown curly hair?	**¿Han visto una niña pequeña de pelo moreno rizado?**	An bees-to oo-na nee-nya pe-ke-nya de pe-lo mo-re-no ree-tha-do
I've lost my wife	**Se me ha perdido mi esposa**	Se may a pair-dee-do mee es-po-sa
Could you please ask for Sra . . . over the loudspeaker?	**¿Podría llamar a la Señora . . . por los altavoces?**	Po-**dree**-a llya-mar a la Se-nyo-ra . . . por los al-ta-bo-thes

Theft

I've been robbed/ mugged	**Me han robado**	May an ro-ba-do
Did you have any jewellery/valuables on you?	***¿Llevaba encima joyas u objetos de valor?**	Llye-ba-ba en-thee-ma ho-yas oo ob-he-tos de ba-lor
Were there any witnesses?	***¿Hay testigos?**	Eye tes-tee-gos
My bag/wallet/ passport has been stolen	**Me han robado el bolso/la cartera/el pasaporte**	May an ro-ba-do el bol-so/la kar-te-ra/ el pa-sa-por-te
It was stolen from our room	**Me lo robaron de la habitación**	May lo ro-ba-ron de la a-bee-ta-**thyon**
Some things have been stolen from our car	**Nos han robado unas cosas del coche**	Nos an ro-ba-do oo-nas ko-sas del ko-che

My car has been broken into	**Me han abierto el coche**	May an a-bee-air-to el ko-che
Apply to the insurance company	***Diríjase a la compañía de seguros**	Dee-**ree**-ha-se a la kom-pa-**nyee**-a de se-goo-ros
I'd like to report a theft	**Quiero denunciar un robo**	Kee-e-ro de-noon-thee-ar oon ro-bo

ENTERTAINMENT

Key Phrases

Is there an entertainment guide?	¿Hay una guía del ocio?	Eye oo-na **gee**-a del o-thyo
What is there for children?	¿Qué cosas hay para niños?	Kay ko-sas eye pa-ra nee-nyos
Do you have a programme for the festival?	¿Tiene un programa del festival?	Tee-e-ne oon pro-gra-ma del fest-ee-bal
The cheapest seats, please	Por favor las entradas más baratas	Por fa-bor las en-tra-das mas ba-ra-tas

What is there to see/ to do here?	¿Qué se puede ver/ hacer aquí?	Kay se pwe-de ber/ a-thair a-**kee**
Is there a playground nearby?	¿Hay un parque infantil por aquí?	Eye oon par-ke een-fant-eel por a-**kee**
Is the circus on?	¿Hay circo?	Eye theer-ko
What time is the firework display?	¿A qué hora son los fuegos artificiales?	A kay o-ra son los fwe-gos ar-tee-fee-thya-les
How far is it to the amusement park?	¿A qué distancia está el parque de atracciones?	A kay dees-tan-thya es-**ta** el par-ke de a-tra-thyo-nes

What age is the show for?	¿Para qué edades es este espectáculo?	Pa-ra kay e-da-des es es-te es-pec-**ta**-koo-lo
What do the local festivities celebrate?	¿Qué se celebra en las fiestas?	Kay se the-le-bra en las fee-es-tas
What time does the karaoke start/finish?	¿A qué hora empieza/termina el karaoke?	A kay o-ra em-pee-e-tha/tair-mee-na el ka-ra-o-kay
cabaret, night club	el café cantante	ka-fe kan-tan-te
casino	el casino	ka-see-no
concert	el concierto	kon-thee-air-to
disco	la discoteca	dees-ko-te-ka
water park	el parque acuático	par-ke a-**kwa**-tee-ko
zoo	el zoo	tho-o

Booking Tickets

I want two seats for tonight	Quiero dos entradas para esta noche	Kee-e-ro dos en-tra-das pa-ra es-ta no-che
I want to book seats for thursday?	Quiero reservar entradas para el jueves	Kee-e-ro re-sair-bar en-tra-das pa-ra el hwe-bes
Are there tickets for the matinée?	¿Hay entradas para el matiné?	Eye en-tra-das pa-ra el ma-tee-**ne**
Where do you want to sit?	*¿Dónde quieren sentarse?	don-de kee-e-ren sen-tar-se

I'd like seats	**Quiero entradas**	Kee-e-ro en-tra-das
near the stage/the screen	**cerca del escenario/la pantalla**	thair-ka del es-the-na-ryo/ la pant-a-llya
by the aisle	**en el pasillo**	en el pa-see-llyo
in the stalls	**de platea**	de pla-tai-a
in the circle	**de anfiteatro**	de an-fee-te-a-tro
in the gallery	**de tribuna**	de tree-boo-na
The cheapest seats, please	**Por favor las entradas más baratas**	Por fa-bor las en-tra-das mas ba-ra-tas
Are they good seats?	**¿Son buenas estas entradas?**	Son bwe-nas es-tas en-tra-das
Where are these seats?	**¿Dónde están estas butacas?**	Don-de es-**tan** es-tas boo-ta-kas
That performance is sold out	***No hay entradas para esta sesión**	No eye en-tra-das pa-ra es-ta se-**syon**
Everything is sold out	***Está todo vendido**	Es-**ta** to-do ben-dee-do
Pick the tickets up before the performance	***Recoja las entradas antes de la función**	Re-ko-ha las en-tra-das an-tes de la foon-**thyon**
This is your seat	***Esta es su butaca**	Es-ta es soo boo-ta-ka
What time is the floorshow?	**¿A qué hora es el espectáculo?**	A kay o-ra es el es-pek-**ta**-koo-lo

Cinema, Theatre and Live Music

chamber music	la música de cámara	moo-see-ka de ka-ma-ra
film	la película	pe-lee-koo-la
modern dance	la danza contemporánea	dan-tha kon-tem-por-a-nea
musical	el musical	moo-see-kal
opera	la ópera	o-pai-ra
play	la obra de teatro	o-bra de te-a-tro
recital	el recital	re-thee-tal
Can you recommend a film/musical?	¿Qué película/ musical me recomienda?	Kay pe-lee-koo-la/ moo-see-kal may re-ko-mee-en-da
What's on at the theatre/cinema?[1]	¿Qué hay en los teatros/cines?	Kay eye en los te-a-tros/ thee-nes
Is it the original version?	¿Es en versión original?	Es en ber-syon or-ee-hee-nal
Are there subtitles?	¿Está subtitulada?	Es-ta soob-tee-too-la-da
Is it dubbed?	¿Está doblada?	Es-ta do-bla-da
Is there a concert?	¿Hay algún concierto?	Eye al-goon kon-thee-air-to
Is there a support band?	¿Quienes son los teloneros?	Kee-e-nes son los te-lo-ne-ros

1. There is usually one performance daily in theatres at around 7 or 8 p.m. and two on Sundays. Cinemas have three sessions at about 5, 7.30 and 10.30 p.m. In a few cinemas the show goes on continuously, starting at 4.30 p.m.

What time does the band start?	¿A qué hora toca el grupo?	A kay o-ra to-ka el groo-po
Who is	¿Quién	Kee-en
acting?	actúa?	ak-**too**-a
conducting?	es el director de la orquesta?	es el dee-rek-tor de la or-kes-ta
directing?	es el director?	es el dee-rek-tor
singing?	canta?	kan-ta
What time does the performance start?	¿A qué hora empieza la función?	A kay o-ra em-pee-e-tha la foon-**thyon**
What time does it end?	¿A qué hora termina?	A kay o-ra tair-mee-na
Where is the cloakroom?	¿Dónde está el guardarropa?	Don-de es-**ta** el gwar-dar-ro-pa
A programme, please	Un programa, por favor	Oon pro-gra-ma por fa-bor

Clubs and Discos

Can you recommend a good cabaret?	¿Puede recomendarme algún espectáculo?	Pwe-de re-ko-men-dar-me al-**goon** es-pek-**ta**-koo-lo
Which is the best club/disco?	¿Cuál es la mejor sala de fiestas/discoteca?	Kwal es la me-hor sa-la de fee-es-tas/dees-ko-te-ka
Where can we go dancing?	¿Dónde podemos ir a bailar?	Don-de po-de-mos eer a ba-ee-lar
Would you like to dance?	¿Quiere bailar?	Kee-e-re ba-ee-lar
Is there a jazz club here?	¿Hay alguna sala/ algún club de jazz?	Eye al-goo-na sa-la/ al-**goon** kloob de jazz

HEALTH

Dentist

I want to go to the dentist	**Quiero ir al dentista**	Kee-e-ro eer al den-tees-ta
Can you recommend one?	**¿Puede recomendarme uno?**	Pwe-de re-ko-men-dair-me oo-no
I've lost a filling	**Se me ha caído un empaste**	Se may a ka-**ee**-do oon em-pas-te
Can you do it now?	**¿Puede hacérmelo ahora?**	Pwe-de a-**thair**-me-lo a-ora
Can you fix it (temporarily)?	**¿Puede arreglármelo (temporalmente)?**	Pwe-de ar-reg-**lar**-me-lo (tem-po-ral-men-te)

Can I make an appointment?	**¿Pueden darme hora?**	Pwe-den dar-me o-ra
As soon as possible	**Lo antes posible**	Lo an-tes po-see-ble
I have toothache	**Me duelen las muelas**	May dwe-len las mwe-las
This tooth hurts	**Me duele este diente**	May dwe-le es-te dyen-te
I have a broken tooth	**Se me ha roto un diente/una muela**	Se may a ro-to oon dyen-te/oon-a mwe-la

Can you fill it?	¿Puede empastarme un diente?	Pwe-de em-pas-tar-me oon dyen-te
Will you take the tooth out?	¿Tiene que sacarme la muela?	Tee-e-ne ke sa-kar-me la mwe-la
I do not want the tooth taken out	No quiero sacarme el diente	No kee-e-ro sa-kar-me el dyen-te
Please give me an anaesthetic	Por favor déme un anestésico	Por fa-bor de-me oon a-nes-te-see-ko
My gums are swollen/keep bleeding	Tengo las encías inflamadas/Me sangran las encías	Ten-go las en-thee-as een-fla-ma-das/May san-gran las en-thee-as
I have broken my dentures	Se me ha roto la dentadura	Se may a ro-to la den-ta-doo-ra
You're hurting me	Me está haciendo mucho daño	May es-ta a-thee-en-do moo-cho da-nyo
How much do I owe you?	¿Cuánto es, por favor?	Kwan-to es por fa-bor
When should I come again?	¿Cuándo tengo que volver?	Kwan-do ten-go ke bol-bair
Please rinse your mouth	*Enjuáguese	En-hwa-ge-se
I have to X-ray your teeth	*Tengo que hacerle una radiografía	Ten-go ke a-thair-le oon-a ra-dee-o-gra-fee-a
You have an abscess	*Tiene usted un absceso	Tee-e-ne oos-te oon abs-the-so
The nerve is exposed	*El nervio está al descubierto	El nair-byo es-ta al des-koo-bee-air-to
This tooth can't be saved	*Esta muela no se puede salvar	Es-ta mwe-la no se pwe-de sal-bar

Doctor

Key Phrases

I want to see a doctor. Can you recommend one?	**Quiero que me vea un médico. ¿Puede recomendarme alguno?**	Kee-e-ro ke may bai-a oon **me**-dee-ko. Pwe-de re-ko-men-dar-me al-goo-no
Please call a doctor	**Llame un médico, por favor**	Llya-me oon **me**-dee-ko por fa-bor
I suffer from ...; here is a list of my medication	**Sufro de ...; ésta es la medicación que tengo que tomar**	Soo-fro de ...; es-ta es la me-dee-ka-**thyon** ke ten-go ke to-mar
I have a cardiac condition	**Sufro del corazón**	Soo-fro del ko-ra-**thon**
I am diabetic	**Soy diabético**	Soy dee-a-**be**-tee-ko
I suffer from asthma	**Tengo asma**	Ten-go as-ma
I've had a high temperature since yesterday	**Tengo fiebre desde ayer**	Ten-go fee-e-brai des-de a-yer
My stomach is upset	**Tengo mal el estómago**	Ten-go mal el es-**to**-ma-go

Is there a doctor's surgery/health centre nearby?	**¿Hay algún ambulatorio/centro de salud cerca?**	Eye al-**goon** am-boo-la-to-ryo/then-tro de sa-lood thair-ka
When can the doctor come?	**¿Cuándo puede venir el médico?**	Kwan-do pwe-de be-neer el **me**-dee-ko
Does the doctor speak English?	**¿Habla inglés el médico?**	Ab-la een-**gles** el **me**-dee-ko

| Can I make an appointment for as soon as possible? | ¿Puedo tener hora lo antes posíble? | Pwe-do te-nair o-ra lo an-tes po-see-ble |
| I'd like to find a paediatrician | Necesito encontrar un pediatra | Ne-thai-see-to en-kon-trar oon pai-dee-a-tra |

Medication

I take daily medication for . . .	Todos los días tomo medicina para . . .	To-dos los dee-as to-mo me-dee-thee-na pa-ra
I suffer from . . . ; here is a list of my medication	Sufro de . . . ; ésta es la medicación que tengo que tomar	Soo-fro de . . . ; es-ta es la me-dee-ka-thyon ke ten-go ke to-mar
This is a copy of my UK prescription. Could you please prescribe this for me?	Aquí tiene una receta de mi médico en el Reino Unido. Puede hacerme una receta, por favor?	A-kee tee-e-ne oo-na rai-thai-ta de mee me-dee-ko en el ray-no oo-nee-do. Pwe-de a-ther-me oo-na re-the-ta por fa-bor

Symptoms and conditions

I am ill	No me encuentro bien	No may en-kwen-tro bee-en
I have high/low blood pressure	Tengo la tensión alta/baja	Ten-go la ten-syon al-ta/ba-ha
I am allergic to . . .	Soy alérgico a . . .	Soy a-ler-hee-ko a
I have a fever	Tengo fiebre	Ten-go fee-e-brai
I've had a high temperature since yesterday	Tengo fiebre desde ayer	Ten-go fee-e-brai des-de a-yer

I have a cardiac condition	**Sufro del corazón**	Soo-fro del ko-ra-**thon**
I am diabetic	**Soy diabético**	Soy dee-a-**be**-tee-ko
I suffer from asthma	**Tengo asma**	Ten-go as-ma
I am . . . months pregnant	**Estoy embarazada de . . . meses**	Es-toy em-ba-ra-tha-da de . . . mai-ses
I think it is infected	**Creo que está infectado**	Kre-o ke es-**ta** een-fek-ta-do
I've a pain in my right/left arm	**Me duele el brazo derecho/izquierdo**	May dwe-le el bra-tho de-re-cho/ eeth-kyair-do
It's a sharp pain/a persistent pain	**Es un dolor fuerte/ persistente**	Es oon do-lor fwer-te/ pair-sees-ten-te
My wrist hurts	**Me duele la muñeca**	May dwe-e-le la moo-nye-ka
I think I've sprained/ broken my ankle	**Creo que me he dislocado/roto el tobillo**	Kre-o ke may ay dees-lo-ka-do/ro-to el to-bee-llyo
I fell down and my back hurts	**Me he caído y me duele la espalda**	May ay ka-**ee**-do ee may dwe-le la es-pal-da
My foot is swollen	**Tengo el pie hinchado**	Ten-go el pee-e een-cha-do
I've burned/cut/ bruised myself	**Me he quemado/ cortado/dado un golpe**	May ay ke-ma-do/ kor-ta-do/da-do oon gol-pe
I've developed a rash/ an inflammation	**Me ha salido una erupción**	May a sal-ee-do oo-na ai-roop-**thyon**
My stomach is upset	**Tengo mal el estómago**	Ten-go mal el es-**to**-ma-go

I have indigestion	**No hago bien la digestión/Tengo indigestión**	No a-go bee-en la dee-hes-**tyon**/Ten-go een-dee-hes-**tyon**
My appetite's gone	**No tengo apetito**	No ten-go a-pe-tee-to
I've eaten something bad	**He comi do algo que estaba mal**	Ay ko-mee-do al-go kay es-ta-ba mal
I can't eat/sleep	**No puedo comer/dormir**	No pwe-do ko-mer/dor-meer
My nose keeps bleeding	**Sangro por la nariz frecuentemente**	San-gro por la nar-eeth fre-kwen-te-men-te
I have earache	**Me duelen los oídos**	May dwe-len los o-**ee**-dos
I have difficulty in breathing	**Me cuesta respirar**	May kwes-ta res-pee-rar
I feel dizzy	**Me siento mareado**	May see-en-to ma-re-a-do
I feel shivery	**Tengo escalofríos**	Ten-go es-ka-lo-**free**-os
I feel sick	**Tengo náuseas/ganas de devolver**	Ten-go **now**-se-as/ga-nas de de-bol-bair
I keep vomiting	**Tengo vómitos**	Ten-go **bo**-mee-tos
I think I've caught flu	**Creo que tengo gripe**	Kre-o ke ten-go gree-pe
I've got a cold	**Tengo catarro**	Ten-go ka-tar-ro
I've had it since yesterday/for a few hours	**Lo tengo desde ayer/desde hace unas horas**	Lo ten-go des-de a-yair/des-de a-the oon-as o-ras
abscess	**el absceso**	ab-the-so
ache	**el dolor**	do-lor
allergy	**la alergia**	al-air-hya

appendicitis	**la apendicitis**	a-pen-dee-thee-tees
asthma	**el asma**	as-ma
back pain	**el dolor de espalda**	do-lor de es-pal-da
blister	**la ampolla**	am-po-llya
boil	**el forúnculo**	for-**oon**-koo-lo
bruise	**el moratón**	mo-ra-**ton**
burn	**la quemadura**	ke-ma-doo-ra
chill	**el enfriamiento**	en-free-a-myen-to
constipation	**el estreñimiento**	es-tre-nyee-myen-to
cough	**la tos**	toss
cramp	**el calambre**	ka-lam-bray
diabetic	**diabético**	dya-**be**-tee-ko
diarrhoea	**la diarrea**	dee-ah-ray-a
earache	**el dolor de oídos**	do-lor de o-**ee**-dos
epilepsy	**la epilepsia**	e-pee-lep-sya
fever	**la fiebre**	fye-bre
food poisoning	**la intoxicación**	een-tok-see-ka-**thyon**
fracture	**la fractura**	frak-too-ra
hay fever	**la alergia al polen**	al-air-hya al po-len
headache	**el dolor de cabeza**	do-lor de ka-be-tha
heart condition	**sufro del corazón**	soo-fro del ko-ra-**thon**
high blood pressure	**la tensión alta**	ten-**syon** al-ta
ill/sick	**enfermo**	en-fair-mo

illness	la enfermedad	en-fair-me-dad
indigestion	la indigestión	een-dee-hes-**tyon**
infection	la infección	een-fek-**thyon**
influenza	la gripe	gree-pe
insect bite	la picadura de insecto	pee-ka-doo-ra de een-sek-to
insomnia	el insomnio	een-som-nyo
nausea	la náusea	**now**-se-a
nose bleed	la hemorragia nasal	e-mo-rra-hya na-sal
pain	el dolor	do-lor
rheumatism	el reumatismo	ray-oom-at-ees-mo
sore throat	la garganta irritada	gar-gan-ta ee-ree-ta-da
sting	la picadura	pee-ka-doo-ra
stomach ache	el dolor de estómago	do-lor de es-**to**-ma-go
sunburn	la quemadura de sol	ke-mah-doo-ra de sol
sunstroke	la insolación	een-so-la-**thyon**
swelling	el hinchazón	een-cha-**thon**
toothache	el dolor de muelas	do-lor de mwe-las
ulcer	la úlcera	**ool**-ther-a
wound	la herida	ay-ree-da

Diagnosis and treatment

Do you have a temperature?	*¿Tiene fiebre?	Tee-e-ne fee-e-brai
Where does it hurt?	*¿Dónde le duele?	Don-de le dwe-le

Have you a pain here?	*¿Le duele aquí?	Le dwe-le a-**kee**
How long have you had the pain?	*¿Desde cuándo le duele?	Des-de kwan-do le dwe-le
Open your mouth	*Abra la boca	Ab-ra la bo-ka
Put out your tongue	*Saque la lengua	Sa-ke la len-gwa
Breathe in	*Respire fuerte	Res-pee-re fwer-te
Breathe out	*Expire	Es-pee-re
Cough	*Tosa	To-sa
Does that hurt?	*¿Le duele ahí?	Le dwe-le a-**ee**
A lot?	*¿Mucho?	Moo-cho
A little?	*¿Un poco?	Oon po-ko
Please lie down	*Acuéstese	A-**kwes**-te-se
I need a specimen	*Necesito tomar una muestra	Ne-the-see-to tomar oon-a mwes-tra
You must have urine test/blood test while fasting	*Hay que hacerle un análisis de orina/de sangre en ayunas	Eye ke a-ther-le oon a-na-lee-sis de o-ree-na/de sang-re en a-yoo-nas
Are you being treated for this?	*¿Le están tratando ésto?	Le es-**tan** tra-tan-do es-to
Do you take medication for this?	*¿Toma medicación para ésto?	To-ma me-dee-ka-**thyon** pa-ra es-to
What medicines have you been taking?	*¿Qué medicinas ha estado tomando?	Kay me-dee-thee-nas a es-ta-do to-man-do
I will give you	*Le voy a dar	Le boy a dar
an antibiotic	un antibiótico	oon an-tee-bee-**o**-tee-ko
an injection	una inyección	oo-na een-yek-**thyon**

a painkiller	**un calmante**	oon kal-man-te
a sedative	**un sedante**	oon se-dan-te
some pills/ medicine	**unas píldoras/una medicina**	oon-as peel-do-ras/ oon-a me-dee-thee-na
Are you allergic to antibiotics?	*¿Es usted alérgico a los antibióticos?**	Es oos-te a-lair-hee-ko a los an-tee-bee-o-tee-kos
Do you have any allergies?	*¿Es usted alérgico a alguna cosa?**	Es oos-te a-lair-hee-ko a al-goo-na ko-sa
Take this prescription to the chemist's	*Lleve esta receta a la farmacia**	Llye-be es-ta re-the-ta a la far-ma-thya
Take this three times a day	*Tómelo tres veces al día**	To-me-lo tres be-thes al dee-a
I'll put you on a diet	*Voy a ponerle un régimen**	Boy a po-nair-le oon re-hee-men
You must go to hospital	*Tiene usted que ir a un hospital/una clínica**	Tee-e-ne oos-te kay eer a oon os-pee-tal/oon-a klee-nee-ka
You must be X-rayed	*Tiene que hacerse una radiografía**	Tee-e-ne kay a-thair-se oon-a ra-dee-o-gra-fee-a
You've pulled a muscle	*Tiene un tirón muscular**	Tee-e-ne oon tee-ron moos-koo-lar
You have a fracture/ sprain	*Tiene una fractura/ un esguince**	Tee-e-ne oo-na frak-too-ra/oon es-geen-the
You need a few stitches	*Necesita unos puntos**	Ne-the-see-ta oo-nos poon-tos
Come and see me again in two days	*Vuelva dentro de dos días**	Bwel-ba den-tro de dos dee-as
You're hurting me	**Me hace daño**	May a-the da-nyo

Must I stay in bed?	¿Tengo que estar en la cama?	Ten-go kay es-tar en la ka-ma
Will you call again?	¿Volverá usted?	Bol-bair-a oos-te
When can I travel again?	¿Cuándo podré viajar?	Kwan-do po-dre bee-a-har
You should not travel until ...	*No debería viajar hasta ...	No de-be-ree-a bee-a-har as-ta
Is it serious/contagious?	¿Es grave/contagioso?	Es gra-be/kon-ta-hee-o-so
Nothing to worry about	*No hay de que preocuparse	No eye de ke pre-o-koo-par-se
I feel better now	Estoy mejor	Es-toy me-hor
Do you have your E111 card? (EU Health Card)	*Tiene la tarjeta E111?	Tee-e-ne la tar-he-ta thee-en-to on-thay
How much do I owe you?	¿Cuánto le debo?	Kwan-to le de-bo
I'd like a receipt for the health insurance	Necesito un recibo para mi seguro	Ne-the-see-to oon re-thee-bo pa-ra mee se-goo-ro
ambulance	la ambulancia	am-boo-lan-thya
anaesthetic	el anestésico	a-nes-tes-ee-ko
aspirin	la aspirina	as-pee-ree-na
bandage	la venda	ben-da
chiropodist	el pedicuro	pe-dee-koo-ro
first aid station/A&E	primeros auxilios/ urgencias	pree-me-ros ow-see-lyos/ oor-hen-thyas
hospital	el hospital	os-pee-tal
injection	la inyección	een-yek-thyon

laxative	**el laxante**	lak-san-te
nurse	**la enfermera**	en-fair-mair-a
operation	**la operación**	o-pair-a-**thyon**
optician	**el óptico**	**op**-tee-ko
osteopath	**el osteópata**	ost-ai-**o**-pa-ta
paediatrician	**el pediatra**	pe-dya-tra
pill	**la píldora**	**peel**-do-ra
(adhesive) plaster	**el esparadrapo/la tirita**	es-pa-ra-dra-po/ tee-ree-ta
prescription	**la receta**	re-the-ta
X-ray	**la radiografía**	ra-dyo-gra-**fee**-a

Optician

Key Phrases

I have broken my glasses	**Se me han roto las gafas**	Se me an ro-to las ga-fas
Can you repair them?	**¿Me las puede arreglar?**	May las pwe-de ar-reg-lar
Can you give me a new pair of glasses with the same prescription?	**¿Podría hacerme unos lentes nuevos con la misma graduación?**	Po-**dree**-a a-thair-me oo-len-tes-fas nwe-bas kon la mees-ma gra-dwa-**thyon**
Please test my eyes	**Por favor necesito que me revise la vista**	Por fa-bor ne-the-see-to ke me re-bee-se la bees-ta
I am short-sighted	**Soy corto de vista**	Soy kor-to de bees-ta
I am long-sighted	**Tengo presbicia**	Ten-go pres-bee-thya

When will the glasses be ready?	**¿Para cuándo estarán las gafas?**	Pa-ra kwan-do es-ta-**ran** las ga-fas
I have difficulty with reading	**Me cuesta leer**	May kwest-a lay-eer
I have difficulty with long distance vision	**No veo bien de lejos**	No be-o bee-en de le-hos
I have lost one of my contact lenses	**He perdido una de mis lentillas**	Ay pair-dee-do oo-na de mees len-tee-llyas
I should like to have contact lenses	**Quiero un par de lentillas**	Kee-e-ro oon par de len-tee-llyas
My vision is blurred	**Veo borroso**	Beo bo-rro-so
I can't see clearly	**No veo con claridad**	No be-o kon kla-ree-dad

Parts of the Body

ankle	**el tobillo**	to-bee-llyo
arm	**el brazo**	bra-tho
artery	**la arteria**	ar-te-rya
back	**la espalda**	es-pal-da
bladder	**la vejiga**	be-hee-ga
blood	**la sangre**	san-gre
body	**el cuerpo**	kwair-po
bone	**el hueso**	way-so
brain	**el cerebro**	the-re-bro
breast	**el pecho**	pe-cho

cheek	la mejilla	me-hee-llya
chest	el pecho	pe-cho
chin	la barbilla	bar-bee-llya
ear	la oreja	or-ay-ha
elbow	el codo	ko-do
eye	el ojo	o-ho
face	la cara	ka-ra
finger	el dedo de la mano	de-do de la ma-no
foot	el pie	pee-ay
forehead	la frente	fren-te
gall bladder	la vesícula	bes-**ee**-ko-la
gums	las encías	en-**thee**-as
hand	la mano	ma-no
head	la cabeza	kab-ay-tha
heart	el corazón	ko-ra-**thon**
heel	el talón	ta-**lon**
hip	la cadera	ka-dair-a
jaw	la mandíbula	man-**dee**-boo-la
kidney	el riñón	ree-**nyon**
knee	la rodilla	ro-dee-llya
knee cap	la rótula	**ro**-too-la
leg	la pierna	pee-air-na
lip	el labio	la-byo

liver	el hígado	ee-ga-do
lung	el pulmón	pool-mon
mouth	la boca	bo-ka
muscle	el músculo	moos-koo-lo
nail	la uña	oo-nya
neck	el cuello	kwe-llyo
nerve	el nervio	nair-byo
nose	la nariz	na-reeth
pelvis	la pelvis	pel-vis
pulse	el pulso	pool-so
rib	la costilla	kos-tee-llya
shoulder	el hombro	om-bro
skin	la piel	pee-el
spine	la espina dorsal	es-pee-na dor-sal
stomach	el estómago	es-to-ma-go
thigh	el muslo	moos-lo
throat	la garganta	gar-gan-ta
thumb	el pulgar	pool-gar
toe	el dedo del pie	de-do del pee-ay
tongue	la lengua	len-gwa
tonsils	las amígdalas	a-meeg-da-las
tooth	el diente	dyen-te
vein	la vena	be-na
wrist	la muñeca	moo-nye-ka

MEETING PEOPLE

Key Phrases

Pleased to meet you	**Encantado/Mucho gusto**	En-kan-ta-do/Moo-cho goos-to
How are you?	**¿Qué tal?**	Kay tal
My name is ...	**Soy ... /Me llamo ...**	Soy ... /May Ilya-mo
I'm on holiday/a business trip	**Estoy de vacaciones/ de negocios**	Es-toy de ba-ka-thyo-nes/de ne-go-thyos
What is your telephone number?	**¿Cuál es su teléfono?**	Kwal es soo te-le-fono
Yes, I'd like to come	**Sí, me gustaría ir**	See me goos-ta-ree-a eer
Thanks for the invitation	**Gracias por la invitación**	Grath-yass por la een-bee-ta-thyon
I'm sorry, I can't go	**Lo siento, no puedo ir**	Lo syen-to no pwe-do eer

Introductions

May I introduce ...?	**Permítame que le presente ...**	Pair-mee-ta-me ke le pre-sen-te
Have you met ...?	**¿Conoce usted a ...?**	Ko-no-the oos-te a
Fine, thanks, and you?	**Muy bien, gracias, y usted?**	Mwee bee-en grath-yass ee oos-te

What is your name?	**¿Cómo se llama?**	Ko-mo se llya-ma
This is . . .	**Este señor/Esta señora es . . .**	Es-te se-nyor/Es-ta se-nyo-ra es . . .
Am I disturbing you?	**¿Le molesto?**	Le mo-les-to
Sorry to have trouble you	**Siento haberle molestado**	See-en-to a-bair-le mo-les-ta-do

Getting Acquainted

Do you live/Are you staying here?	**¿Vive/Está usted aquí?**	Bee-be/Es-ta oos-te a-kee
Do you travel a lot?	**¿Viaja usted mucho?**	Bee-a-ha oos-te moo-cho
We've been here a week	**Llevamos aquí ya una semana**	Llye-ba-mos a-kee ya oon-a se-ma-na
Is this your first time here?	**¿Es la primera vez que está aquí?**	Es la pree-mair-a beth ke es-ta a-kee
Do you like it here?	**¿Le gusta esto?**	Le goo-sta es-to
Are you on your own?	**¿Está solo/sola?**	Es-ta so-lo/so-la
I am travelling alone	**Viajo solo/sola**	Bee-a-ho so-lo/so-la
Where do you come from?	**¿De dónde es usted?**	De don-de es oos-te
I come from . . .	**Soy de . . .**	Soy de
Have you been to England/America?	**¿Ha estado usted en Inglaterra/Estados Unidos?**	A es-ta-do oos-te en een-gla-te-rra/es-ta-dos oo-nee-dos

I hope to see you again	**Espero volver a verlo**	Es-pe-ro bol-bair a bair-lo
It was nice talking to you	**Ha sido muy agradable charlar con usted**	A see-do mwee a-gra-da-ble char-lar kon oos-te

Personal Information

I am with	**Estoy con**	Es-toy kon
a colleague	**un colega**	oon ko-lai-ga
a friend	**un amigo**	oon a-mee-go
my family	**mi familia**	mee fa-mee-lya
my husband	**mi esposo**	mee es-po-so
my parents	**mis padres**	mees pa-dres
my wife	**mi esposa**	mee es-po-sa
I have a boyfriend/ girlfriend	**Tengo novio/novia**	Ten-go no-byo/no-bya
I live with my partner	**Vivo con mi pareja**	Bee-bo kon mee pa-rai-ha
I am separated/ divorced	**Estoy separado/ divorciado**	Es-toy se-par-a-do/ dee-bor-thya-do
I am a widow(er)	**Estoy viuda/viudo**	Es-toy bee-oo-da/ bee-oo-do
Are you married/ single?	**¿Está usted casado/ soltero?**	Es-ta oos-te ka-sa-do/ sol-tair-o

Do you have children/ grandchildren?	¿Tiene hijos/nietos?	Tee-e-ne ee-hos/nye-tos
What do you do?	¿Qué hace usted?	Kay a-the oos-te
I work in . . .	Trabajo en . . .	Tra-ba-ho en
I am	Soy	Soy
an accountant	contable	kont-ab-le
a consultant	consultor	kon-sool-ton
a nurse	enfermero	en-fair-mair-o
a student	estudiante	es-too-dyan-te
I work freelance	Trabajo por cuenta propia	Tra-ba-jo por kwen-ta pro-pya
We're retired	Estamos jubilados	Es-ta-mos hoo-bee-la-dos
What are you studying?	¿Qué estudia?	Kay es-too-dya
What do you do in your spare time?	¿Qué le gusta hacer en su tiempo libre?	Kay le goos-ta a-ther en soo tee-em-po lee-bre
I like sailing/ swimming/walking	Me gusta navegar/ nadar/caminar	May goos-ta na-be-gar/ na-dar/ka-mee-nar
I don't like cycling/ tennis	No me gusta andar en bicicleta/el tenis	No may goos-ta an-dar en bee-thee-kle-ta/el te-nees
I'm interested in art/ music	Me interesa el arte/ la música	May een-te-re-sa el ar-te/la **moo**-see-ka

Going Out[1]

Would you like to have a drink/coffee?	¿Quieres tomar algo/un café?	Kee-e-res to-mar al-go/oon ka-fe
I'd like a . . ., please	Quisiera un . . ., por favor	Kee-see-er-a oon . . . por fa-bor
Would you like to have lunch tomorrow?	¿Te gustaría comer conmigo mañana?	Te goos-tar-ee-a ko-mair kon-mee-go ma-nya-na
Can you come to dinner/for a drink?	¿Puedes venir a cenar/a tomar algo?	Pwe-des be-neer a the-nar/a to-mar al-go
We are giving a party/There is a party	Damos una fiesta/Hay una fiesta	Da-mos oon-a fee-es-ta/Eye oon-a fee-es-ta
Would you like to come?	¿Quieres venir?	Kee-e-res be-neer
May I bring a (girl) friend?	¿Puedo traer un amigo (una amiga)?	Pwe-do tra-yer oon a-mee-go (oon-a a-mee-ga)
Are you doing anything tonight/tomorrow afternoon?	¿Tienes algún plan para esta noche/para mañana por la tarde?	Tee-e-nes al-goon plan pa-ra es-ta no-che/pa-ra ma-nya-na por la tar-de
Could we have a drink/coffee somewhere?	¿Podemos ir a tomar algo/un café a algún sitio?	Po-de-mos eer a to-mar al-go/oon ka-fe a al-goon see-tyo
Shall we go to the cinema/theatre/beach?	¿Vamos al cine/al teatro/a la playa?	Ba-mos al thee-ne/al te-a-tro/a la pla-ya

1. Elsewhere in the book the polite form for 'you' has been used. Since this section deals with close personal relationships we have usually used the familiar form *tú*.

Would you like to go dancing/for a drive?	¿Quieres que vayamos a bailar/a dar una vuelta en coche?	Kee-e-res ke ba-ya-mos a ba-ee-lar/a dar oon pa-se-o en ko-che
Do you know a good disco/restaurant?	¿Conoces una discoteca/un restaurante que esté bien?	Ko-no-thes oon-a dees-ko-te-ka/oon res-tow-ran-te ke es-te bee-en
Let's go to a gay bar	Vamos a un bar gay	Ba-mos a oon bar gay

Arrangements

Where shall we meet?	¿Dónde nos encontramos?	Don-de nos en-kon-tra-mos
What time shall I/ we come?	¿A qué hora vengo/ venimos?	A ke o-ra ben-go/ be-nee-mos
I could pick you up at (place/time)	Puedo recogerte en . . . a las . . .	Pwe-do re-ko-her-te en . . . a las
Could you meet me at the hotel?	¿Quedamos en el hotel?	Ke-da-mos en el o-tel
May I see you home?	¿Puedo acompañarte a casa?	Pwe-do a-kom-pa-nyar-te a ka-sa
Can we give you a lift home/to your hotel?	¿Podemos llevarte en coche a tu casa/ al hotel?	Po-de-mos llye-bar-te en ko-che a too ka-sa/ al o-tel
Can we see each other again?	¿Podemos vernos otra vez?	Po-de-mos bair-nos ot-ra beth
Where do you live?	¿Dónde vives?	Don-de bee-bes
What is your telephone number?	¿Cuál es tu teléfono?	Kwal es too te-le-fono
Thanks for the drinks/ride	Gracias por la copa/ el paseo	Grath-yass por la ko-pa/ el pa-se-o

It was lovely	**Ha sido muy agradable**	A see-do mwee a-gra-da-ble
Hope to see you again soon	**Espero verte pronto**	Es-pair-o bair-te pron-to
See you soon/ tomorrow	**Hasta luego/Hasta mañana**	As-ta lwe-go/As-ta ma-nya-na
Are you free at the weekend?	**¿Estás libre el fin de semana?**	Es-**tas** lee-bre el feen de se-ma-na

Accepting and declining

Yes, I'd like to come	**Sí, me gustaría ir**	See me goos-ta-**ree**-a eer
Thanks for the invitation	**Gracias por la invitación**	Grath-yass por la een-bee-ta-**thyon**
Did you enjoy it?	**¿Te ha gustado?/¿Lo has pasado bien?**	Te a goos-ta-do/Lo as pa-sa-do bee-en
I'd love to go with you	**Me encantaría ir contigo**	May en-kan-ta-**ree**-a eer kon-tee-go
I've enjoyed myself very much	**Me he divertido mucho**	May ai dee-ber-tee-do moo-cho
It was very interesting/funny/ fantastic	**Ha sido muy interesante/ divertido/fantástico**	A see-do mwee een-te-re-san-te/dee-ber-tee-do/fan-**tas**-tee-ko
I'm sorry, I can't go	**Lo siento, no puedo ir**	Lo syen-to no pwe-do eer
Maybe another time	**Tal vez en otra ocasión**	Tal beth en o-tra o-ka-**syon**
No thanks, I'd rather not	**No gracias, mejor no**	No grath-yass mai-hor no
Go away	**Vete**	Beh-teh
Leave me alone	**Déjame en paz**	**Deh**-ha-may en path

MONEY[1]

Key Phrases

Where is the nearest ATM?	**¿Dónde está el cajero más cercano?**	Don-de es-**ta** el ka-hair-o mas thair-ka-no
Do you take credit cards?	**¿Aceptan tarjetas de crédito?**	A-thep-tan tar-het-as de **kre**-dee-to
Is there a bank that changes money near here?	**¿Hay algún banco cerca para cambiar dinero?**	Eye al-**goon** ban-ko thair-ka pa-ra kam-bee-ar dee-ne-ro
Please give me some small change	**Déme algo de dinero suelto, por favor**	**Day**-may al-go de dee-ne-ro swel-to por fa-bor
I want to open a bank account	**Quiero abrir una cuenta**	Kee-e-ro a-breer oon-a kwen-ta

Credit and Debit Cards

I'd like to get some cash with my credit card	**Quiero sacar dinero con mi tarjeta de crédito**	Kee-er-o sa-kar dee-ne-ro kon mee tar-he-ta de **kre**-dee-to

1. Banks and Cajas de Ahorros (savings banks) usually open 8.30 or 9 a.m. to 2 p.m., Monday to Friday. Additionally some banks or Cajas may open once a weet, 4 to 6 p.m., and on Saturday morning. Opening hours vary and are normally displayed on the door.

| Please enter your pin number | *Por favor, teclee su número PIN | Por fa-bor te-klai-e soo noo-me-ro peen |
| The ATM has swallowed my card | El cajero se ha tragado mi tarjeta | El ka-hair-o se a tra-ga-do mee tar-he-ta |

Exchange

Exchange	Cambio	Kam-byo
Do you cash travellers' cheques?	¿Aquí cambian cheques de viaje?	A-kee kam-byan che-kes de bya-hai
Where can I cash travellers' cheques?	¿Dónde puedo cambiar cheques de viaje?	Don-de pwe-do kam-bee-ar che-kes de bya-hai
I want to change	Quiero cambiar	Kee-e-ro kam-bee-ar
dollars	dólares	do-la-res
euros	euros	a-oo-ros
pounds	libras	lee-bras
some English/ American money	dinero inglés/ americano	dee-ne-ro een-gles/ amer-ee-ka-no
Do you have identification?	*¿Tiene algo que le identifique?	Tee-e-ne al-go ke le ee-den-tee-fee-ke
Your passport, please	*Su pasaporte, por favor	Soo pa-sa-por-te por fa-bor
Where do I sign?	¿Dónde firmo?	Don-de feer-mo
Sign here, please	*Firme aquí, por favor	Feer-me a-kee por fa-bor
Go to the cashier	*Vaya a la caja	Ba-ya a la ka-ha

How much do I get for a pound/dollar?	¿A cuánto está la libra/el dólar?	A kwan-to es-**ta** la lee-bra/el **dol**-ar
What is the rate of exchange?	¿A cuánto está el cambio?	A kwan-to es-**ta** el kam-byo
How much is your commission?	¿Cuánto cobran de comisión?	Kwan-to ko-bran de ko-mee-**syon**
Please give me some small change	Déme algo de dinero suelto, por favor	**Day**-may al-go de dee-ne-ro swel-to por fa-bor
I'd like small notes, please	Por favor, déme billetes pequeños	Por fa-bor **day**-may bee-llye-tes pe-ke-nyos

General Banking

I arranged for money to be transferred from the UK. Has it arrived yet?	Me han hecho una transferencia desde el Reino Unido. ¿Ha llegado ya?	May an e-cho oon-a trans-fe-rain-thya des-de el ray-ee-no oo-nee-do. A llye-ga-do ya
I want to open a bank account	Quiero abrir una cuenta	Kee-e-ro a-breer oon-a kwen-ta
Please credit this to my account	Por favor ponga esto en mi cuenta	Por fa-bor pon-ga es-to en mee kwen-ta
I'd like to withdraw some cash with my debit card	Quiero sacar dinero con mi tarjeta de débito	Kee-e-ro sa-kar dee-ne-ro kon mee tar-he-ta de **de**-bee-to
I want to make a transfer	Quiero hacer una transferencia	Kee-e-ro a-ther oon-a trans-fe-rain-thya

balance	**el balance**	ba-lan-the
bank card	**la tarjeta de banco**	tar-he-ta de ban-ko
cheque book	**el talonario de cheques**	ta-lo-na-ryo de che-kes
current account	**la cuenta corriente**	kwen-ta kor-ree-en-te
deposit account	**la cuenta de ahorro**	kwen-ta de a-or-ro
foreign currency	**la moneda extranjera**	mo-ne-da es-tran-he-ra
statement	**el extracto de cuenta**	es-trak-to de kwen-ta

SHOPS AND SERVICES[1]

Where to Go

antique shop	**la tienda de antigüedades**	tee-en-da de an-tee-gwe-da-des
audio equipment shop	**la tienda de sonido y hi-fi**	tee-en-da de so-nee-do ee ee-fee
bakery	**la panadería**	pa-na-dair-**ee**-a
bank	**el banco**	bank-o
barber (see p. 196)	**la barbería/el barbero**	bar-bair-**ee**-a/ bar-bair-o
beauty treatments (see p. 184)	**el salón de belleza**	sa-**lon** de bai-llye-tha
bicycle repair shop (see p. 46)	**la tienda de reparación de bicicletas**	tee-en-da de re-pa-ra-**thyon** de bee-thee-kle-tas
bookshop (see p. 185)	**la librería**	lee-brai-**ree**-a
builder	**el albañil**	al-ba-nyeel
butcher (see pp. 125 and 199)	**la carnicería**	kar-nee-thair-**ee**-a
cake shop (see p. 113)	**la pastelería**	pas-te-le-**ree**-a

1. Shopping hours vary across regions. Generally speaking, shops open between 9 and 10 a.m. and close between 1 and 2 p.m. They are usually closed for 2–2½ hours and then reopen between 4 and 5 p.m.

camping equipment (see p. 198)	el equipo de camping	e-kee-po de kam-ping
carpenter	el carpintero	kar-peen-tair-o
chemist (see pp. 188 and 207)	la farmacia	far-ma-thya
consulate (see p. 135)	el consulado	kon-soo-la-do
craft shop	la tienda de artesanía	tee-en-da de ar-te-sa-nee-a
decorator/painter	el decorador/el pintor	de-ko-ra-dor/peen-tor
delicatessen (see p. 121)	la tienda delicatessen	tee-en-da de-lee-ka-tes-sen
dentist (see p. 147)	el dentista	den-tees-ta
department stores (see p. 283)	los grandes almacenes	gran-des alma-then-es
DIY shop (see p. 75)	la tienda de bricolage	tee-en-da de bree-ko-la-he
doctor (see p. 149)	el médico	me-dee-ko
dry cleaner (see p. 200)	la tintorería	teen-tor-air-ee-a
electrical appliances	los electrodomésticos	e-lek-tro-do-mes-tee-kos
electrician	el electricista	e-lek-tree-thees-ta
embassy	la embajada	em-ba-ha-da
fishmonger (see pp. 123 and 199)	la pescadería	pes-ka-dair-ee-a
florist	la floristería	flo-ris-tair-ee-a
furniture shop (see p. 77)	la tienda de muebles	tee-en-da de mwe-bles

garden centre	la tienda de jardinería	tee-en-da de har-dee-nai-ree-a
gift shop	la tienda de regalos	tee-en-da de re-ga-los
greengrocer (see pp. 128, 131 and 199)	la frutería	froo-te-ree-a
grocery (see pp. 130 and 135)	la alimentación/ los comestibles/los ultramarinos	a-lee-men-ta-thyon/ ko-mes-tee-bles/ ool-tra-ma-ree-nos
haberdashery (for fabrics see p. 185)	la mercería	mair-thair-ee-a
hairdresser (see p. 196)	la peluquería	pe-loo-kair-ee-a
hardware shop (see p. 198)	la ferretería	fer-re-te-ree-a
health food shop	la tienda de productos naturales	tee-en-da de pro-dook-tos na-too-ra-les
home entertainment shop	la tienda de electrónica	tee-en-da de e-lek-tro-nee-ka
interior design shop	la tienda de interiorismo y decoración	tee-en-da de een-tair-ryo-rees-mo ee de-ko-ra-thyon
ironmonger	la cerrajería/ la ferretería	ther-ra-he-ree-a/ fer-re-te-ree-a
jeweller (see p. 301)	la joyería	hoy-air-ree-a
kitchen shop (see p. 80)	(la tienda de menaje de cocina	tee-en-da de me-na-he de ko-thee-na
launderette/laundry (see p. 200)	la lavandería	la-ban-dair-ee-a

light fittings shop	la tienda de iluminación	tee-en-da de ee-loo-mee-na-**thyon**
market (see p. 201)	el mercado	mair-ka-do
mobile/cell phone shop (see p. 94)	la tienda de telefonía móvil	tee-en-da de te-le-fo-**nee**-a mo-beel
newsagent (see p. 185)	el quiosco de periódicos	kyos-ko de pe-ree-**o**-dee-kos
notary	el notario	no-ta-ryo
optician (see p. 158)	el óptico	**op**-tee-ko
outdoor equipment shop (see p. 198 and 220)	la tienda para deportes al aire libre	tee-en-da pa-ra de-por-tes al eye-ray lee-bre
pastry shop (see p. 113)	la repostería/ la pastelería	re-pos-tair-**ree**-a/ pas-te-le-**ree**-a
photographer (see p. 206)	el fotógrafo	fo-**to**-gra-fo
plasterer	el yesero	ye-se-ro
plumber	el fontanero	fon-ta-ne-ro
police (see p. 137)	la policía	po-lee-**thee**-a
post office (see p. 92)	los correos	ko-rre-os
shoe repairs	el zapatero/la reparación de calzado	tha-pa-tair-o/rai-pa-ra-**thyon** de kal-tha-do
shoe shop (see pp. 190 and 192)	la zapatería	tha-pa-tair-**ee**-a
shopping centre	el centro comercial	then-tro ko-mer-thyal
souvenir shop	la tienda de recuerdos	tee-en-da de re-kwer-dos
sports shop	la tienda de deportes	tee-en-da de de-por-tes
stationery	la papelería	pa-pe-le-**ree**-a

supermarket	**el supermercado**	soo-per-mair-ka-do
sweet shop	**la confitería**	kon-fee-te-**ree**-a
tobacconist	**el estanco**	es-tan-ko
tourist information office	**la oficina de información turística**	o-fee-thee-na de een-for-ma-**thyon** too-**rees**-tee-ka
toy shop	**la juguetería/la tienda de juguetes**	hoo-ge-tair-**ee**-a/ tee-en-da de hoo-ge-tes
travel agent	**la agencia de viajes**	a-hen-thya de bya-hes
travel goods shop	**la tienda de artículos de viaje**	tee-en-da de art-**ee**-koo-los de bya-he
wine merchant	**la bodega/el almacén de vinos**	bo-de-ga/al-ma-**then** de bee-nos

Key Phrases

Which is the best . . . ?	**¿Cuál es el mejor . . . ?**	Kwal es el me-hor
Can you recommend a . . . ?	**¿Puede usted recomendarme un/ una . . . ?**	Pwe-de oos-te re-ko-men-dar-me oon/ oo-na
Where is the market?	**¿Dónde está el mercado?**	Don-de es-**ta** el mer-ka-do
Is there a market every day?	**¿Hay mercado todos los días?**	Eye mer-ka-do to-dos los **dee**-as
Where's the nearest chemist?	**¿Dónde está la farmacia más próxima?**	Don-de es-**ta** la far-ma-thya mas **pro**-see-ma
Where can I buy . . . ?	**¿Dónde puedo comprar . . . ?**	Don-de pwe-do kom-prar
When are the shops open?	**¿A qué hora abren las tiendas?**	A kay o-ra a-bren las tee-en-das

In the Shop

cash desk	**la caja**	ka-ha
manager	**el encargado/ la encargada**	en-kar-ga-do/en-kar-ga-da
self-service	**el autoservicio**	ow-to-sair-bee-thyo
sale (clearance)	**las rebajas/la liquidación**	rai-ba-has/lee-kee-da-thyon
shop assistant	**el dependiente/ la dependienta**	de-pen-dee-en-te/ de-pen-dee-en-ta
Where can I get a trolley/a shopping basket?	**¿Dónde están los carritos de la compra/las cestas de la compra?**	Don-de es-**tan** los kar-ree-tos de la kom-pra/las thest-as de la kom-pra
Can I help you?	***¿Qué desea?**	Kay de-se-a
I want to buy . . .	**Quiero comprar . . .**	Kee-e-ro kom-prar
Do you sell . . .?	**¿Venden ustedes . . .?**	Ben-den oos-te-des
I'm just looking around	**Sólo estoy mirando**	So-lo es-toy mee-ran-do
I don't want to buy anything now	**Ahora no voy a comprar nada**	A-o-ra no boy a kom-prar na-da
Could you show me . . .?	**¿Puede enseñarme . . .?**	Pwe-de en-sai-nyar-me
I don't like this	**Este no me gusta**	Es-te no may goos-ta
I'll have this	**Me quedo con éste**	May ke-do kon es-te
Will you gift wrap it, please?	**¿Me lo envuelve para regalo, por favor?**	May lo en-bwel-be pa-ra re-ga-lo por fa-bor

We do not have that	*No tenemos eso	No te-ne-mos e-so
You'll find them in the ... department	*Eso lo encontrará en el departamento de ...	E-so lo en-kon-tra-ra en el de-par-ta-men-to de
We've sold out but we'll have more tomorrow	*Se nos han terminado pero tendremos mañana	Se nos an tair-mee-na-do pe-ro ten-dre-mos ma-nya-na
Can I order one?	¿Puedo encargar uno?	Pwe-do en-kar-gar oon-o
Anything else?	*¿Algo más?	Al-go mas
That will be all	Esto es todo	Es-to es to-do
Shall we send it, or will you take it with you?	*¿Se lo mandamos, o se lo lleva usted?	Se lo man-da-mos o se lo llye-ba oos-te
I will take it with me	Me lo llevo	May lo llye-bo
Please send them to ...	Mándenlos a ...	Man-den-los a ...

Choosing

I like the one in the window	Me gusta el del escaparate	May goos-ta el del es-ka-pa-ra-te
Could I see that one, please?	¿Puedo ver ése, por favor?	Pwe-do bair e-se por fa-bor
Is it handmade?	¿Está hecho a mano?	Es-ta e-cho a ma-no
What is it made of?	¿De qué es?/¿De qué está hecho?	De kay es/De kay es-ta e-cho
I like the colour but not the style	Me gusta el color pero no el estilo	May goo-sta el ko-lor pe-ro no el es-tee-lo

I want a darker/ lighter shade	Quiero un tono más oscuro/más claro	Kee-e-ro oon to-no mas os-koo-ro/mas kla-ro
Do you have one in another colour/size?[1]	¿Lo tienen en otro color/talla?	Lo tee-e-nen en o-tro ko-lor/ta-llya
It's for a three-year-old boy/girl	Es para un niño/una niña de tres años	Es pa-ra oon nee-nyo/ oo-na nee-nya de-tres a-nyos
How much is this?	¿Cuánto cuesta?	Kwan-to kwes-ta
Have you anything better/cheaper?	¿Tienen algo mejor/ más barato?	Tee-en-en al-go me-hor/ mas ba-ra-to
That is too much	Es demasiado	Es de-ma-see-a-do
For how long is it guaranteed?	¿Por cuánto tiempo está garantizado?	Por kwan-to tee-em-po es-ta ga-ran-teé-tha-do

Colours

beige	beige	bezh
black	negro	ne-gro
blue	azul	a-thool
brown	marrón	mar-ron
cream	crema	kre-ma
gold	dorado	dor-a-do
green	verde	bair-de
grey	gris	grees
mauve	malva	mal-ba

1. See clothing sizes (p. 192).

orange	**naranja**	na-ran-ha
pink	**rosa**	ro-sa
purple	**morado**	mo-ra-do
red	**rojo**	ro-ho
silver	**plateado**	pla-tai-a-do
white	**blanco**	blan-ko
yellow	**amarillo**	a-ma-ree-llyo
colourful	**colorido/multicolor**	ko-lo-ree-do/ mool-tee-ko-lor
dark	**oscuro**	os-koo-ro
light	**claro**	kla-ro
pale/soft colours	**colores pálidos/ suaves**	ko-lo-res **pa**-lee-dos/ swa-bes
strong colours	**colores fuertes**	ko-lo-res fwer-tes

Materials

canvas	**la loneta**	lo-ne-ta
cotton	**el algodón**	al-go-**don**
glass	**el cristal**	krees-tal
lace	**el encaje**	en-ka-he
leather	**el cuero/la piel**	kwe-ro/pee-ail
linen	**el lino**	lee-no
muslin	**la gasa/la muselina**	ga-sa/moo-sai-lee-na

plastic	**el plástico**	**plas**-tee-ko
silk	**la seda**	se-da
suede	**el ante**	an-te
synthetic	**sintético**	seen-**te**-tee-ko
velvet	**el terciopelo**	tair-thyo-pai-lo
wood	**la madera**	ma-dair-a
wool	**la lana**	la-na

Paying

How much is this?	**¿Cuánto cuesta ésto?**	Kwan-to kwes-ta es-to
That's … euros	***Son … euros**	Son … a-oo-ros
They are … euros each	***Son … euros cada uno**	Son … a-oo-ros ka-da oon-o
It's too expensive	**Es demasiado caro**	Es de-ma-see-a-do ka-ro
Is that your best price?	**¿Es el mejor precio que me puede ofrecer?**	Es el me-hor pre-thyo ke me pwe-de o-fre-ther
How much does that come to?	**¿Cuánto es en total?**	Kwan-to es en to-tal
How would you like to pay?	***¿Cómo va a pagar?**	Ko-mo ba a pa-gar
Do you take credit cards/travellers' cheques?	**¿Aceptan tarjetas de crédito/cheques de viaje?**	A-thep-tan tar-he-tas de **kre**-dee-to/che-kes de bya-hai
Cash only	**Sólo aceptamos efectivo**	So-lo a-thep-ta-mos ai-faik-tee-bo

Do you give any discount?	**¿Hacen descuento?**	A-then des-kwen-to
Do I have to pay VAT?	**¿Tengo que pagar IVA?**	Ten-go ke pa-gar ee-ba
Please pay at the check out/cash desk	***Pague en la caja**	Pa-ge en la ka-ha
May I have a receipt, please	**Quiero un recibo, por favor**	Kee-e-ro oon re-thee-bo por fa-bor
You've given me the wrong change	**Creo que el cambio no está bien**	Kreo ke el kam-byo no es-**ta** bee-en

Complaints

I want to see the manager	**Quiero hablar con el encargado**	Kee-e-ro ab-lar kon el en-kar-ga-do
I bought this yesterday	**Compré esto ayer**	Kom-**pre** es-to a-yair
It doesn't work/fit	**No funciona/No me vale**	No foon-thyo-na/ No me ba-le
This is	**Está**	Es-**ta**
bad	**en malas condiciones**	en mal-as kon-dee-thyo-nes
broken	**estropeado**	es-tro-pe-ad-o
cracked	**roto**	ro-to
dirty	**sucio**	soo-thyo
stained	**manchado**	man-cha-do
torn	**rasgado**	ras-ga-do

I want to return this	**Quiero devolver esto**	Kee-e-ro de-bol-bair es-to
Will you change it, please?	**¿Pueden cambiármelo?**	Pwe-den kam-bee-**ar**-me-lo
Will you refund my money?	**¿Pueden devolverme el dinero?**	Pwe-den de-bol-bair-me el dee-ne-ro

Beauty and Spa Treatments

I'd like to make an appointment for tomorrow	**¿Pueden darme hora para mañana?**	Pwe-den dar-me o-ra pa-ra ma-nya-na
I'd like a manicure/pedicure	**Quería hacerme la manicura/la pedicura**	Ke-**ree**-a a-ther-may la ma-nee-koo-ra/la pe-dee-koo-ra
I'd like a facial/massage	**Quería una limpieza de cutis/un masaje**	Ke-**ree**-a oo-na leem-pee-e-tha de koo-tis/oon ma-sa-he
Do you do waxing?	**¿Hacen depilación a la cera aquí?**	A-then de-pee-la-**thyon** a la thai-ra a-**kee**
I'd like my eyebrows shaped	**Quería que me arreglaran las cejas**	Ke-**ree**-a kay may ar-re-gla-ran las the-has
Do you do aromatherapy?	**¿Hacen aromaterapia?**	A-then a-ro-ma-tai-ra-pya
Is there a sauna?	**¿Hay sauna?**	Eye sa-oo-na
What spa packages are available?	**¿Qué tratamientos tienen en el balneario?**	Kay tra-ta-mee-en-tos tee-en-en en el bal-nai-a-ryo

How much does it cost?	¿Cuánto cuesta?	Kwan-to kwes-ta
How long does it take?	¿Cuánto tiempo necesita?	Kwan-to tee-em-po ne-the-see-ta
body massage	masaje corporal	ma-sa-he kor-po-ral
hydromassage	hidromasaje	hee-dro-ma-sa-he
full-leg waxing	depilación de piernas	de-pee-la-thyon de pee-air-nas

Books, Newspapers and Stationery

Do you sell English/American newspapers?	¿Venden periódicos ingleses/americanos?	Ben-den pe-ree-o-dee-kos een-gle-ses/a-mer-ee-ka-nos
Can you get ... newspaper/magazine for me?	¿Pueden conseguirme el diario ... /la revista ...?	Pwe-den kon-se-geer-me el dee-a-ryo/la re-bees-ta
Where can I get the ...?	¿Dónde puedo comprar ...?	Don-de pwe-do kom-prar
I want a map of the city/a road map	Quiero un mapa de la ciudad/de carreteras	Kee-e-ro oon ma-pa de la thee-oo-dad/de kar-re-te-ras
I'd like a guide to the city in English	Quisiera la guía de la ciudad en inglés	Kee-see-e-ra la gee-a de la thee-oo-dad en een-gles
Is there an entertainment/amusements guide?	¿Hay una guía del ocio?	Eye oon-a gee-a del o-thyo

Do you have any books in English?	¿Tienen libros en inglés?	Tee-e-nen lee-bros en een-**gles**
Have you any books by . . .?	¿Tienen algún libro de . . .?	Tee-e-nen al-**goon** lee-bro de
I want some picture postcards	Quiero unas postales	Kee-e-ro oon-as pos-ta-les
Do you sell souvenirs/toys?	¿Venden objetos de recuerdo/ juguetes?	Ben-den ob-he-tos de re-kwer-do/ hoo-ge-tes
ballpoint pen	el bolígrafo	bol-**ee**-gra-fo
calculator	la calculadora	kal-koo-la-do-ra
card	la tarjeta	tar-he-ta
crayon	la lápiz de cera	**la**-peeth de thera
dictionary	el diccionario	dee-thee-o-na-ryo
drawing paper	el papel para dibujar	pa-pel pa-ra dee-boo-har
drawing pins	las chinchetas	cheen-che-tas
envelope	el sobre	so-bre
felt-tip pen	el rotulador	ro-too-la-dor
file	la carpeta	kar-pe-ta
glue	el pegamento	pe-ga-men-to
guide book	la guía de la ciudad	**gee**-a de la thee-oo-dad
ink	la tinta	teen-ta
label	la etiqueta	e-tee-ke-ta

notebook	**el bloc/el cuaderno**	blok/kwa-der-no
paperclip	**el clip**	kleep
pen	**la pluma/el bolígrafo**	ploo-ma/bol-**ee**-gra-fo
pen cartridge	**el recambio**	re-kam-byo
pencil	**el lápiz**	la-peeth
pencil sharpener	**el sacapuntas**	sa-ka-poon-tas
postcard	**la tarjeta postal**	tar-he-ta pos-tal
rubber/eraser	**la goma**	go-ma
sellotape	**el cello**	the-lo
sketch pad	**el bloc de dibujo**	blok de dee-boo-ho
string	**la cuerda**	kwer-da
wrapping paper	**el papel de envolver**	pa-pel de en-bol-ber
writing paper	**el papel de cartas**	pa-pel de kar-tas

CDs and DVDs

Do you have any CDs of local music?	**¿Venden CDs de la música de aquí?**	Ben-den thay-days de la **moo**-see-ka de a-**kee**
Are there any new CDs by . . .?	**¿Ha sacado . . . algún CD nuevo?**	A sa-ka-do . . . al-**goon** thay-day nwe-bo
Have you any CDs by . . .?	**¿Tiene CDs de . . .?**	Tee-ne thay-days de
I'm looking for DVDs of . . .	**Estoy buscando DVDs de . . .?**	Es-toy boos-kan-do day-bay-days de

Chemist[1]

Can you prepare this prescription for me, please?	¿Pueden servirme esta receta, por favor?	Pwe-den ser-beer-me es-ta re-the-ta por fa-bor
Have you a small first-aid kit?	¿Venden botiquines pequeños?	Ben-den bo-tee-**kee**-nes pe-ke-nyos
I want	Quiero	Kee-e-ro
a packet of adhesive plasters	una caja de tiritas	oo-na ka-ha de tee-ree-tas
an antiseptic cream	una crema antiséptica	oo-na kre-ma an-tee-**sep**-tee-ka
some aspirin	aspirinas	as-pee-ree-nas
a disinfectant	un desinfectante	oon de-seen-fek-tan-te
a mosquito repellent	algo contra los mosquitos	al-go kon-tra los mos-kee-tos
a mouthwash	un enjuague bucal	oon en-hoo-a-ge boo-kal
some nose drops	gotas nasales	go-tas na-sa-les
paracetamol	paracetamol	pa-ra-the-ta-mol
sun cream (for children)	crema para el sol (infantil)	kre-ma pa-ra el sol (een-fan-teel)
throat lozenges	pastillas para la garganta	pas-tee-llyas pa-ra la gar-gan-ta

1. See also DOCTOR (p. 149). Chemists in Spain sell full boxes, packets or jars of ready-prepared drugs. No waiting time is needed for prescriptions.

Could you give me something for	¿Puede darme algo para	Pwe-de dar-me al-go pa-ra
diarrhoea?	la diarrea?	la dee-a-rre-a
indigestion?	la indigestión?	la een-dee-hes-tyon
an insect bite?	las picaduras de insecto?	las pee-ka-doo-ras de in-sek-to
a jellyfish sting?	las picaduras de medusa?	las pee-ka-doo-ras de me-doo-sa
sunburn?	las quemaduras del sol?	las ke-ma-doo-ras del sol
an upset stomach?	el dolor de estómago?	el do-lor de es-to-ma-go
Do you sell	¿Venden	Ben-den
condoms?	condones?	kon-do-nes
contraceptives?	anticonceptivos?	an-tee-kon-thep-tee-bos
cotton wool?	algodón?	al-go-don
sanitary towels?	compresas?	kom-pre-sas
tampons?	tampones?	tam-po-nes
I need something for	Necesito algo para	Ne-the-see-to al-go pa-ra
a hangover	la resaca	la re-sa-ka
a headache	el dolor de cabeza	el do-lor de ca-be-tha
travel sickness	el mareo	el ma-re-o

Clothes, Shoes and Accessories[1]

I want a hat/sunhat	Quiero un sombrero/un sombrero para el sol	Kee-e-ro oon som-brair-o/oon som-brair-o pa-ra el sol
Where are beach clothes?	¿Dónde está la ropa de playa?	Don-de es-ta la ro-pa de pla-ya
I want a short/long-sleeved shirt	Quiero una camisa de manga corta/larga	Kee-e-ro oo-na ka-mee-sa de man-ga kor-ta/lar-ga
Where can I find	¿Dónde puedo encontrar	Don-de pwe-do en-kon-trar
blouses?	blusas?	bloo-sas
bras?	sujetadores?	soo-he-ta-do-res
socks?	calcetines?	kal-the-teen-es
tights?	un per de medias?	oon par day me-dyas
I am looking for	Busco	Boos-ko
a dress	un vestido	oon best-ee-do
a jacket	una chaqueta	oo-na cha-ke-ta
a sweater	una prenda de punto	oo-na pren-da de poon-to
I need	Necesito	Ne-the-see-to
a coat	un abrigo	oon a-bree-go
a raincoat	un impermeable	oon eem-pair-me-a-ble
a pair of trousers	unos pantalones	oo-nos pan-ta-lo-nes
a pair of gloves	un par de guantes	oon par de gwan-tes

1. For sizes see p. 192.

Do you have other colours?	¿Tienen de otros colores?	Tee-en-en de o-tros ko-lo-res
I need it to match this	Quiero que combine con esto	Kee-e-ro ke kom-bee-ne kon es-to
I need something warmer/thinner	Necesito algo que abrigue más/algo más fino	Ne-the-see-to al-go ke a-bree-ge mas/al-go mas fee-no
What size is this?	¿Qué talla es ésta?	Kay ta-llya es es-ta
I need a size XS	Uso una (talla) XS	Oo-so oo-na (ta-llya) e-kees-e-se
I am a size 12	Soy una (talla) 42	Soy oo-na (ta-llya) kwa-ren-ta
Can you measure me?	¿Me puede medir?	May pwe-de me-deer
The English/ American size is . . .	La talla inglesa/ americana es . . .	La ta-llya een-gle-sa/. a-me-ree-ka-na es
May I try it on?	¿Puedo probármelo?	Pwe-do pro-**bar**-me-lo
Is there a mirror?	¿Hay un espejo?	Eye oon es-pe-ho
This doesn't fit	Esto no me vale	Es-to no may ba-le
It's too	Es demasiado	Es de-ma-see-a-do
short	corto	kor-to
long	largo	lar-go
tight	estrecho	es-tre-cho
loose	ancho	an-cho
Have you a larger/ smaller one?	¿Tienen mayor/más pequeña?	Tee-en-en ma-yor/mas pe-ke-nya
Will it hold its colour?	¿Desteñirá?	Des-te-nyee-**ra**

Is it machine-washable?	¿Se puede lavar en la lavadora?	Se pwe-de la-bar en la la-ba-do-ra
Will it shrink?	¿Encogerá?	En-ko-he-ra
I need a pair of walking shoes	Necesito unos zapatos cómodos	Ne-the-see-to oo-nos tha-pa-tos ko-mo-dos

I want	Quiero	Kee-e-ro
beach sandals	unas sandalias de playa/unas chanclas	oo-nas san-da-lyas de pla-ya/oo-nas chan-klas
black shoes	unos zapatos negros	oo-nos tha-pa-tos ne-gros
a pair of boots	unas botas	oo-nas bo-tas
trainers	unas playeras/unas-bambas/unas-zapatillas de deporte	oo-nas pla-ye-ras/oo-nas bam-bas/oo-nas tha-pa-tee-llyas de de-por-te

Clothing sizes[1]

XS	XS	e-kees-e-se
S	S	e-se
M	M	e-me
L	L	e-le
XL	XL	e-kees-e-le
XXL	XXL	e-kees-e-kees-e-le

1. These tables are only intended as a rough guide, since sizes vary from manufacturer to manufacturer.

WOMEN'S CLOTHING

Coats, dresses, shirts, tops, trousers

UK/Australia	8	10	12	14	16	18
USA/Canada	6	8	10	12	14	16
EU	38	40	42	44	46	48

Shoes

UK	4	5	6	7	8	9	10
USA/Canada	5$\frac{1}{2}$	6$\frac{1}{2}$	7$\frac{1}{2}$	8$\frac{1}{2}$	9$\frac{1}{2}$	10$\frac{1}{2}$	11$\frac{1}{2}$
EU	37	38	39/40	41	42	43	44

MEN'S CLOTHING

Suits and coats

UK/USA/Canada	36	38	40	42	44	46
EU	46	48	50	52	54	56

Shirts

UK/USA/Canada	14	14$\frac{1}{2}$	15	15$\frac{1}{2}$	16	16$\frac{1}{2}$	17
EU	36	37	38	39	40	41	42

Shoes

UK	9$\frac{1}{2}$	10	10$\frac{1}{2}$	11	11$\frac{1}{2}$
USA/Canada	10	10$\frac{1}{2}$	11	11$\frac{1}{2}$	12
EU	43	44	44	45	45

Food[1]

Give me a kilo/half a kilo of . . ., please	**Un kilo/medio kilo de . . ., por favor**	Oon kee-lo/me-dyo kee-lo de . . . por fa-bor
100 grammes of sweets	**Cien gramos de caramelos**	Thee-en gra-mos de ka-ra-me-los
250 grammes of sliced ham/mature cheese	**Un cuarto de jamón en lonchas/de queso curado**	Oon kwar-to de ha-**mon** en lon-chas/de ke-so koo-ra-do
A bottle of	**Una botella de**	Oon-a bo-te-llya de
beer	**cerveza**	thair-be-tha
mineral water	**agua mineral**	a-gwa mi-ne-ral
wine	**vino**	bee-no
A litre of semi-skimmed/full-fat milk	**Un litro de leche semidesnatada/ entera**	Oon lee-tro de le-che se-mee-des-na-ta-da/ en-te-ra
A carton of plain yogurt	**Un bote de yogur natural**	Oon bo-te de yo-goor na-too-ral
A dozen/ half a dozen eggs	**Una docena/media docena de huevos**	Oo-na do-the-na/me-dya do-the-na de we-bos
I want	**Quiero**	Kee-e-ro
a jar of marmalade/ instant coffee	**un tarro de mermelada/de nescafé**	oon tar-ro de mair-me-la-da/de nes-ka-**fe**
a can of tomato sauce/tuna	**una lata de tomate frito/de atún**	oon-a la-ta de to-ma-te free-to/de a-**toon**
a packet of biscuits/ spaghetti	**un paquete de galletas/de espaguetis**	oon pa-ke-te de ga-llye-tas/ de es-pa-ge-tees

1. See also the various MENU sections (p. 118 ff) and WEIGHTS AND MEASURES (p. 246).

Do you sell frozen food?	**¿Venden congelados?**	Ben-den kon-he-la-dos
Is it fresh or frozen?	**¿Es fresco o congelado?**	Es fres-ko o kon-he-la-do
These pears are very hard/soft	**Estas peras están muy duras/blandas**	Es-tas pe-ras es-**tan** mwee doo-ras/ blan-das
Is it fresh?	**¿Está fresco?**	Es-**ta** fres-ko
Are they ripe?	**¿Están maduros?**	Es-**tan** ma-doo-ros
This is bad/off	**Esto está malo/ pasado**	Es-to es-**ta** ma-lo/ pa-sa-do
A loaf of bread, please[1]	**Una barra de pan, por favor**	Oo-na bar-ra de pan por fa-bor
How much a kilo/ a bottle?	**¿Cuánto cuesta el kilo/la botella?**	Kwan-to kwes-ta el kee-lo/la bo-te-llya
A kilo of chicken sausages	**Un kilo de salchichas de pollo**	Oon kee-lo de sal-chee-chas de po-llyo
Four pork chops	**Cuatro chuletas de cerdo**	Kwa-tro chu-le-tas de ther-do
Will you mince the meat?	**¿Me puede picar la carne?**	May pwe-de pee-kar la kar-ne
Will you bone it?	**¿Me quita el hueso?**	May kee-ta el oo-e-so
I'll take the bones	**Me llevo los huesos**	May llye-bo los oo-e-sos
Will you clean the fish?	**¿Me limpia el pescado?**	May leem-pya el pes-ka-do
Leave/Take off the head	**Deje/Quite la cabeza**	De-he/Kee-te la ka-be-tha

1. Spanish bread: *un pan de kilo/medio kilo* – a loaf weighing 1 kilo/½ kilo; *una barra de pan* – a French loaf/baguette; *bollos/panecillos* – rolls.

Please fillet the fish	¿Me quita la espina del pescado?	May kee-ta la es-pee-na del pes-ka-do
Is there any shellfish?	¿Tiene marisco?	Tee-e-ne ma-rees-ko
Shall I help myself?	¿Me sirvo yo?	May seer-bo yo

Hairdresser and Barber

May I make an appointment for this morning/tomorrow afternoon?	¿Pueden darme hora para esta mañana/para mañana por la tarde?	Pwe-den dar-me o-ra pa-ra es-ta ma-nya-na/pa-ra ma-nya-na por la tar-de
What time?	¿A qué hora?	A kay o-ra
I want my hair cut/trimmed	Quiero cortarme el pelo/cortarme las puntas	Kee-e-ro kor-tar-me el pe-lo/kor-tar-me las poon-tas
No shorter than this	No más corto que esto	No mas kor-to ke es-to
Not too short at the sides	No demasiado corto de los lados	No de-ma-see-a-do kor-to de los la-dos
I'll have it shorter at the back/on top	Más corto por atrás/por arriba	Mas kor-to por a-**tras**/por ar-ree-ba
That's fine	Así está bien	A-**see**-es-**ta** bee-en
My hair is oily/dry	Tengo el pelo graso/seco	Ten-go el pe-lo gra-so/se-ko
I want a shampoo	Quiero que me laven la cabeza	Kee-e-ro ke may la-ben la ka-be-tha
Please use conditioner	Por favor póngame suavizante	Por fa-bor **pon**-ga-me soo-a-bee-than-te

I want my hair washed, styled and blow-dried	**Quiero lavar y marcar (secado a mano)**	Kee-e-ro la-bar ee mar-kar (se-ka-do a ma-no)
Please do not use any hairspray	**No me ponga laca**	No may pon-ga la-ka
I want a colour rinse	**Quiero unos reflejos**	Kee-e-ro oo-nos re-fle-hos
I'd like to see a colour chart	**¿Puedo ver los colores?**	Pwe-do bair los ko-lo-res
I want a darker/ lighter shade	**Quiero un tono más oscuro/más claro**	Kee-e-ro oon to-no mas os-koo-ro/mas kla-ro
I'd like a tint/ highlights	**Quería teñirme/ unas mechas**	Ke-**ree**-a te-nyeer-me/ oo-nas me-chas
I'd like a shave, please	**Aféiteme, por favor**	A-**fay**-ee-te-me por fa-bor
Please trim my beard/my moustache	**Córteme un poco la barba/el bigote**	**Kor**-te-me oon po-ko la bar-ba/ el bee-go-te
The water is too cold	**El agua está demasiado fría**	El a-gwa es-**ta** de-ma-see-a-do **free**-a
The dryer is too hot	**El secador calienta demasiado**	El se-ka-dor ka-lee-en-ta de-ma-see-a-do
I want a manicure, please	**¿Pueden hacerme la manicura, por favor?**	Pwe-den a-thair-me la ma-nee-koo-ra por fa-bor
Thank you, I like it very much	**Me gusta mucho**	May goos–ta moo-cho

Hardware and Outdoors[1]

Where is the camping equipment?	¿El equipo de camping, por favor?	El e-kee-po de kam-ping por fa-bor
Do you have batteries for this?	¿Tienen pilas para esto?	Tee-e-nen pee-las pa-ra es-to
Where can I get butane gas/paraffin?	¿Dónde se puede comprar butano/parafina?	Don-de se pwe-de kom-prar boo-ta-no/pa-ra-fee-na
I need	Necesito	Ne-the-see-to
a bottle-opener	un abrebotellas	oon a-bre-bo-te-llyas
a corkscrew	un sacacorchos	oon sa-ka-kor-chos
a small/large screwdriver	un destornillador pequeño/grande	oon des-tor-nee-llya-dor pe-ke-nyo/gran-de
a tin-opener	un abrelatas	oon a-bre-la-tas
Some candles/matches, please	Una velas/cerillas, por favor	Oo-nas be-las/thair-ee-llyas por fa-bor
I want	Quiero	Kee-e-ro
a knife	un cuchillo	oon koo-chee-llyo
a pair of scissors	unas tijeras	oon-as tee-hair-as
a penknife	una navaja	oo-na na-ba-ha
a torch	una linterna	oon-a leen-ter-na
Do you sell string/rope?	¿Venden cuerda/soga?	Ben-den kwer-da/so-ga

1. See also CAMPING (p. 64) and APARTMENTS AND VILLAS (p. 73).

Where can I find washing-up liquid/ soap pads?	¿Dónde puedo comprar líquido lavavajillas/ estropajos?	Don-de pwe-do kom-prar **lee**-kee-do la-ba-ba-hee-llyas/ es-tro-pa-hos
Do you have dishcloths/brushes?	¿Tienen paños de cocina/cepillos?	Tee-e-nen pa-nyos de ko-thee-na/the-pee-llyos
I need	Necesito	Ne-the-see-to
a bucket	un cubo	oon koo-bo
a frying pan	una sartén	oon-a sar-**ten**
a groundsheet	una lona impermeable	oo-na lo-na eem-pair-me-a-ble
I want to buy a portable barbecue	Quiero comprar una barbacoa portátil	Kee-e-ro kom-prar oo-na bar-ba-ko-a por-**ta**-teel
Do you sell charcoal?	¿Venden carbón?	Ben-den kar-**bon**
adaptor	el adaptador	a-dap-ta-dor
basket	la cesta	thes-ta
duster	la bayeta para el polvo	ba-ye-ta pa-ra el pol-bo
extension lead	el alargador	a-lar-ga-dor
fuse	el fusible	foo-see-ble
insulating tape	la cinta aislante	theen-ta a-ees-lan-te
lightbulb	la bombilla	bom-bee-llya
plug (bath)	el tapón del baño	ta-**pon** del ba-nyo
plug (electric)	el enchufe	en-choo-fe

Laundry and Dry Cleaning

Where is the nearest dry cleaner?	¿Dónde está la tintorería más próxima?	Don-de es-**ta** la teen-to-rair-**ee**-a mas **pro**-see-ma
I want to have these things drycleaned	Quería que me limpiaran esto en seco	Ke-**ree**-a kay may leem-pee-ar-an es-to en se-ko
Can you get this stain out?	¿Se quitará esta mancha?	Se kee-ta-**ra** es-ta man-cha
It is	Es de	Es de
coffee	café	ka-**fe**
grease	grasa	gra-sa
wine	vino	bee-no
These stains won't come out	*Estas manchas no se quitan	Es-tas man-chas no se kee-tan
It only needs to be pressed	Sólo necesita plancharse	So-lo ne-the-see-ta plan-char-se
This is torn; can you mend it?	Esto está roto. ¿Pueden cosérmelo?	Es-to es-**ta** ro-to. Pwe-den ko-**sair**-me-lo
There's a button missing	Me falta un botón	May fal-ta oon bo-**ton**
Will you sew on another one?	¿Pueden ponerme otro?	Pwe-den po-nair-me o-tro
When will they be ready?	¿Cuándo estarán?	Kwan-do es-ta-**ran**
I need them by this evening/tomorrow	Los necesito para esta noche/para mañana	Los ne-the-see-to pa-ra es-ta no-che/pa-ra ma-nya-na

Call back at five o'clock	*Vuelva a las cinco	Bwel-ba a las theen-ko
We can't do it before Thursday	*No podemos hacerlo antes del jueves	No po-de-mos a-thair-lo an-tes del hwe-bes
It will take three days	*Estará dentro de tres días	Es-ta-ra den-tro de tres dee-as
This isn't mine	Esto no es mío	Es-to no es mee-o
I've lost my ticket	He perdido mi recibo	Ay pair-dee-do mee re-thee-bo

Household laundry

bath towel	la toalla de baño	to-a-llya de ba-nyo
blanket	la manta	man-ta
napkin	la servilleta	sair-bee-llye-ta
pillow case	el almohadón	al-mo-a-don
sheet	la sábana	sa-ba-na
tablecloth	el mantel	man-tel
tea towel	el paño de cocina	pa-nyo de ko-thee-na

Markets

Is there a market?	¿Hay mercado?	Eye mair-ka-do
Where is the market?	¿Dónde está el mercado?	Don-de es-ta el mair-ka-do
Is it a covered market or a street market?	¿Es un mercado cubierto o un mercadillo en la calle?	Es oon mair-ka-do koo-bee-er-to o oon mair-ka-dee-llyo en la ka-llye

Is the market held every day?	¿Hay mercado todos los días?	Eye mair-ka-do to-dos los **dee**-as
Which day is market day?	¿Que día es el mercado?	Ke **dee**-a es el mair-ka-do
Where is the market held?	¿Dónde ponen el mercadillo?	Don-de po-nen el mair-ka-dee-llyo
What time does it start/finish?	¿A qué hora empieza/termina?	A kay o-ra em-pee-e-tha/tair-mee-na
Is there a market today in a nearby town?	¿Hay mercado hoy en algún pueblo alrededor?	Eye mair-ka-do oy en al-**goon** pwe-blo al-re-re-dor

Photography

I want to buy a . . .	Quería una máquina fotográfica	Ke-**ree**-a oon-a ma-kee-na fo-to-**gra**-fee-ka
digital camera	digital	dee-hee-tal
disposable camera	de usar y tirar	de oo-sar ee tee-rar
camcorder	de video	de bee-de-o
Do you have a memory card for this camera?	¿Venden tarjetas de memoria para esta cámara?	Ben-den tar-he-tas de me-mo-rya pa-ra es-ta ka-ma-ra
Can you print photos from this card/disk/USB?	¿Se pueden imprimir fotos desde esta tarjeta/este CD/este lápiz?	Se pwe-den eem-pree-meer fo-tos des-de es-ta tar-he-ta/es-te thay-day/es-te **la**-peeth
I'd like prints/an enlargement of this image	Quería hacer copias/una ampliación de esta foto	Ke-**ree**-a a-ther ko-pyas/oo-na am-plee-a-**thyon** de es-ta fo-to

I'd like the express service	Quería el servicio rápido	Ke-ree-a el sair-bee-thyo ra-pee-do
When will it be ready?	¿Cuándo estará?	Kwan-do es-ta-ra
Will it be done tomorrow?	¿Estará mañana?	Es-ta-ra ma-nya-na
My camera's not working. Could you have a look at it?	Mi máquina no funciona. ¿Pueden mirar qué le pasa?	Mee ma-kee-na no foon-thyo-na. Pwe-den mee-rar ke le pa-sa
You will have to leave the camera for a few days	*Tendrá que dejarnos la cámara unos días	Ten-dra ke de-har-nos la ka-ma-ra oo-nos dee-as
battery	la pila	pee-la
camera case	la funda de la cámara	foon-da de la ka-ma-ra
film	la película	pe-lee-koo-la
filter	el filtro	feel-tro
glossy	con brillo	kon bree-llyo
lens	la lente	len-te
lens cap	la tapa de la lente	ta-pa de la len-te
light meter	el medidor de la luz	me-dee-dor de la looth
matt	mate/sin brillo	ma-te/seen bree-llyo

Repairs

| This is broken. Can you mend it? | Esto está estropeado. ¿Puede repararlo? | Es-to es-ta es-tro-pe-a-do. Pwe-de re-pa-rar-lo |
| Could you do it now? | ¿Podría hacerlo ahora? | Po-dree-a a-thair-lo a-or-a |

When should I come back for it?	¿Cuándo puedo recogerlo?	Kwan-do pwe-do re-ko-hair-lo
I want these shoes soled with leather/ heeled with rubber	Quiero que me pongan mediasuelas de cuero/tacones de goma	Kee-e-ro ke may pon-gan me-dee-a-soo-e-las de kwe-ro/ta-ko-nes de go-ma
Do you sell shoelaces?	¿Venden cordones de zapatos?	Ben-den kor-do-nes de tha-pa-tos
Can you repair this watch?	¿Pueden arreglarme este reloj?	Pwe-den ar-re-glar-me es-te re-loh
I have broken the	Se me ha roto	Se may a ro-to
glass	el cristal	el krees-tal
spring	el muelle	el mwe-llye
strap	la correa	la kor-re-a
Could you mend this bag/suitcase for me?	¿Me pueden arreglar esta bolsa/maleta?	May pwe-den ar-re-glar es-ta bol-sa/ma-le-ta
Could you put in a new zip?	¿Puede ponerle una cremallera nueva?	Pwe-de po-ner-le oo-na kre-ma-llye-ra nwe-ba
The stone/charm/ screw has come loose	La piedra/El colgante/La tuerca se ha soltado	La pee-e-dra/El kol-gan-te/La twer-ka se a sol-ta-do
The fastener/clip/ chain is broken	El cierre/El clip/La cadena se ha roto	El thee-er-re/El kleep/ La ka-de-na se a ro-to
It can't be repaired	*No tiene arreglo	No tee-e-ne ar-re-glo
You need a new one	*Necesita uno nuevo/una nueva	Ne-the-see-ta oo-no nwe-bo/oon-a nwe-ba
How much would a new one cost?	¿Cuánto costaría una nueva?	Kwan-to kos-tar-ee-a oon-a nwe-ba

Toiletries

A razor, please	**Una maquinilla de afeitar, por favor**	Oo-na ma-kee-nee-llya de a-fay-tar por fa-bor
A pack of razor blades, please	**Un paquete de cuchillas de afeitar, por favor**	Oon pa-ke-te de koo-chee-llyas de a-fay-tar por fa-bor
How much is this after-shave lotion?	**¿Cuánto cuesta esta loción para el afeitado?**	Kwan-to kwes-ta es-ta lo-**thyon** pa-ra el a-fay-ta-do
A tube of toothpaste, please	**Un tubo de pasta de dientes/Un dentífrico, por favor**	Oon too-bo de pas-ta de dee-en-tes/Oon den-**tee**-free-ko por fa-bor
A box of paper handkerchiefs/A roll of toilet paper, please	**Una caja de pañuelos de papel/Un rollo de papel higiénico, por favor**	Oon-a ka-ha de pa-nwe-los de pa-pel/Oon ro-llyo de pa-pel ee-hee-**e**-nee-ko por fa-bor
I'd like	**Quiero**	Kee-e-ro
a bar of soap	**una pastilla de jabón de manos**	oo-na past-ee-llya de ha-**bon** de ma-nos
some cleansing cream/lotion	**crema/loción limpiadora**	kre-ma/lo-**thyon** leem-pee-a-do-ra
some hair conditioner	**suavizante para el pelo**	soo-a-bee-than-te pa-ra el pe-lo
some hand cream	**crema de manos**	kre-ma de ma-nos
a lipsalve	**una barra de cacao**	oo-na ba-rra de ka-ka-o
a moisturizer	**una crema hidratante**	oo-na kre-ma ee-dra-tan-te

I want some eau-de-cologne/perfume, please	Un frasco de colonia/perfume, por favor	Oon fras-ko de ko-lo-nya/pair-foo-me por fa-bor
May I try it?	¿Puedo probarlo?	Pwe-do pro-bar-lo
A shampoo for dry/greasy hair, please	Champú para pelo seco/graso, por favor	Cham-**poo** pa-ra pe-lo se-ko/gra-so por fa-bor

SIGHTSEEING[1]

What should we see here?	¿Qué hay para ver aquí?	Kay eye pa-ra bair a-**kee**
I want a good guide book	Quiero una guía turística buena	Kee-e-ro oon-a **gee**-a too-**rees**-tee-ka bwe-na
Does the coach stop at . . . hotel?	¿Para el autocar en el hotel . . .?	Pa-ra el ow-to-kar en el o-tel

1. See also GETTING AROUND (p. 12) and DIRECTIONS (p. 52).

Can you suggest an interesting half-day excursion?	¿Puede aconsejarnos una excursión interesante de medio día?	Pwe-de a-kon-se-har-nos oo-na es-koor-**syon** een-te-re-san-te de me-dyo **dee**-a
Can we take a boat cruise/a balloon flight?	¿Podemos hacer un crucero/un vuelo en globo?	Po-de-mos a-ther oon kroo-the-ro/oon bwe-lo en glo-bo
We want to go hiking	Queremos hacer senderismo	Ke-rai-mos a-ther sen-de rees-mo
Do we need a guide?	¿Necesitamos un guía?	Ne-the-see-ta-mos oon **gee**-a
It's	Es	Es
beautiful	**precioso**	prai-thee-o-so
funny	**divertido**	dee-bair-tee-do
impressive	**impresionante**	eemp-rai-syon-an-tai
romantic	**romántico**	ro-**man**-te-ko
stunning	**sorprendente**	sor-pren-den-te
unusual	**inusual**	een-oo-swal

Exploring

I'd like to walk round the old town	Quiero dar una vuelta por la parte vieja	Kee-e-ro dar oon-a bwel-ta por la par-te bee-e-ha
Is there a good street plan showing the buildings?	¿Hay algún buen callejero con los edificios?	Eye al-**goon** bwen ka-llye-he-ro kon los e-dee-fee-thyos

We want to visit the	Queremos visitar	Ke-rai-mos bee-see-tar
cathedral	la catedral	la ka-te-dral
cloister	el claustro	el klaws-tro
fortress	la fortaleza/el castillo	la fort-al-ai-tha/el kas-tee-llyo
library	la biblioteca	la bee-blee-o-te-ka
monastery	el monasterio	el mo-nas-te-ryo
palace	el palacio	el pa-la-thyo
ruins	las ruinas	las roo-ee-nas
May we walk around the walls?	¿Podemos andar por las murallas?	Po-de-mos an-dar por las moo-ra-llyas
May we go up the tower?	¿Podemos subir a la torre?	Po-de-mos soo-beer a la to-rre
Where is the antiques market/flea market?	¿Dónde está el mercado de antigüedades/el rastro?	Don-de es-ta el mair-ka-do de an-tee-gwe-da-des/el ras-tro

Gardens, Parks and Zoos

Where is the botanic garden/zoo?	¿Dónde está el jardín botánico/zoológico?	Don-de es-ta el har-deen bo-ta-nee-ko/tho-lo-hee-ko
How do I get to the park?	¿Cómo puedo ir hasta el parque?	Ko-mo pwe-do eer as-ta el par-ke
Can we walk there?	¿Podemos ir andando?	Po-de-mos eer an-dan-do

Can we drive through the park?	¿Se puede ir en coche por el parque?	Se pwe-de eer en ko-che por el par-ke
Are the gardens open to the public?	¿Los jardines están abiertos al público?	Los har-dee-nes es-tan a-bee-er-tos al poo-blee-ko
What time do the gardens close?	¿A qué hora cierran los jardines?	A kay o-ra thee-e-rran los har-dee-nes
Is there a plan of the gardens?	¿Hay un plano de los jardines?	Eye oon pla-no de los har-dee-nes
Who designed the gardens?	¿Quién diseñó los jardines?	Kee-en dee-se-nyo los har-dee-nes
Where is the tropical plant house/lake?	¿Dónde está el invernadero/el lago?	Don-de es-ta el een-bair-na-de-ro/el la-go

Historic Sites

We want to visit . . . Can we get there by car?	Queremos visitar . . . ¿Podemos ir en coche?	Ke-rai-mos bee-see-tar . . . Po-de-mos eer en ko-che
Is there far to walk?	¿Hay que andar mucho?	Eye ke an-dar moo-cho
Is it an easy walk?	¿El camino es fácil?	El ka-mee-no es fa-theel
Is there access for wheelchairs?	¿Hay acceso para silla de ruedas?	Eye ath-ais-o pa-ra see-llya de rwe-das
Is it far to the	¿Está(n) lejos	Es-ta(n) le-hos
aqueduct?	el acueducto?	el a-kwe-dook-to
castle?	el castillo?	el kas-tee-llyo
cathedral?	la catedral?	la ka-te-dral

caves?	**las cuevas?**	las kwe-bas
fort?	**la fortaleza?**	la for-ta-le-tha
fortifications?	**las fortificaciones?**	las for-tee-fee-ka-thyo-nes
fountain?	**la fuente?**	la fwen-te
gate?	**la puerta/la entrada?**	la pwer-ta/la en-tra-da
walls?	**las murallas?**	las moo-ra-llyas
When was it built?	**¿Cuándo fue construido?**	Kwan-do fwe kons-troo-ee-do
Who built it?	**¿Quién lo construyó?**	Kee-en lo kons-troo-**yo**
Where is the old part of the city?	**¿Dónde está la parte vieja de la ciudad?**	Don-de es-**ta** la par-te bee-e-ha de la thee-oo-dad
What is this building?	**¿Qué es este edificio?**	Kay es es-te e-dee-fee-thyo
Where is the	**¿Dónde está**	Don-de es-**ta**
cemetery of...?	**el cementerio de...?**	el the-men-te-ryo de
church of...?	**la iglesia de...?**	la ee-gle-sya de
house of...?	**la casa de...?**	la ka-sa de

Museums and Galleries

| When does the museum open/close? | **¿A qué hora abren/cierran el museo?** | A kay o-ra a-bren/thee-e-ran el moo-se-o |
| Is it open every day? | **¿Está abierto todos los días?** | Es-**ta** a-bee-er-to to-dos los **dee**-as |

The gallery is closed on Mondays	*La galería está cerrada los lunes	La ga-le-**ree**-a es-**ta** the-rra-da los loo-nes
How much does it cost?	¿Cuánto cuesta?	Kwan-to kwes-ta
Are there reductions for	¿Hay descuento para	Eye des-kwen-to pa-ra
children?	los niños?	los nee-nyos
students?	los estudiantes?	los es-too-dee-an-tes
seniors	los de la tercera edad?	los de la ter-the-ra e-dad
Are admission fees lower on any special day?	¿Hay precios reducidos algún día en especial?	Eye pre-thyos re-doo-thee-dos al-**goon dee**-a en es-pe-thee-al
Admission free	*Entrada gratuita	En-tra-da gra-too-ee-ta
Have you got a ticket?	*¿Tiene usted entrada?	Tee-e-ne oos-te en-tra-da
Where do I buy a ticket?	¿Dónde compro la entrada?	Don-de kom-pro la en-tra-da
Is there a family ticket?	¿Hay entradas para familias?	Eye en-tra-das pa-ra fa-mee-lyas
Are there guided tours of the museum?	¿Hay visitas guiadas al museo?	Eye bee-see-tas gee-a-das al moo-se-o
Does the guide speak English?	¿Habla inglés el guía?	A-bla een-**gles** el **gee**-a
Is there an audio guide in English?	¿Hay una audio guía en inglés?	Eye oo-na a-oo-dyo **gee**-a en een-**gles**
We don't need a guide	No necesitamos un guía	No ne-the-see-ta-mos oon **gee**-a
I would prefer to go round alone; is that all right?	Prefiero ir yo solo; ¿se puede?	Pre-fee-e-ro eer yo so-lo; se pwe-de

Where is the . . . collection/exhibition?	¿Dónde está la colección/exposición (de) . . .?	Don-de es-**ta** la ko-lek-**thyon**/ es-po-see-**thyon** (de)
Please leave your bags in the cloakroom	*Por favor dejen los bolsos en el guardarropa	Por fa-bor de-hen los bol-sos en el gwar-dar-ro-pa
It's over there	Está allí	Es-**ta** à-**llyee**
Can I take photographs?	¿Se pueden hacer fotografías?	Se pwe-den a-ther fo-to-gra-**fee**-as
Can I use a tripod?	¿Puedo utilizar un trípode?	Pwe-do oo-tee-lee-thar oon **tree**-po-de
Flash photography	Fotografía con flash	Fo-to-gra-**fee**-a kon flash
Photographs are not allowed	*Prohibido hacer fotos	Pro-ee-bee-do a-ther fo-tos
I want to buy a catalogue	Quiero comprar un catálogo	Kee-e-ro kom-prar oon ka-**ta**-lo-go

Places of Worship

Is there a protestant church?	¿Hay una iglesia protestante?	Eye oo-na ee-gle-sya pro-tes-tan-te
Where is the	¿Dónde está la	Don-de es-**ta** la
cathedral?	catedral?	ka-te-dral
catholic church?	iglesia católica?	ee-gle-sya ka-**to**-lee-ka
mosque?	mezquita?	meth-kee-ta
synagogue?	sinagoga?	see-na-go-ga

What time is mass/ the service?	¿A qué hora hay misa/servicio?	A kay o-ra eye mee-sa/ ser-bee-thyo
I'd like to look round the church	Me gustaría ver la iglesia	May goos-ta-**ree**-a bair la ee-gle-sya
When was the church built?	¿Cuándo se construyó la iglesia?	Kwan-do se kons-troo-**yo** la ee-gle-sya

Tours

Is there a coach tour round the sights?	¿Hay una visita a los sitios de interés en autocar?	Eye oo-na bee-see-ta a los see-tyos de een-te-**res** en ow-toh-kar
Is there a sightseeing tour?	¿Hay un recorrido turístico/una excursión?	Eye oon re-kor-ee-do too-**rees**-tee-ko/oon-a es-koor-**syon**
Is there an excursion to...?	¿Hay una excursión a...?	Eye oon-a es-koor-**syon** a...
Is there a guided walking tour of the town?	¿Hay visitas guiadas a pie por la ciudad?	Eye bee-see-tas gee-a-das a pee-ai por la thee-oo-dad
How long does the tour take?	¿Cuánto dura la excursión?	Kwan-to doo-ra la es-koor-**syon**
When does it leave/ return?	¿A qué hora se sale/ se vuelve?	A kay o-ra se sa-le/ se bwel-be
Does the bus/coach stop at our hotel?	¿El autobús/autocar para en nuestro hotel?	El ow-toh-**boos**/ow-toh-kar pa-ra en nwes-tro o-tel
How much does the tour cost?	¿Cuánto cuesta la excursión?	Kwan-to kwes-ta la es-koor-**syon**

Are all admission fees included?	¿Están incluidas las entradas a los monumentos?	Es-**tan** een-kloo-ee-das las en-tra-das a los mo-noo-men-tos
Does it include lunch?	¿Está incluida la comida?	Es-**ta** een-kloo-ee-da la ko-mee-da
Could we stop here to	¿Podemos parar	Po-de-mos pa-rar
take photographs?	a hacer unas fotos?	a a-ther oo-nas fo-tos
buy souvenirs?	a comprar unos recuerdos?	a kom-prar oo-nos re-kwer-dos
get a bottle of water?	a comprar una botella de agua?	a kom-prar oo-na bo-te-llya de a-gwa
use the toilets?	para ir al servicio?	pa-ra eer al sair-bee-thyo
How long do we stay here?	¿Cuánto vamos a parar aquí?	Kwan-to ba-mos a pa-rar a-**kee**

SPORTS AND LEISURE[1]

Where is the nearest tennis court/golf course?	**¿Dónde hay una pista de tenis/un campo de golf?**	Don-de eye oo-na pees-ta de te-nees/ oon kam-po de golf
Is there a gym/ a running track?	**¿Hay un gimnasio/ una pista para correr?**	Eye oon him-na-syo/ oo-na pis-ta pa-ra ko-rrer
What is the charge per	**¿Cuánto cuesta**	Kwan-to kwes-ta
day?	**por día?**	por **dee**-a
game?	**por partida?**	por par-tee-da
hour?	**la hora?**	la o-ra
Is it a members' club?	**¿Es un club de socios?**	Es oon kloob de so-thyos
Do I need temporary membership?	**¿Tengo que hacerme socio temporalmente?**	Ten-go ke a-thair-me so-thyo tem-po-ral-men-te
Where can I go fishing?	**¿Dónde puedo ir a pescar?**	Don-de pwe-do eer a pes-kar
Can I hire	**¿Puedo alquilar**	Pwe-do al-kee-lar
a racket?	**una raqueta?**	oo-na ra-ke-ta
clubs?	**palos de golf?**	pa-los de golf
fishing tackle?	**equipo de pesca?**	e-kee-po de pes-ka
skates?	**patines?**	pa-tee-nes
Do I need a permit?	**¿Necesito permiso/ licencia?**	Ne-the-see-to per-mee-so/lee-then-thya

1. See also BY BIKE OR MOPED (p. 46).

Where do I get a permit?	¿Dónde puedo sacar la licencia?	Don-de pwe-do sa-kar la lee-then-thya
Is there a skating rink?	¿Hay pista de patinaje sobre hielo?	Eye pees-ta de pa-tee-na-he so-bre ee-e-lo
I'd like to ride	Me gustaría montar a caballo	May goos-ta-ree-a mon-tar a ka-ba-llyo
Is there a riding stable nearby?	¿Hay escuela hípica cerca?	Eye es-koo-e-la ee-pee-ka thair-ka
Do you give lessons?	¿Dan lecciones?	Dan le-thee-o-nes
I am a good rider	Monto bien a caballo	Mon-to beé-en a ka-ba-llyo

Winter Sports

Do you hire skis/ski boots?	¿Alquilan esquís/ botas de esquí?	Al-kee-lan es-kee-es/ bo-tas de es-kee
Do you give lessons here?	¿Dan clases?	Dan kla-ses
I've never skied before	No he esquiado nunca	No e es-kee-a-do noon-ka
Are there ski runs for beginners?	¿Tienen pistas para principiantes?	Tee-e-nen pees-tas pa-ra preen-thee-pee-an-tes
I'd like to go cross-country skiing	Quiero hacer esquí de fondo	Kee-e-ro a-ther es-kee de fon-do
Are there ski lifts?	¿Hay telesilla?	Eye te-le-see-llya
Can we go snowboarding?	¿Podemos hacer snowboarding?	Po-de-mos a-ther es-now-bor-deen

Can I buy a ski pass?	¿Puedo comprar un forfait?	Pwe-do kom-prar oon for-fait
helmet	el casco	kas-ko
rope tows	el remonte	re-mon-te
ski bindings	las fijaciones	fee-ha-thyo-nes
ski instructor	el monitor de esquí	mo-nee-tor de es-**kee**
ski pistes	las pistas de esquí	pees-tas de es-**kee**
ski poles	los bastones	bast-o-nes
ski resort	la estación de esquí	es-ta-**thyon** de es-**kee**
sledge	el trineo	tree-ne-o
snowboard	la tabla de snowboarding	ta-bla de es-now-bor-deen

At the Beach

Which is the best beach?	¿Cuál es la mejor playa?	Kwal es la me-hor pla-ya
How do we get to the cove?	¿Como se llega a la cala?	Ko-mo se llye-ga a la ka-la
Is there a quiet beach near here?	¿Hay por aquí alguna playa tranquila?	Eye por a-**kee** al-goo-na pla-ya tran-kee-la
Can I walk there?	¿Se puede ir andando?	Se pwe-de eer an-dan-do
Is there a bus to the beach?	¿Hay autobús a la playa?	Eye ow-toh-**boos** a la pla-ya

Is the beach of	¿Es la playa de	Es la pla-ya de
pebbles?	piedras?	pee-e-dras
rocks?	rocas?	ro-kas
sand?	arena?	a-re-na
Is it safe for swimming?	¿Se puede nadar sin peligro?	Se pwe-de na-dar sin pe-lee-gro
Is there a lifeguard?	¿Hay socorrista/ salvavidas?	Eye so-kor-rees-ta/sal-ba-bee-das
Is it safe for small children?	¿Es seguro para niños pequeños?	Es se-goo-ro pa-ra nee-nyos pe-ke-nyos
Does it get very rough?	¿Se pone el mar muy revuelto?	Se po-ne el mar mwee re-bwel-to
Bathing prohibited	*Prohibido bañarse	Pro-ee-bee-do ba-nyar-se
Nudist beach	Playa nudista	Pla-ya noo-dees-ta
Naturist/clothes free area	Zona naturista/anti-textil	Tho-na na-too-rees-ta/ an-tee-tes-teel
It's dangerous	*Hay peligro	Eye pel-ee-gro
What time is high/ low tide?	¿A qué hora es la marea alta/baja?	A kay o-ra es la ma-re-a al-ta/ba-ha
Is the tide rising/ falling?	¿Está la marea subiendo/bajando?	Es-ta la ma-re-a soo-bee-en-do/ba-han-do
Are there toilets?	¿Hay aseos?	Eye a-sai-os
I want to hire a deck chair/sunshade for	Quiero alquilar una hamaca/una sombrilla para	Kee-e-ro al-kee-lar oon-a a-ma-ka/oon-a som-bree-llya pa-ra
the day	todo el día	to-do el dee-a
the morning	la mañana	la ma-nya-na
two hours	dos horas	dos o-ras

Where can I buy a	¿Dónde puedo comprar	Don-de pwe-do kom-prar
ball?	una pelota de playa?	oon-a pe-lo-ta de pla-ya
beach bag?	un bolso playero?	oon bol-so pla-ye-ro
bucket and spade?	un cubo y una pala?	oon koo-bo ee oo-na pa-la
snorkel?	un tubo de bucear?	oon too-bo de boo-the-ar
beach bar	el bar de playa/ el chiringuito	bar de pla-ya/chee-reeng-ee-to
crab	el cangrejo	kan-gre-ho
first aid	los primeros auxilios	pree-me-ros a-oo-see-lyos
fishing net	la red de pescar	red de pes-kar
flippers	las aletas	a-le-tas
jellyfish	la medusa	me-doo-sa
lifeguard	el socorrista/el salvavidas	so-kor-rees-ta/sal-ba-bee-das
lifejacket	el chaleco salvavidas	cha-le-ko sal-ba-bee-das
lighthouse	el faro	fa-ro
outboard motor	el motor fueraborda	mo-tor fwe-ra-bor-da
rock	la roca	ro-ka
rockpool	el charco	char-ko
sand	la arena	a-re-na
sandbank	el banco de arena	ban-ko de a-re-na

sandcastle	**el castillo de arena**	kas-tee-llyo de a-re-na
shell	**la concha**	kon-cha
suncream	**la crema para el sol**	kre-ma pa-ra el sol
sunglasses	**las gafas de sol**	ga-fas de sol
swimming trunks	**el bañador**	ba-nya-dor
swimsuit	**el traje de baño**	tra-he de ban-yo
towel	**la toalla**	to-a-llya
wave	**la ola**	o-la

Swimming

Is there an indoor/ outdoor swimming pool?	**¿Hay piscina cubierta/al aire líbre?**	Eye pees-thee-na koo-bee-air-ta/ al a-ee-re lee-bre
Is it heated?	**¿Está climatizada?**	Es-**ta** klee-ma-tee-tha-da
Is the water cold?	**¿Está el agua fría?**	Es-**ta** el a-gwa **free**-a
It's warm	**Está caliente**	Es-**ta** ka-lee-en-te
Is it salt or fresh water?	**¿Es agua dulce o salada?**	Es a-gwa dul-the o sa-la-da
Can one swim in the lake/river?	**¿Se puede nadar en el lago/río?**	Se pwe-de na-dar en el la-go/**ree**-o
There's a strong current here	***Aquí hay mucha corriente**	A-**kee** eye moo-cha kor-ree-en-te
Is it deep?	**¿Hay mucha profundidad?**	Eye moo-cha pro-foon-dee-dad
You will be out of your depth	***No se hace pie**	No se a-the pee-ay

Are you a strong swimmer?	*¿Es usted buen nadador?	Es oos-ted bwen na-da-dor
Are there showers?	¿Hay duchas?	Eye doo-chas
No lifeguard on duty	*No hay salvavidas	No eye sal-ba-bee-das
armbands	los manguitos	man-gee-tos
goggles	las gafas de piscina/ de bucear	ga-fas de pis-thee-na/de boo-the-ar
rubber ring	el flotador	flo-ta-dor

Watersports

I'd like to try waterskiing	Quería hacer esquí aquático	Ke-ree-a a-thair es-kee a-kwa-tee-ko
I haven't tried it before	Nunca lo he hecho antes	Noon-ka lo e e-cho an-tes
Can I hire a wetsuit?	¿Puedo alquilar un traje de neopreno?	Pwe-do al-kee-lar oon tra-he de ne-o-pre-no
Do you have a course in windsurfing for beginners?	¿Tienen cursillos de windsurfing para principiantes?	Tee-en-en koor-see-llyos de ween-ser-fin pa-ra preen-thee-pyan-tes
Should I wear a life jacket?	¿Tengo que llevar chaleco salvavidas?	Ten-go ke llye-bar cha-le-ko sal-ba-bee-das
Can I hire	¿Puedo alquilar	Pwe-do al-kee-lar
diving equipment?	equipo de buceo?	e-kee-po de boo-the-o
a motor boat?	una motora?	oo-na mo-to-ra

a rowing boat?	**una barca de remos?**	oo-na bar-ka de re-mos
a surf board?	**una tabla de surf?**	oo-na ta-bla de soorf
a waterskiing board?	**una tabla de esquí acuático?**	oo-na ta-bla de es-**kee** a-**kwa**-tee-ko
Is there a map of the river?	**¿Tiene un mapa del río?**	Tee-e-ne oon ma-pa del **ree**-o
Can we get fuel here?	**¿Podemos repostar combustible aquí?**	Po-de-mos re-pos-tar kom-boos-tee-ble a-**kee**
Where's the harbour?	**¿Dónde está el puerto?**	Don-de es-**ta** el pwe-to
Can we go out in a fishing boat?	**¿Se puede salir a pescar en barca?**	Se pwe-de sa-leer a pes-kar en bar-ka
What does it cost by the hour?	**¿Cuánto cuesta por hora?**	Kwan-to kwes-ta por or-a

Walking[1]

I'd like a map of the area showing walking trails	**Quiero un mapa con las rutas a pie de la zona**	Kee-e-ro oon ma-pa kon las roo-tas a pee-ai de la tho-na
Can we walk?	**¿Podemos ir andando?**	Po-de-mos eer an-dan-do
How far is the next village?	**¿A cuánto está el próximo pueblo?**	A kwan-to es-**ta** el pro-see-mo pwe-blo
How long is the walk to ...?	**¿Qué distancia hay a ...?**	Ke dees-tan-thya eye a
It's an hour's walk to ...	***Hay una hora de camino a ...**	Eye oon-a o-ra de ka-mee-no a

1. See also DIRECTIONS (p. 52).

Which way is the	¿Por dónde se va	Por don-de se ba
lake?	al lago?	al la-go
nature reserve?	a la reserva natural?	a la re-sair-ba na-too-ral
waterfall?	a la cascada?	a la kas-ka-da
Is there a scenic walk to ...?	¿Hay una ruta panorámica a ...?	Eye oo-na roo-ta pa-no-ra-mee-ka a
Is it far?	¿Está lejos?	Es-ta le-hos
Is it steep?	¿Hay mucha cuesta?	Eye moo-cha kwes-ta
Is it difficult?	¿Es difícil?	Es dee-fee-theel
Is there a footpath to ...?	¿Hay un camino a ...?	Eye oon ka-mee-no a
Is it possible to go across country?	¿Se puede ir campo a través?	Se pwe-de eer kam-po a tra-bes
Is there a shortcut?	¿Hay algún atajo?	Eye al-goon a-ta-ho
Is there a bridge across the stream?	¿Hay un puente para cruzar el arroyo?	Eye oon pwen-te pa-ra kroo-thar el ar-roy-o
Can you give me a lift to ...?	¿May puede llevar a ...?	May pwe-de llye-bar a

Spectator Sports and Indoor Games

We want to go to a	Queremos ir a	Ke-rai-mos eer a
basketball match	un partido de baloncesto	oon par-tee-do de ba-lon-thest-o
bullfight	una corrida de toros	oo-na ko-rre-da de to-ros

football match	**un partido de fútbol**	oon par-**tee**-do de **foot**-bol
tennis match	**un partido de tenis**	oon par-**tee**-do de te-nees
Who's fighting the bull today?	**¿Quién torea hoy?**	Kee-en to-re-a oy
Can you get us tickets?	**¿Nos puede sacar entradas?**	Nos pwe-de sa-kar en-tra-das
Are there seats in the grandstand?	**¿Tienen entradas de tribuna?**	Tee-e-nen en-tra-das de tree-boo-na
How much are the cheapest seats?	**¿Cuánto valen las entradas más baratas?**	Kwan-to ba-len las en-tra-das mas ba-ra-tas
Are they in the sun or the shade?	**¿Son de sol o sombra?**	Son de sol o som-bra
Who is playing?	**¿Quién juega?**	Kee-en hwe-ga
When does it start?	**¿A qué hora empieza?**	A kay o-ra em-pee-e-tha
Who is winning?	**¿Quién gana?**	Kee-en ga-na
What is the score?	**¿Cómo van?**	Ko-mo ban
Where is the racecourse?	**¿Dónde está el hipódromo?**	Don-de es-**ta** el ee-**po**-dro-mo
Which is the favourite?	**¿Cuál es el favorito?**	Kwal es el fa-bo-ree-to
Who is the jockey?	**¿Quién es el jinete?**	Kee-en es el he-ne-tay
Where can I place a bet?	**¿Dónde puedo hacer una apuesta?**	Don-de pwe-do a-ther oo-na a-pwes-ta

Do you play cards?	**¿Juega a las cartas?**	Hwe-ga a las kar-tas
Would you like a game of chess?	**¿Quiere jugar una partida de ajedrez?**	Kee-e-re hoo-gar oo-na par-tee-da de a-he-dreth

TRAVELLING WITH CHILDREN

Key Phrases

Are children allowed?	¿Pueden entrar los niños?	Pwe-den en-trar los nee-nyos
Is there a lower price for children?	¿Hay descuento para niños?	Eye des-kwen-to pa-ra nee-nyos
Are there any organized activities for children?	¿Se organizan juegos para los niños?	Se or-ga-nee-than hwe-gos pa-ra los nee-nyos
Can you put a child's bed/cot in our room?	¿Puede poner una camita/cuna en nuestra habitación?	Pwe-de po-nair oon-a ka-mee-ta/koo-na en nwes-tra a-bee-ta-**thyon**
Where can I feed/change my baby?	¿Dónde puedo dar de comer al niño/cambiar mi bebé?	Don-de pwe-do dar de ko-mair al nee-nyo/kam-byar mee be-**be**
My son/daughter is missing	Se ha perdido mi hijo/hija	Se ah per-dee-do mee ee-ho/ee-ha

Out and About[1]

Is there	¿Hay	Eye
an amusement park?	un parque de atracciones?	oon par-ke de a-trak-thee-o-nes
a fair?	una feria/las barracas?	oo-na fai-rya/ las bar-ra-kas
a games room?	una sala de juegos recreativos?	oo-na sa-la de hwe-gos re-kre-a-tee-bos
a playground?	algún parque infantil?	al-**goon** par-ke een-fan-teel
a toyshop?	una tienda de juguetes?	oo-na tee-en-da de hoo-ge-tes
a zoo?	un parque zoológico?	oon par-ke tho-**lo**-hee-ko
Where is the aquarium?	¿Dónde está el acuario?	Don-de es-**ta** el a-kwa-ryo
Is there a paddling pool/ children's swimming pool?	¿Tienen piscina pequeña/piscina de niños?	Tee-e-nen pees-thee-na pe-ke-nya/pees-thee-na de nee-nyos
Is the beach safe for children?	¿Es segura la playa para los niños?	Es se-goo-ra la pla-ya pa-ra los nee-nyos
Can we hire a canoe/ paddle boat?	¿Puedo alquilar una canoa/patín acuático?	Pwe-do al-kee-lar oo-na ka-no-a/oon pa-**teen** a-**kwa**-tee-ko
Are there snorkeling/ skiing/(horse)riding lessons for children?	¿Hay clases de buceo/de esquiar/de montar (a caballo) para niños?	Eye kla-ses de boo-thai-o/de es-kee-ar/ de mon-tar (a ka-ba-llyo) pa-ra nee-nyos

1. See also AT THE BEACH (p. 218).

I'd like	Quiero	Kee-e-ro
a doll	una muñeca	oon-a moo-nye-ka
some playing cards	una baraja	oon-a ba-ra-ha
a pair of roller skates	unos patines	oon-os pa-tee-nes
He has lost his toy	Ha perdido su juguete	A pair-dee-do soo hoo-ge-te
I'm sorry if they have bothered you	Perdone si le han molestado	Pair-do-ne see le an mo-les-ta-do

Everyday Needs

Can you put a child's bed/cot in our room?	¿Puede poner una camita/cuna en nuestra habitación?	Pwe-de po-nair oon-a ka-mee-ta/koo-na en nwes-tra a-bee-ta-**thyon**
Can you give us adjoining rooms?	¿Nos puede dar habitaciones contiguas?	Nos pwe-de dar a-bee-ta-thyo-nes kon-tee-gwas
Does the hotel have a babysitting service?	¿Tiene este hotel servicio de niñeras/canguros?	Tee-e-ne es-te o-tel sair-bee-thyo de nee-nye-ras/kan-goo-ros
Can you find me a babysitter?	¿Puede buscarme una niñera/canguro?	Pwe-de boos-kar-me oon-a nee-nye-ra/kan-goo-ro
We shall be out for a couple of hours	Estaremos fuera dos horas	Es-ta-re-mos fwe-ra dos o-ras
We shall be back at ...	Volveremos a las ...	Bol-be-rai-mos a las
You can reach me at ...	Me puede localizar en ...	May pwe-de lo-ka-lee-thar en

This is my mobile (cell) number	**Este es mi número de móvil**	Este es mee **noo**-me-ro de **mo**-beel
Is there a children's menu?	**¿Hay menú de niños?**	Eye me-**noo** de nee-nyos
Do you have small portions for children?	**¿Tiene raciones pequeñas para niños?**	Tee-e-ne ra-thee-o-nes pe-ke-nyas pa-ra nee-nyos
Have you got a high chair?	**¿Tiene sillita de niños/una trona?**	Tee-e-ne see-llyee-ta de nee-nyos/oo-na tro-na
Where can I feed/ change my baby?	**¿Dónde puedo dar de comer al niño/ cambiar mi bebé?**	Don-de pwe-do dar de ko-mair al nee-nyo/kam-byar mee be-**be**
Can you heat the bottle for me?	**¿Puede calentarme el biberón?**	Pwe-de ka-len-tar-me el bee-be-**ron**
I want	**Quiero**	Kee-e-ro
baby food	**potitos de niño**	po-tee-tos de nee-nyo
baby wipes	**toallitas de bebé**	to-a-llyee-tas de be-**be**
a bib	**un babero**	oon ba-be-ro
a feeding bottle	**un biberón**	oon bee-be-**ron**
disposable nappies	**pañales desechables**	pa-nya-les de-se-cha-bles

Health and Emergencies[1]

| My daughter suffers from travel sickness | **Mi hija se marea en los viajes** | Mee ee-ha se ma-re-a en los bee-a-hes |
| She has hurt herself | **Se ha hecho daño** | Se a e-cho da-nyo |

1. See also DOCTOR (p. 149).

My son is ill	**Mi hijo está enfermo**	Mee ee-ho es-**ta** en-fair-mo
He is allergic to . . .	**Es alérgico a . . .**	Es al-**air**-hee-ko a
My son/daughter is missing	**Se ha perdido mi hijo/hija**	Se ah per-dee-do mee ee-ho/ee-ha
He/she is . . . years old	**Tiene . . . años**	Tee-e-ne . . . a-nyos
He/she is wearing . . .	**Lleva . . .**	Llye-ba

WORK[1]

I am here on business	**Estoy aquí de negocios**	Es-toy a-**kee** de ne-go-thyos
Where is the conference centre/ exhibition centre?	**¿Dónde está el centro de congresos/ recinto ferial/centro de exposiciones y congresos?**	Don-de es-**ta** el then-tro de kon-gre-sos/ re-theen-to fair-ee-al/ then-tro de es-po-see-thyo-nes ee kon-gre-sos
I'm here for the . . . trade fair	**He venido por la feria de . . .**	Ay be-nee-do por la fai-rya de
I've come to a conference/a seminar	**He venido a una conferencia/un seminario/un congreso**	Ay be-nee-do a oo-na kon-fe-ren-thya/ oon se-mee-na-ryo/ oon kon-gre-so
This is my colleague	**Este es mi colega**	Es-te es mee ko-le-ga
I have an appointment with . . .	**Tengo una cita con . . .**	Ten-go oo-na thee-ta kon
Here is my card	**Tenga mi tarjeta**	Ten-ga mee tar-he-ta
Can you provide an interpreter?	**¿Puede traer un intérprete?**	Pwe-de tra-er oon een-**tair**-pre-te

1. See also TELEPHONE, MOBILES AND SMS (p. 91).

TIME AND DATES

Time

What time is it?	¿Qué hora es?	Kay o-ra es
It's one o'clock	Es la una	Es la oon-a
It's	Son las	Son las
two o'clock	dos	dos
quarter to ten	diez menos cuarto	dy-eth me-nos kwar-to
quarter past five	cinco y cuarto	theen-ko ee kwar-to
half past four	cuatro y media	kwa-tro ee me-dya
five past eight	ocho y cinco	o-cho ee theen-ko
twenty to three	tres menos veinte	tres me-nos beyn-te
twenty-five past eight	ocho y veinticinco	o-cho ee beyn-tee-theen-ko
It's early/late	Es temprano/tarde	Es tem-pra-no/tar-de
My watch is slow/fast	Mi reloj está atrasado/ adelantado	Mee re-loh es-ta a-tra-sa-do/a-de-lan-ta-do
The clock has stopped	Se ha parado el reloj	Se a pa-ra-do el re-loh
I am late	Llego tarde	Llye-go tar-de
Sorry I am late	Perdone el retraso	Pair-do-ne el re-tra-so

Days

Sunday	**domingo**	do-meen-go
Monday	**lunes**	loo-nes
Tuesday	**martes**	mar-tes
Wednesday	**miércoles**	mee-**air**-ko-les
Thursday	**jueves**	hwe-bes
Friday	**viernes**	bee-air-nes
Saturday	**sábado**	**sa**-ba-do

Months

January	**enero**	e-nair-o
February	**febrero**	feb-rair-o
March	**marzo**	mar-tho
April	**abril**	ab-reel
May	**mayo**	ma-yo
June	**junio**	hoo-nyo
July	**julio**	hoo-lyo
August	**agosto**	a-gos-toh
September	**setiembre**	se-tyem-bre
October	**octubre**	ok-too-bre
November	**noviembre**	no-byem-bre
December	**diciembre**	dee-thyem-bre

Seasons

spring	**la primavera**	pree-ma-bair-a
summer	**el verano**	bair-ra-no
autumn	**el otoño**	oto-nyo
winter	**el invierno**	een-byair-no

Periods of Time

second	**el segundo**	se-goon-do
minute	**el minuto**	mee-noo-to
hour	**la hora**	o-ra
morning	**la mañana**	ma-nya-na
this morning	**esta mañana**	es-ta ma-nya-na
in the morning	**por la mañana**	por la ma-nya-na
at midday/noon	**al mediodía**	al me-dee-o-**dee**-a
afternoon	**la tarde**	tar-de
yesterday afternoon	**ayer por la tarde**	a-yair por la tar-de
at dusk/nightfall¹	**al anochecer**	al a-no-che-thair
tomorrow night	**mañana por la noche**	ma-nya-na por la no-che
midnight	**la medianoche**	me-dee-a-no-che
night	**la noche**	no-che

1. Spanish has no exact equivalent of the English word 'evening': *la tarde* is used if the time is before sunset; *la noche* if it is after.

at night	por la noche/de noche	por la no-che/de no-che
day	el día	dee-a
by day	de día	de dee-a
today	hoy	oy
tonight	esta noche	es-ta no-che
yesterday	ayer	a-yair
day before yesterday	anteayer	an-te-a-yair
four days ago	hace cuatro días	a-the kwa-tro dee-as
tomorrow	mañana	ma-nya-na
day after tomorrow	pasado mañana	pa-sa-do ma-nya-na
in ten days' time	dentro de diez días	den-tro de dyeth dee-as
on Tuesday	el martes	el mar-tes
on Sundays	los domingos	los do-meen-gos
week	la semana	se-ma-na
weekend	el fin de semana	feen de se-ma-na
on weekdays	los días de diario	los dee-as de dee-a-ryo
every week	todas las semanas	to-das las se-ma-nas
once a week	una vez a la semana	oo-na beth a la se-ma-na
fortnight	quince días/dos semanas	keen-the dee-as/dos se-ma-nas
month	el mes	mes
in January	en enero	en e-ne-ro

since March	**desde marzo**	des-de mar-tho
this year	**este año**	es-te an-yo
last year	**el año pasado**	el an-yo pa-sa-do
next year	**el próximo año/el año que viene**	el **pro**-see-mo an-yo/ el an-yo kay bye-ne
in spring	**en primavera**	en pree-ma-bair-a
during the summer	**durante el verano**	doo-ran-te el bai-ra-no
sunrise	**el amanecer**	a-ma-ne-thair
at sunrise	**al amanecer**	al a-ma-ne-thair
dawn	**la madrugada**	ma-droo-ga-da
at dawn	**de madrugada**	de ma-droo-ga-da
sunset/twilight	**el crepúsculo**	kre-**poos**-koo-lo

Dates

What's the date?	**¿A cuántos estamos?/¿Qué día es hoy?**	A kwan-tos es-ta-mos/ Kay **dee**-a es oy
It's 9 December[1]	**Hoy es el nueve de diciembre**	Oy es el nwe-be de dee-thyem-bre
We're leaving on 5 January	**Nos marchamos el cinco de enero**	Nos mar-cha-mos el theen-ko de e-nair-o
We got here on 27 July	**Llegamos el veintisiete de julio**	Llye-ga-mos el beyn-tee-sye-te de hoo-lyo

1. Cardinal numbers are used for dates in Spanish, except for 1st which is *primero*.

Public Holidays[1]

1 Jan – New Year's Day	1 de enero – Año Nuevo
6 Jan – Epiphany	6 de enero – Día de Reyes
Good Friday	Viernes Santo – Pascua
1 May – Labour Day	1 de mayo – Día del Trabajo
15 Aug – Assumption Day	15 de agosto – Día de la Asunción de la Virgen
12 Oct	12 de octubre – Día de la Hispanidad
1 Nov – All Saints' Day	1 de noviembre – Día de Todos los Santos
6 Dec – Constitution Day	6 de diciembre – Día de la Constitución Española
8 December – Immaculate Conception Day	8 de diciembre – Día de la Inmaculada Concepción
25 December – Christmas	25 de diciembre – Navidad

1. Apart from the 10 national holidays, every Autonomous Region has a 'Día de la Comunidad' as well as other local holidays; towns and villages celebrate particular festivities, e.g. the day of the patron saint.

WEATHER

What is the weather forecast?	**¿Cuál es la previsión del tiempo?**	Kwal es la pre-bee-**syon** del tee-em-po
What is the temperature?	**¿Qué temperatura hay?**	Kay tem-pe-ra-too-ra eye
Is it usually as hot as this?	**¿Hace tanto calor normalmente?**	A-the tan-to ka-lor nor-mal-men-te
It's going to be hot/ cold today	***Hoy va a hacer calor/frío**	Oy ba a a-thair ka-lor/ **free**-o
The weather is good/bad	**Hace buen/mal tiempo**	A-the bwen/mal tee-em-poo
The weather is very good/very bad	**Hace muy bueno/ malísimo**	A-the mwee bwe-no/ ma-**lee**-see-mo
It's windy	**Hace viento**	A-the vee-en-to
It's misty/foggy	**Hay niebla**	Eye nee-e-bla
It's sunny	**Hay sol**	Eye sol
The mist will clear later	***Luego se levanta la niebla**	Lwe-go se le-ban-ta la nee-e-bla
It's raining	**Llueve**	Llwe-bay
Will it be fine tomorrow?	**¿Hará buen tiempo mañana?**	A-**ra** bwen tee-em-po ma-nya-na
Do you think it's going to rain/snow?	**¿Cree que va a llover/nevar?**	Kre-e ke ba a llyo-ber/ ne-bar

clear	**claro**	kla-ro
cloudy	**nublado**	noo-bla-do
frost	**la escarcha**	es-kar-cha
hail	**el granizo**	gra-nee-tho
humid	**húmedo**	oo-me-do
ice	**el hielo**	ye-lo
storm	**la tormenta**	tor-men-ta

OPPOSITES

before/after	**antes/después**	an-tes/des-**pwes**
early/late	**temprano, pronto/ tarde**	tem-pra-no, pron-to/ tar-de
first/last	**primero/último**	pree-me-ro/**ool**-tee-mo
now/then	**ahora/antes, entonces**	a-or-a/an-tes, en-ton-thes
far/near	**lejos/cerca**	le-hos/thair-ka
here/there	**aquí/allí**	a-**kee**/a-**llyee**
in/out	**dentro/fuera**	den-tro/fwer-a
inside/outside	**dentro/fuera**	den-tro/fwer-a
under/over	**debajo/encima**	de-ba-ho/en-thee-ma
big, large/small	**grande/pequeño**	gran-de/pe-ke-nyo
deep/shallow	**profundo/poco profundo, superficial**	pro-foon-do/po-co pro-foon-do, soo-per-fee-thyal
empty/full	**vacío/lleno**	ba-**thee**-oh/llye-no
fat/thin *(material)*	**grueso/fino**	groo-eh-so/fee-no
fat/thin *(person)*	**gordo/delgado**	gor-do/del-ga-do
heavy/light	**pesado/ligero**	pe-sa-doh/lee-hair-o
high/low	**alto/bajo**	al-to/ba-ho
long/short	**largo/corto**	lar-go/kor-to

tall/short	**alto/bajo**	al-to/ba-ho
narrow/wide	**estrecho/ancho**	es-tre-cho/an-cho
many/few	**muchos/pocos**	moo-chos/po-kos
more/less	**más/menos**	mas/me-nos
much/little	**mucho/poco**	moo-cho/po-ko
beautiful/ugly	**bonito/feo**	bo-nee-to/fay-o
better/worse	**mejor/peor**	me-hor/pe-or
cheap/expensive	**barato/caro**	ba-ra-to/ka-ro
clean/dirty	**limpio/sucio**	leem-pyo/soo-thyo
cold/hot, warm	**frío/caliente**	**free**-o/ka-lee-en-te
easy/difficult	**fácil/difícil**	fa-theel/dee-**fee**-theel
fresh/stale	**fresco/pasado**	fres-ko/pa-sa-do
good/bad	**bueno/malo**	bwe-no/ma-lo
young/old	**joven/viejo**	ho-ben/bye-ho
new/old	**nuevo/viejo**	nwe-bo/bye-ho
right/left	**derecha/izquierda**	de-re-cha/eeth-kee-air-da
right/wrong	**correcto/incorrecto**	ko-rek-to/een-ko-rek-to
vacant/occupied	**libre/ocupado**	lee-bre/o-koo-pa-do
open/closed, shut	**abierto/cerrado**	a-byer-to/ther-ra-do
quick/slow	**rápido/lento**	**ra**-pee-do/len-to
quiet/noisy	**tranquilo/ruidoso**	tran-kee-lo/roo-ee-do-so

NUMBERS

Cardinal

0	cero	the-ro
1	uno/un, una	oo-no/oon, oo-na
2	dos	dos
3	tres	tres
4	cuatro	kwa-tro
5	cinco	theen-ko
6	seis	says
7	siete	sye-te
8	ocho	o-cho
9	nueve	nwe-be
10	diez	dyeth
11	once	on-the
12	doce	do-the
13	trece	tre-the
14	catorce	ka-tor-the
15	quince	keen-the
16	diez y seis/dieciséis	dyeth ee says
17	diez y siete/diecisiete	dyeth ee sye-te

18	**diez y ocho/dieciocho**	dyeth ee o-cho
19	**diez y nueve/diecinueve**	dyeth ee nwe-be
20	**veinte**	bain-te
21	**veintiuno**	bain-tee-oo-no
22	**veintidós**	bain-tee-**dos**
30	**treinta**	train-ta
31	**treinta y uno**	train-ta ee oo-no
40	**cuarenta**	kwa-ren-ta
41	**cuarenta y uno**	kwa-ren-ta ee oo-no
50	**cincuenta**	theen-kwen-ta
51	**cincuenta y uno**	theen-kwen-ta ee oo-no
60	**sesenta**	se-sen-ta
61	**sesenta y uno**	se-sen-ta ee oo-no
70	**setenta**	se-ten-ta
71	**setenta y uno**	se-ten-ta ee oo-no
80	**ochenta**	o-chen-ta
81	**ochenta y uno**	o-chen-ta ee oo-no
90	**noventa**	no-ben-ta
91	**noventa y uno**	no-ben-ta ee oo-no
100	**cien/ciento**	thyen/thyen-to
101	**ciento uno**	thyen-to oo-no
200	**doscientos**	dos-thyen-tos
500	**quinientos**	kin-yen-tos

700	setecientos	se-te-thyen-tos
1,000	mil	meel
2,000	dos mil	dos meel
1,000,000	un millón	oon mee-llyon

Ordinal

1st	primero/primer, primera	pree-mair-o/pree-mair, pree-mair-a
2nd	segundo, -a	se-goon-do
3rd	tercero, -a	tair-thair-o
4th	cuarto, -a	kwar-to
5th	quinto, -a	keen-to
6th	sexto, -a	ses-to
7th	séptimo, -a	sep-tee-mo
8th	octavo, -a	ok-ta-bo
9th	noveno, -a	no-be-no
10th	décimo, -a	de-thee-mo
half	medio, -a/la mitad	me-dyo/mee-ta
quarter	un cuarto	oon kwar-to
three quarters	tres cuartos	tres kwar-tos
a third	un tercio	oon tair-thyo
two thirds	dos tercios	dos tair-thyos

WEIGHTS AND MEASURES

Distance

kilometres – miles

km	miles or km	miles		km	miles or km	miles
1.6	1	0.6		14.5	9	5.6
3.2	2	1.2		16.1	10	6.2
4.8	3	1.9		32.2	20	12.4
6.4	4	2.5		40.2	25	15.3
8.0	5	3.1		80.5	50	31.1
9.7	6	3.7		160.9	100	62.1
11.3	7	4.4		804.7	500	310.7
12.9	8	5.0				

A rough way to convert from miles to km: divide by 5 and multiply by 8; from km to miles, divide by 8 and multiply by 5.

Length and Height

centimetres – inches

cm	ins or cm	ins	cm	ins or cm	ins
2.5	1	0.4	17.8	7	2.8
5.1	2	0.8	20.3	8	3.2
7.6	3	1.2	22.9	9	3.5
10.2	4	1.6	25.4	10	3.9
12.7	5	2.0	50.8	20	7.9
15.2	6	2.4	127.0	50	19.7

A rough way to convert from inches to cm: divide by 2 and multiply by 5; from cm to inches, divide by 5 and multiply by 2.

metres – feet

m	ft or m	ft	m	ft or m	ft
0.3	1	3.3	2.4	8	26.2
0.6	2	6.6	2.7	9	29.5
0.9	3	9.8	3.0	10	32.8
1.2	4	13.1	6.1	20	65.6
1.5	5	16.4	15.2	50	164.0
1.8	6	19.7	30.5	100	328.1
2.1	7	23.0			

A rough way to convert from feet to m: divide by 10 and multiply by 3; from m to feet, divide by 3 and multiply by 10.

metres – yards

m	yds or m	yds	m	yds or m	yds
0.9	1	1.1	7.3	8	8.7
1.8	2	2.2	8.2	9	9.8
2.7	3	3.3	9.1	10	10.9
3.7	4	4.4	18.3	20	21.9
4.6	5	5.5	45.7	50	54.7
5.5	6	6.6	91.4	100	109.4
6.4	7	7.7	457.2	500	546.8

A rough way to convert from yards to m: subtract 10 per cent from the number of yards; from m to yards, add 10 per cent to the number of metres.

Liquid Measures

litres – gallons

litres	galls or litres	galls	litres	galls or litres	galls
4.6	1	0.2	36.4	8	1.8
9.1	2	0.4	40.9	9	2.0
13.6	3	0.7	45.5	10	2.2
18.2	4	0.9	90.9	20	4.4
22.7	5	1.1	136.4	30	6.6
27.3	6	1.3	181.8	40	8.8
31.8	7	1.5	227.3	50	11.0

A rough way to convert from gallons to litres: divide by 2 and multiply by 9; from litres to gallons, divide by 9 and multiply by 2.

Weight

kilogrammes – pounds

kg	lb or kg	lb	kg	lb or kg	lb
0.5	1	2.2	3.2	7	15.4
0.9	2	4.4	3.6	8	17.6
1.4	3	6.6	4.1	9	19.8
1.8	4	8.8	4.5	10	22.0
2.3	5	11.0	9.1	20	44.1
2.7	6	13.2	22.7	50	110.2

A rough way to convert from pounds to kg: divide by 11 and multiply by 5; from kg to pounds, divide by 5 and multiply by 11.

grammes – ounces

grammes	oz	oz	grammes
100	3.5	2	56.7
250	8.8	4	113.4
500	17.6	8	226.8
1,000 (1 kg)	35.0	16 (1 lb)	453.6

Temperature

centigrade (°C) – fahrenheit (°F)

°C	°F	°C	°F	°C	°F
- 10	14	15	59	37	98.4
- 5	23	20	68	38	100.5
0	32	25	77	39	102.0
5	41	30	86	40	104.0
10	50	35	95	100	212.0

To convert °F to °C: deduct 32, divide by 9 and multiply by 5; to convert °C to °F, divide by 5, multiply by 9 and add 32.

BASIC GRAMMAR

Nouns

Nouns in Spanish are either masculine or feminine. Nouns denoting males are masculine, as are most nouns ending in **-o**. Nouns denoting females are feminine, as are most nouns ending in **-a**.

e.g. **tío** – uncle; **vaso** – glass; **tía** – aunt; **playa** – beach.

Plural

The plural is formed by adding **-s** if the word ends in a vowel; **-es** if it ends in a consonant.

e.g. ventana (window) – ventana**s**; tren (train) – tren**es**.

Definite Article

the

el before a masculine singular noun	**el banco** (the bank)
los before a masculine plural noun	**los bancos**
la before a feminine singular noun	**la cesta** (the basket)
las before a feminine plural noun	**las cestas**

Indefinite Article

a, an

| un before a masculine singular noun | **un banco** (a bank) |
| una before a feminine singular noun | **una cesta** (a basket) |

Adjectives

Adjectives agree in number and gender with the noun.

Those ending in **-o** change to **-a** in the feminine.

e.g. fresco – fresca (fresh, cool).

Those ending in **-e** and most of those ending in a consonant are the same in the masculine and the feminine.

e.g. el coche grande; la casa grande (the big car; the big house).

The plural is formed by adding **-s** if the word ends in a vowel, **-es** if it ends in a consonant.

e.g. fresco – frescos; azul (blue) – azules.

The comparative and superlative are formed by putting **más** before the adjective.

un hotel barato	a cheap hotel
un hotel **más** barato	a cheaper hotel
el hotel **más** barato de la ciudad	the cheapest hotel in the town

Possessive Adjectives

	singular	*plural*
my	mi	mis
your (*familiar*)	tu	tus
his, her	su	sus
our	nuestro	nuestros
your (*familiar*)	vuestro	vuestros
their, your (*polite*)	su	sus

Personal Pronouns

	subject	*direct object*	*indirect object*
I	yo	me	me
you (*familiar*)	tú	te	te
you (*polite*)	usted	lo (*m*), la (*f*)	le
he	él	lo	le
she	ella	la	le
it	él/ella	lo (*m*), la (*f*)	le
we	nosotros/-as	nos	nos
you (*familiar*)	vosotros/-as	os	os
you (*polite*)	ustedes	los (*m*), las (*f*)	les
they *m*	ellos	los	les
they *f*	ellas	las	les

Personal pronouns are usually omitted before the verb.

e.g. **voy** – I go; **viene** – he (she) comes.

Direct object pronouns are usually placed before the verb.

e.g. **me ve** – he sees me.

Indirect object pronouns are the same as direct object pronouns except that **le** is used to mean to him, to her, to it, to you (*polite*), and **les** means to them and to you (*polite*). If a direct and an indirect object pronoun are used together, the indirect one is placed first.

e.g. me **lo** da – he gives it to me.

If both pronouns are in the third person, **se** is used as indirect object.

e.g. **se** lo da – he gives it to him.

When speaking to strangers always use the forms **usted** and **ustedes. Tú** and **vosotros** are used to close friends and to children.

Demonstrative Pronouns

this one, that one

	m	*f*
this (*one*)	éste	ésta
these	éstos	éstas
that (*one*)	ése	ésa
those	ésos	ésas
that (*one*) over there	aquél	aquella
those	aquellos	aquellas

They agree in number and gender with the nouns they represent.

   e.g. **éste** es mi bolígrafo – this is my ball-point.

      quiero **esta** postal, **ésa,** y **aquélla** – I want this postcard, that one, and that one over there.

The demonstrative adjectives have the same form as the pronouns, except that they are not written with accents.

   e.g. **este** libro – this book; **esa** casa – that house; **aquellos** árboles – those trees over there.

Verbs

'To be' is translated by **ser** and **estar**.

When it is followed by a noun, or when it indicates an origin or a permanent or inherent quality, **ser** is used.

la nieve **es** fría y blanca	snow is cold and white
soy inglés	I am English
Inglaterra **es** una isla	England is an island

When it indicates position or a temporary state, **estar** is used.

el hotel **está** en la calle principal	the hotel is in the main street
estamos en España	we are in Spain

Present tense of **ser** and **estar**

	ser	**estar**
I am	soy	estoy
you (*familiar*) are	eres	estás
he, she is	es	está
you (*polite*) are	es	está
we are	somos	estamos
you (*familiar*) are	sois	estáis
they, you (*polite*) are	son	están

'To have, to possess' is translated by **tener**.

I have, etc.	tengo
	tienes
	tiene
	tenemos
	tenéis
	tienen

e.g. **tengo** mi pasaporte – I have my passport.

'To have' is translated by **haber** only to form compound tenses of other verbs.

e.g. **he** visto el hotel – I've seen the hotel.

I have, etc.	he
	has
	ha
	hemos
	habéis
	han

In Spanish there are three types of verbs, distinguished by the endings of the infinitives.

-ar	hablar – to speak
-er	vender – to sell
-ir	vivir – to live

The present tense is formed as follows:

hablar	vender	vivir
hablo	vendo	vivo
hablas	vendes	vives
habla	vende	vive
hablamos	vendemos	vivimos
habláis	vendéis	vivís
hablan	venden	viven

The present tense of some common irregular verbs:

dar – to give	**decir** – to say	**hacer** – to do, to make
doy	digo	hago
das	dices	haces
da	dice	hace
damos	decimos	hacemos
dais	decís	hacéis
dan	dicen	hacen

ir – to go	**poder** – can, to be able	**poner** – to put
voy	puedo	pongo
vas	puedes	pones
va	puede	pone
vamos	podemos	ponemos
vais	podéis	ponéis
van	pueden	ponen

querer – to want, to love	**traer** – to bring	**venir** – to come
quiero	traigo	vengo
quieres	traes	vienes
quiere	trae	viene
queremos	traemos	venimos
queréis	traéis	venís
quieren	traen	vienen

The past participle is formed by dropping the infinitive ending and adding the following endings to the stem of the verb.

ar	hablar – to speak	**ado**	hablado – spoken
er	vender – to sell	**ido**	vendido – sold
ir	vivir – to live	**ido**	vivido – lived

Some common irregular past participles:

abierto from abrir – opened

dicho from decir – said

escrito from escribir – written

hecho from hacer – made, done

puesto from poner – put

visto from ver – seen

The imperfect tense

hablar – I was speaking, used to speak, spoke, etc.	**vender** – I was selling, used to sell, sold, etc.
hablaba	vendía
hablabas	vendías
hablaba	vendía
hablábamos	vendíamos
hablabais	vendíais
hablaban	vendían

Verbs ending in -**ir** (**vivir**) have the same endings in the imperfect as those in -**er** (**vender**).

Irregular imperfect tense of **ser** – to be:

era
eras
era
éramos
erais
eran

The future is formed by adding the following endings to the infinitives of all regular verbs:

hablar	vender	vivir
hablaré	venderé	viviré
hablarás	venderás	vivirás
hablará	venderá	vivirá
hablaremos	venderemos	viviremos
hablaréis	venderéis	viviréis
hablarán	venderán	vivirán

The Negative

The negative is formed by putting **no** before the verb.

e.g. **no** hablo español – I don't speak Spanish.

VOCABULARY

Specific vocabulary lists are given elsewhere in this book and these words are not usually repeated in the vocabulary:

A

a/an	**un/una**	oon/oon-a
abbey	**la abadía**	a-ba-**dee**-a
able (to be)	**poder**	po-dair
about	**alrededor de**	al-re-de-dor de
above	**encima (de)**	en-thee-ma
abroad	**el extranjero**	es-tran-hair-o
accept (to)	**aceptar**	a-thep-tar
accident	**el accidente**	ak-thee-den-te
accommodation	**el alojamiento**	al-lo-ha-mee-en-to
account	**la cuenta**	kwen-ta
ache (to)	**doler**	do-lair

acquaintance	**el conocido**	ko-no-thee-do
across	**a través de**	a tra-**bes** de
act (to)	**actuar**	ak-too-ar
add	**añadir**	a-nya-deer
address	**la dirección**	dee-rek-**thyon**
admire (to)	**admirar**	ad-mee-rar
admission	**la admisión/ la entrada**	ad-mee-**syon**/ en-tra-da
adventure	**la aventura**	a-ben-too-ra
advertisement	**el anuncio**	a-noon-thyo
advice	**el consejo**	kon-say-ho
aeroplane	**el avión**	a-**byon**
afford (to)	**costear**	kos-tai-ar
afraid (to be)	**tener miedo**	ten-air myay-do
after	**después (de)**	des-**pwes**
afternoon	**la tarde**	tar-de
again	**otra vez**	o-tra beth
against	**contra**	kon-tra
age	**la edad**	ay-dad
agency	**la agencia**	a-hen-thya
agent	**el agente**	a-hen-te
agree (to)	**estar de acuerdo**	es-tar de a-kwair-do
air	**el aire**	a-ee-re
airbed	**el colchón de aire**	kol-**chon** de a-ee-re

air-conditioning	**el aire acondicionado**	a-ee-re a-kon-dee-thyon-ado
alarm clock	**el (reloj) despertador**	(re-loh) des-pair-ta-dor
alcoholic	**alcohólico**	al-**ko**-lee-ko
alike	**parecido/similar**	pa-re-thee-do/see-mee-lar
alive	**vivo**	bee-bo
all	**todo**	to-do
all right	**bueno/bien**	bwe-no/bee-en
allow (to)	**permitir/dejar**	pair-mee-teer/de-har
almost	**casi**	ka-see
alone	**solo**	so-lo
along	**a lo largo**	a lo lar-go
already	**ya**	ya
also	**también**	tam-**byen**
alternative	**la alternativa**	al-tair-na-tee-ba
although	**aunque**	a-oon-ke
always	**siempre**	syem-pre
ambulance	**la ambulancia**	am-boo-lan-thya
America	**los Estados Unidos (de América)**	es-ta-dos oo-nee-dos (de a-mer-ee-ka)
American	**estadounidense/norteamericano**	es-ta-do-oo-nee-den-se/nor-te-a-mer-ee-ka-no
among	**entre**	en-tre

amuse (to)	**divertir**	dee-bair-teer
amusement park	**el parque de atracciones**	par-ke de a-trak-thyo-nes
amusing	**divertido**	dee-bair-tee-do
ancient	**antiguo/viejo**	an-tee-gwo/bee-e-ho
and	**y**	ee
angry/annoyed	**enfadado**	en-fa-da-do
animal	**el animal**	a-nee-mal
anniversary	**el aniversario**	a-nee-bair-sa-ryo
annoy (to)	**molestar**	mo-les-tar
another	**otro**	ot-ro
answer	**la respuesta**	res-pwes-ta
answer (to)	**contestar**	kon-tes-tar
antique	**antiguo**	an-tee-gwo
any *pron.*	**alguno/alguna**	al-goo-no/al-goo-na
any *adj.*	**algún/alguna**	al-**goon**/al-goo-na
anyone/someone	**alguien**	alg-yen
anything/something	**algo**	al-go
anyway	**de todos modos/ todas formas**	de to-dos mo-dos/ to-das for-mas
anywhere/ somewhere	**en alguna parte**	en al-goo-na par-te
apartment	**el apartamento**	a-par-ta-men-to
apologize (to)	**disculparse**	dees-kool-par-se

appetite	**el apetito/la hambre**	a-pe-tee-to/am-bre
appointment *general*	**la cita**	thee-ta
appointment (to make) *medical etc.*	**pedir hora**	pe-deer o-ra
architect	**el arquitecto**	ar-kee-tek-to
architecture	**la arquitectura**	ar-kee-tek-too-ra
arm	**el brazo**	bra-tho
armchair	**el sillón**	see-llyon
army	**el ejército**	e-hair-thee-to
around	**alrededor de**	al-ray-de-dor de
arrange (to)	**arreglar/colocar**	ar-reg-lar/ko-lo-kar
arrival	**la llegada**	llye-ga-da
arrive (to)	**llegar**	llye-gar
art	**el arte**	ar-te
art gallery	**la galería de arte**	gal-air-ee-a de ar-te
artificial	**artificial**	ar-tee-fee-thee-al
artist	**el artista**	ar-tees-ta
as	**como**	ko-mo
as much as	**tanto como**	tan-to ko-mo
as soon as	**en cuanto**	en kwan-to
as well/also	**también**	tam-byen
ashtray	**el cenicero**	then-ee-thair-o
ask (to)	**preguntar**	pre-goon-tar

asleep	**dormido**	dor-mee-do
at	**en**	en
at last	**al fin**	al feen
at once	**en seguida/pronto**	en se-gee-da/pron-to
atmosphere	**el ambiente**	am-byen-te
attention	**la atención**	a-ten-**thyon**
attractive	**atractivo**	a-trak-tee-bo
auction	**la subasta**	soo-bas-ta
audience	**el público**	**poo**-blee-ko
aunt	**la tía**	**tee**-a
Australia	**Australia f**	ows-tral-ya
Australian	**australiano**	ows-tral-ya-no
author	**el autor**	ow-tor
autumn	**el otoño**	o-to-nyo
available	**disponible/listo**	dees-po-nee-ble/lees-to
avalanche	**la avalancha**	a-ba-lan-cha
avenue	**la avenida**	a-be-nee-da
average	**el promedio**	pro-me-dyo
avoid (to)	**evitar**	e-bee-tar
awake	**despierto**	des-pyair-to
away	**fuera**	fwer-a
awful	**horrible**	or-ree-ble

B

baby	**el bebé**	be-**be**
baby food	**los potitos**	po-tee-tos
babysitter	**la niñera/el canguro**	nee-nye-ra/kan-goo-ro
bachelor	**el soltero**	sol-tair-o
back *returned*	**de vuelta**	de bwel-ta
backpack	**la mochila**	mo-chee-la
bad	**malo**	ma-lo
bag	**la bolsa**	bol-sa
baggage	**el equipaje**	e-kee-pa-he
baggage cart	**el carrito**	kar-ree-to
bait *fishing*	**el cebo**	thay-bo
balcony	**el balcón**	bal-kon
ball *sport*	**la pelota/el balón**	pe-lo-ta/ba-**lon**
balloon	**el globo**	glo-bo
ballpoint pen	**el bolígrafo**	bol-**ee**-gra-fo
band *music*	**la orquesta/la banda**	or-kes-ta/ban-da
bank	**el banco**	ban-ko
bank account	**la cuenta bancaria**	kwen-ta ban-ka-rya
bare	**desnudo/ descubierto**	des-noo-doh/des-koo-byer-to
barn	**el granero**	gra-ne-ro

basket	**la cesta**	thes-ta
bath	**la bañera**	ba-nye-ra
bath essence	**la colonia de baño**	ko-lo-nya de ba-nyo
bathe (to)	**bañar**	ba-nyar
bathing cap	**el gorro de baño**	gor-ro de ba-nyo
bathing suit	**el traje de baño**	tra-he de ba-nyo
bathing trunks	**el bañador**	ba-nya-dor
bathroom	**el cuarto de baño**	kwar-to de ba-nyo
battery	**la pila**	pee-la
bay	**la bahía**	ba-**ee**-a
be (to) *permanent/ temporary*	**ser/estar**	sair/es-tar
beach	**la playa**	pla-ya
beard	**la barba**	bar-ba
beautiful	**hermoso**	air-mo-so
because	**porque**	por-ke
become (to)	**convertirse en**	kon-ber-teer-se en
bed	**la cama**	ka-ma
bedroom	**el dormitorio**	dor-mee-to-ryo
before	**antes**	an-tes
begin (to)	**empezar**	em-pe-thar
beginning	**el principio**	preen-thee-pyo
behind	**atrás**	a-**tras**

believe (to)	**creer**	kray-air
bell	**la campana**	kam-pa-na
belong (to)	**pertenecer**	pair-ten-e-thair
below	**abajo/debajo (de)**	a-ba-ho/de-ba-ho
belt	**el cinturón**	thin-toor-**on**
bench	**el banco**	ban-ko
berth	**la litera**	lee-tair-a
beside	**cerca de/al lado de**	thair-ka de/al la-do de
best	**lo/la/el mejor**	lo/la/el me-hor
better	**mejor**	me-hor
between	**entre**	en-tre
bicycle	**la bicicleta**	bee-thee-klay-ta
big	**grande**	gran-de
bill	**la factura/el recibo**	fak-too-ra/re-thee-bo
binoculars	**los prismáticos**	prees-**ma**-tee-kos
bird	**el pájaro**	**pa**-ha-ro
birthday	**el cumpleaños**	koom-ple-a-nyos
bite (to)	**morder**	mor-dair
bitter	**amargo**	a-mar-go
blanket	**la manta**	man-ta
bleed (to)	**sangrar**	san-grar
blind *person*	**ciego**	thee-e-go
blind *window*	**la persiana**	pair-see-a-na

blister	**la ampolla**	am-po-llya
blond	**rubio**	roo-byo
blood	**la sangre**	san-gre
blouse	**la blusa**	bloo-sa
blow	**el golpe**	gol-pe
(on) board	**a bordo**	a bor-do
boat	**el barco**	bar-ko
body	**el cuerpo**	kwair-po
bone	**el hueso**	way-so
book	**el libro**	lee-bro
book (to)	**reservar**	res-air-bar
boot	**la bota**	bo-ta
border	**la frontera**	fron-tair-a
bored	**aburrido**	a-boor-ree-do
borrow (to)	**pedir prestado**	pe-deer pres-ta-do
both	**ambos**	am-bos
bother (to) *annoy*	**molestar**	mo-les-tar
bottle	**la botella**	bo-te-llya
bottle opener	**el abrebotellas**	abre-bo-te-llyas
bottom	**el fondo**	fon-do
bow tie	**la pajarita**	pa-ha-ree-ta
bowl	**el tazón**	ta-**thon**
box *container*	**la caja**	ka-ha

box *theatre*	el palco	pal-ko
box office	la taquilla	ta-kee-llya
boy	el muchacho/el niño	moo-cha-cho/nee-nyo
bracelet	la pulsera	pool-sair-a
braces	los tirantes	tee-ran-tes
brain	el cerebro	the-re-bro
branch *bank etc.*	la sucursal	soo-koor-sal
branch *tree*	la rama	ra-ma
brand	la marca	mar-ka
brassière	el sujetador	soo-he-ta-dor
break (to)	romper	rom-pair
breakfast	el desayuno	des-a-yoo-no
breathe (to)	respirar	res-pee-rar
brick	el ladrillo	la-dree-llyo
bridge	el puente	pwen-te
bright *colour*	vivo	bee-bo
bring (to)	traer	tra-air
British	británico	bree-**tan**-ee-ko
broadband	la banda ancha	ban-da an-cha
broken	roto	ro-to
brooch	el broche	bro-che
brother	el hermano	air-ma-no
brush	el cepillo	the-pee-llyo

brush (to)	**cepillar**	the-pee-llyar
bucket	**el cubo**	koo-bo
buckle	**la hebilla**	e-bee-llya
build (to)	**construir**	kon-stroo-eer
building	**el edificio**	e-dee-fee-thyo
bullfight	**la corrida de toros**	kor-ree-da de to-ros
bullring	**la plaza de toros**	pla-tha de to-ros
burn (to)	**quemar**	ke-mar
burst (to)	**reventar**	re-ben-tar
bus	**el autobús**	ow-toh-**boos**
bus stop	**la parada**	pa-ra-da
business	**el negocio**	ne-go-thyo
busy	**ocupado**	o-koo-pa-do
but	**pero**	pe-ro
butterfly	**la mariposa**	ma-ree-po-sa
button	**el botón**	bo-**ton**
buy (to)	**comprar**	kom-prar
by	**por**	por

C

cabin	**el camarote**	ka-ma-ro-te
calculator	**la calculadora**	kal-koo-la-do-ra
calendar	**el calendario**	ka-len-da-ryo

call (to) *summon/ name*	**llamar**	llya-mar
(telephone) call	**la llamada (telefónica)**	llya-ma-da te-le-**fo**-nee-ka
call *visit*	**la visita**	bee-see-ta
call (to) *visit*	**visitar**	bee-see-tar
calm	**tranquilo**	tran-kee-lo
camera	**la máquina fotográfica**	**ma**-kee-na fo-to-**gra**-fee-ka
camp (to)	**acampar**	a-kam-par
campsite	**el camping**	kam-peeng
can *to be able*	**poder**	po-dair
can *tin*	**la lata**	la-ta
can opener	**el abrelatas**	a-bre-la-tas
Canada	**Canadá m**	ka-na-**da**
Canadian	**canadiense**	ka-na-dyen-se
cancel (to)	**anular**	a-noo-lar
candle	**la vela/el cirio**	be-la/thee-ryo
canoe	**la canoa**	ka-no-a
cap	**la gorra**	gor-ra
capital city	**la capital**	ka-pee-tal
car	**el coche**	ko-che
car park	**el aparcamiento**	a-par-ka-mee-en-to
carafe	**la garrafa**	gar-ra-fa

caravan	**el remolque**	re-mol-ke
card	**la tarjeta**	tar-he-ta
(playing) card	**la carta**	kar-ta
care	**el cuidado**	kwee-da-do
careful	**cuidadoso**	kwee-da-do-so
careless	**descuidado**	des-kwee-da-do
caretaker	**el portero**	por-tair-o
carpet	**la alfombra**	al-fom-bra
carry (to)	**llevar**	llye-bar
cash	**el metálico**	me-**tal**-ee-ko
cashier	**el cajero**	ka-hair-o
casino	**el casino**	ka-see-no
castle	**el castillo**	kas-tee-llyo
cat	**el gato**	ga-to
catalogue	**el catálogo**	ka-**ta**-lo-go
catch (to)	**coger**	ko-hair
cathedral	**la catedral**	ka-te-dral
Catholic	**católico**	ka-**to**-lee-ko
cause	**la causa**	kaw-sa
cave	**la cueva**	kwe-ba
cement	**el cemento**	the-men-to
central	**central**	then-tral
centre	**el centro**	then-tro

century	**el siglo**	see-glo
ceremony	**la ceremonia**	the-re-mon-ya
certain	**seguro**	se-goo-ro
certainly	**ciertamente**	thyair-ta-men-te
chain	**la cadena**	ka-de-na
chair	**la silla**	see-llya
chambermaid	**la camarera**	ka-ma-rair-a
chance	**la oportunidad**	o-por-too-nee-dad
change	**el cambio**	kam-byo
change (to)	**cambiar**	kam-bee-ar
chapel	**la capilla**	ka-pee-llya
charge	**la tarifa**	ta-ree-fa
charge (to)	**cobrar**	kob-rar
cheap	**barato**	ba-ra-to
check (to)	**examinar**	ek-sam-ee-nar
cheque	**el cheque**	che-ke
chess	**el ajedrez**	a-he-dreth
chess set	**el juego de ajedrez**	hwe-go de a-he-dreth
chief	**el jefe**	he-fe
child	**el niño**	nee-nyo
chill (to)	**enfriar**	en-free-ar
china	**la porcelana**	por-the-la-na
choice	**la selección**	se-lek-**thyon**

choose (to)	elegir	el-e-heer
Christmas	la Navidad	na-bee-dad
church	la iglesia	ee-gle-sya
cigar	el puro	poo-ro
cigarette	el cigarrillo	thee-gar-ree-llyo
cinema	el cine	thee-ne
circus	el circo	theer-ko
city	la ciudad	thee-oo-dad
class	la clase	kla-se
clean	limpio	leem-pyo
clean (to)	limpiar	leem-pyar
cleansing cream	la crema limpiadora	kre-ma leem-pee-a-do-ra
clear	claro	kla-ro
cliff	el acantilado	a-kan-tee-la-do
climb (to)	escalar	es-ka-lar
cloakroom	el guardarropa	gwar-dar-ro-pa
clock	el reloj	re-loh
close (to)	cerrar	ther-rar
closed	cerrado	ther-ra-do
cloth	la tela	te-la
clothes	la ropa	ro-pa
cloud	la nube	noo-be
coach	el autocar	ow-toh-kar

coast	**la costa**	kos-ta
coat	**el abrigo**	a-bree-go
coathanger	**la percha**	pair-cha
coin	**la moneda**	mo-ne-da
cold	**frío**	**free**-o
collar	**el cuello**	kwe-llyo
collect (to)	**recoger**	re-ko-hair
colour	**el color**	ko-lor
comb	**el peine**	pay-ne
come (to)	**venir**	be-neer
come in	**¡adelante!**	a-de-lan-te
comfortable	**cómodo**	**ko**-mo-do
common	**frecuente**	fre-kwen-te
company	**la compañía**	kom-pa-**nyee**-a
compass	**el compás**	kom-**pas**
compensation	**la compensación**	kom-pen-sa-**thyon**
complain (to)	**quejarse**	ke-har-se
complaint	**la queja**	ke-ha
complete	**completo/lleno**	kom-ple-to/llye-no
computer	**la computadora/ el ordenador**	kom-poo-ta-do-ra/or-de-na-dor
concert	**el concierto**	kon-thee-er-to
concert hall	**la sala de conciertos**	sa-la de kon-thee-er-tos

concrete	**el cemento**	the-men-to
condition	**la condición**	kon-dee-**thyon**
condom	**el condón**	kon-**don**
conductor *bus*	**el cobrador**	ko-bra-dor
conductor *orchestra*	**el director de orquesta**	dee-rek-tor de or-kes-ta
congratulations	**¡felicidades!**	fe-lee-thee-da-des
connect (to) *train*	**enlazar**	en-la-thar
connection	**la conexión**	ko-nek-**syon**
consul	**el cónsul**	**kon**-sool
consulate	**el consulado**	kon-soo-la-do
contact lenses	**las lentillas**	len-tee-llyas
contain (to)	**contener**	kon-ten-air
contraceptives	**los anticonceptivos**	an-tee-kon-thep-tee-bos
contrast	**el contraste**	kon-tras-te
convenient	**conveniente**	kon-ben-yen-te
convent	**el convento**	kon-ben-to
conversation	**la conversación**	kon-bair-sa-**thyon**
cook	**el cocinero**	ko-thee-nair-o
cook (to)	**cocer**	ko-thair
cool	**fresco/frío**	fres-ko/**free**-o
copper	**el cobre**	ko-bre
copy	**la copia**	ko-pya

cork	el corcho	kor-cho
corkscrew	el sacacorchos	sa-ka-kor-chos
corner	la esquina	es-kee-na
correct	correcto	kor-rek-to
corridor	el pasillo	pa-see-llyo
cosmetics	los cosméticos	kos-**me**-tee-kos
cost	el precio	pre-thyo
cost (to)	costar	kos-tar
cot	la cuna	koo-na
cotton wool	el algodón	al-go-**don**
couchette	la litera	lee-tair-a
count (to)	contar	kon-tar
country *nation*	el país	pa-**ees**
countryside	el campo	kam-po
courtyard	el patio	pa-tyo
cousin	el primo	pree-mo
cover	la cubierta	koo-bee-air-ta
crash *collision*	el choque	cho-ke
credit	el crédito	**kre**-dee-to
credit card	la tarjeta de crédito	tar-he-ta de **kre**-dee-to
crew	la tripulación	tree-poo-la-**thyon**
cross	la cruz	krooth
cross (to)	atravesar	a-tra-be-sar

crossroads	**el cruce de carreteras**	kroo-the de kar-re-tair-as
crowd	**la multitud**	mool-tee-tood
cry (to)	**llorar**	llyo-rar
cup	**la taza**	ta-tha
cupboard	**el armario**	ar-ma-ryo
cure (to)	**curar**	koo-rar
curious	**curioso**	koo-ree-o-so
curl (to)	**rizar**	ree-thar
current	**la corriente**	kor-ryen-te
curtain	**la cortina**	kor-tee-na
curve	**la curva**	koor-ba
cushion	**el cojín**	ko-**heen**
customs	**la aduana**	a-dwan-a
customs officer	**el oficial de aduana**	off-ee-thyal de a-dwan-a
cut	**la cortadura**	kor-ta-doo-ra
cut (to)	**cortar**	kor-tar
cycle (to)	**ir en bicicleta**	eer en bee-thee-klay-ta
cyclist	**el ciclista**	thee-klees-ta

D

daily	**a diario**	a dee-a-ryo
damaged	**estropeado**	es-tro-pe-a-do
damp	**húmedo**	oo-me-do

dance	**el baile**	ba-ee-le
dance (to)	**bailar**	ba-ee-lar
danger	**el peligro**	pe-lee-gro
dangerous	**peligroso**	pe-lee-gro-so
dark	**oscuro**	os-koo-ro
date *day/year*	**la fecha**	fe-cha
date *appointment*	**la cita**	thee-ta
daughter	**la hija**	ee-ha
day	**el día**	**dee**-a
dead	**muerto**	mwer-to
deaf	**sordo**	sor-do
dealer	**el comerciante**	ko-mair-thee-an-te
dear *price*	**caro**	ka-ro
decanter	**la garrafa**	gar-ra-fa
decide (to)	**decidir**	de-thee-deer
deck	**la cubierta**	koo-byair-ta
deckchair	**la hamaca**	a-ma-ka
declare (to)	**declarar**	de-kla-rar
deep	**profundo**	pro-foon-do
delay	**el retraso**	re-tra-so
deliver (to)	**entregar**	en-tre-gar
delivery	**el reparto**	re-par-to
demi-pension	**la media pensión**	me-dya pen-**syon**

dentist	el dentista	den-tees-ta
deodorant	el desodorante	de-so-dor-an-te
depart (to)	salir	sa-leer
department	el departamento	de-par-ta-men-to
department store	el grande almacén	gran-de al-ma-**then**
departure	la salida	sa-lee-da
dessert	el postre	pos-tre
detour	la desviación	des-bya-**thyon**
dial (to)	marcar	mar-kar
diamond	el brillante	bree-llyan-te
dice	los dados	da-dos
dictionary	el diccionario	deek-thyo-na-ryo
diet	la dieta	dee-e-ta
diet (to)	estar a dieta	es-tar a dee-e-ta
different	differente	dee-fair-en-te
difficult	difícil	dee-**fee**-theel
dine (to)	cenar	the-nar
dining room	el comedor	ko-me-dor
dinner	la cena	the-na
dinner jacket	el smoking	es-mo-keeng
direct	directo	dee-rek-to
direction	la dirección	dee-rek-**thyon**
dirty	sucio	soo-thyo

disappointed	**decepcionado**	de-thep-thee-on-a-do
discount	**el descuento**	des-kwen-to
dish	**el plato**	pla-to
disinfectant	**el desinfectante**	de-seen-fek-tan-te
distance	**la distancia**	dees-tan-thya
disturb (to)	**molestar**	mo-les-tar
ditch	**la cuneta**	koo-ne-ta
dive (to)	**tirarse de cabeza**	tee-rar-se de ka-be-tha
diving board	**el trampolín**	tram-po-**leen**
divorced	**divorciado**	dee-bor-thya-do
do (to)	**hacer**	a-thair
dock (to)	**atracar**	a-tra-kar
doctor	**el médico**	**me**-dee-ko
dog	**el perro**	per-ro
doll	**la muñeca**	moo-nye-ka
door	**la puerta**	pwer-ta
double	**doble**	do-ble
double bed	**la cama doble**	ka-ma-do-ble
double room	**la habitación de matrimonio**	a-bee-ta-**thyon** de mat-ree-mo-nyo
down (stairs)	**abajo**	a-ba-ho
dozen	**la docena**	do-the-na
draughty	**aireado/ con corrientes**	ay-ray-a-do/ kon kor-ree-en-tes
draw (to)	**dibujar**	dee-boo-har

drawer	el cajón	ka-hon
drawing	el dibujo	dee-boo-ho
dream	el sueño	swe-nyo
dress	el vestido	bes-tee-do
dressing gown	la bata/el batín	ba-ta/ba-tin
dressmaker	la modista	mo-dees-ta
drink (to)	beber	be-bair
drinking water	el agua potable	ag-wa po-ta-ble
drive (to)	conducir	kon-doo-theer
driver	el conductor	kon-dook-tor
driving licence	el carnet de conducir	kar-net de kon-doo-theer
drop (to)	dejar caer	de-har ka-yer
drunk	borracho	bor-ra-cho
dry	seco	se-ko
dry (to)	secar	se-kar
during	mientras	myen-tras
duvet	el edredón	e-dre-don
dye	el tinte	teen-te

E

each	cada	ka-da
early	temprano	tem-pra-no
earrings	los pendientes	pen-dyen-tes

east	el este	es-te
Easter	Pascua	pas-koo-a
easy	fácil	fa-theel
eat (to)	comer	ko-mair
edge	el borde	bor-de
elastic	el elástico	e-las-tee-ko
electric point	el enchufe	en-choo-fe
electricity	la electricidad	el-ek-tree-thee-dad
elevator	el ascensor	as-then-sor
embassy	la embajada	em-ba-ha-da
emergency exit	la salida de emergencia	sa-lee-da-dee-mer-hen-thya
empty	vacío	ba-thee-o
end	el fin/el final	feen/fee-nal
engaged *person*	comprometido	kom-prom-e-tee-do
engaged *telephone*	ocupado	o-koo-pa-do
engine	el motor/la máquina	mo-tor/ma-kee-na
England	Inglaterra *f*	een-gla-ter-ra
English	inglés	een-gles
enjoy oneself (to)	divertirse	dee-bair-teer-se
enlargement	la ampliación	amp-lya-thyon
enough	bastante	bas-tan-te
enquiries	información	een-for-ma-thyon

enter (to)	**entrar**	en-trar
entrance	**la entrada**	en-tra-da
entrance fee	**el precio de entrada**	pre-thyo de en-tra-da
envelope	**el sobre**	so-bre
equipment	**el equipo**	e-kee-po
escalator	**la escalera automática**	es-ka-lair-a ow-to-**ma**-tee-ka
escape (to)	**escapar**	es-ka-par
estate agent	**el agente inmobiliario**	a-hen-te een-mo-bee-lee-a-ryo
EU	**Unión Europea** *f*	oon-**yon** e-oo-ro-pe-a
Europe	**Europa** *f*	e-oo-ro-pa
even *opp. odd*	**igual**	ee-gwal
even *smooth*	**liso**	lee-so
evening	**la tarde/la noche**	tar-de/no-che
event	**el acontecimiento**	a-kon-te-thee-myen-to
every	**cada**	ka-da
everybody	**todos**	to-dos
everything	**todo**	to-do
everywhere	**en todas partes**	en to-das par-tes
example	**el ejemplo**	e-hem-plo
excellent	**excelente**	eks-the-len-te
except	**excepto**	eks-thep-to

excess	**el exceso**	eks-the-so
exchange (bureau)	**la oficina de cambio**	o-fee-thee-na de kam-byo
exchange rate	**el cambio**	kam-byo
excursion	**la excursión**	es-koor-**syon**
exhibition	**la exposición**	es-po-see-**thyon**
exit	**la salida**	sa-lee-da
expect (to)	**esperar**	es-pair-ar
expensive	**caro**	ka-ro
express	**urgente**	oor-hen-te
express train	**el rápido**	**ra**-pee-do
eye	**el ojo**	o-ho
eye shadow	**la sombra de ojos**	som-bra de o-hos

F

fabric	**la tela**	te-la
face	**la cara**	ka-ra
face cloth	**la toalla pequeña**	to-a-llya pe-ke-nya
face cream	**la crema de la cara**	kre-ma de la ka-ra
fact	**el hecho**	e-cho
factory	**la fábrica**	**fab**-ree-ka
fade (to)	**decolorar**	de-ko-lor-ar
faint (to)	**desmayarse**	des-ma-yar-se

fair *blond*	rubio	roo-byo
fair *fête*	la feria	fe-rya
fall (to)	caer	ka-air
family	la familia	fa-mee-lya
far	lejos	le-hos
fare	el billete	bee-llye-te
farm	la granja	gran-ha
farmer	el granjero	gran-he-ro
farmhouse	la granja	gran-ha
fashion	la moda	mo-da
fast	rápido	ra-pee-do
fat	gordo	gor-do
father	el padre	pa-dre
fault	la culpa	kool-pa
fear	el temor/el miedo	te-mor/mee-e-do
feed (to)	dar de comer	dar de ko-mer
feeding bottle	el biberón	bee-be-ron
feel (to)	sentir	sen-teer
felt-tip pen	el rotulador	ro-too-la-dor
female *adj.*	femenino	fe-me-nee-no
festival	la fiesta	fee-es-ta
fetch (to)	ir a buscar	eer a boos-kar
few	pocos	po-kos

fiancé(e)	el novio/la novia	no-byo/no-bya
field	el campo	kam-po
fight (to)	luchar	loo-char
fill/fill in (to)	llenar	llye-nar
film *cinema*	la película	pe-**lee**-koo-la
find (to)	encontrar	en-kon-trar
fine	la multa	mool-ta
finish (to)	acabar	a-ka-bar
finished	acabado	a-ka-ba-do
fire	el fuego	fwe-go
fire escape	la escalera de incendios	es-ka-le-ra de een-then-dyos
fire extinguisher	el extintor	es-teen-tor
fireworks	los fuegos artificiales	fwe-gos ar-tee-fee-thyal-es
first	primero	pree-mair-o
first aid	los primeros auxilios	pree-mair-os ow-see-lyos
fish	el pescado	pes-ka-do
fish (to)	pescar	pes-kar
fisherman	el pescador	pes-ka-dor
fishing tackle	el aparejo de pescar	a-pa-re-ho de pes-kar
fit (to)	sentar	sen-tar
flag	la bandera	ban-dair-a
flat	el apartamento	a-par-ta-men-to

flat *level*	llano	llya-no
flavour	**el sabor/el gusto**	sa-bor/goos-to
flea market	**el rastro**	ras-tro
flight	**el vuelo**	bwe-lo
flippers	**las aletas**	a-le-tas
float (to)	**flotar**	flo-tar
flood	**la inundación**	ee-noon-da-**thyon**
floor *room*	**el suelo**	swe-lo
floor *storey*	**el piso**	pee-so
floor show	**el espectáculo**	es-pek-**ta**-koo-lo
flower	**la flor**	flor
fly	**la mosca**	mos-ka
fly (to)	**volar**	bo-lar
fog	**la niebla**	nee-e-bla
fold (to)	**doblar**	dob-lar
follow (to)	**seguir**	se-geer
food	**la comida**	ko-mee-da
foot	**el pie**	pee-ay
football	**el fútbol**	**foot**-bol
footpath	**el camino**	ka-mee-no
for	**por/para**	por/pa-ra
forbid (to)	**prohibir**	pro-ee-beer
foreign	**extranjero**	es-tran-hair-o

forest	**la selva/el bosque**	sel-ba/bos-ke
forget (to)	**olvidar**	ol-bee-dar
fork	**el tenedor**	te-ne-dor
forward	**adelante**	a-de-lan-te
fountain	**la fuente**	fwen-te
fragile	**frágil**	**fra**-heel
free	**libre/gratuito**	lee-bre/gra-twee-to
fresh	**fresco**	fres-ko
fresh water	**el agua dulce** *f*	a-gwa dool-the
friend	**el amigo**	a-mee-go
from	**de/desde**	de/des-de
(in) front	**frente**	fren-te
frontier	**la frontera**	fron-tair-a
frost	**la escarcha**	es-kar-cha
frozen	**congelado**	kon-hel-a-do
frozen food	**los congelados**	kon-he-la-dos
fruit	**la fruta**	froo-ta
full	**lleno**	llye-no
full board	**la pensión completa**	pen-**syon** kom-ple-ta
fun	**la diversión**	dee-bair-**syon**
funny	**cómico/divertido**	**ko**-mee-ko/dee-bair-tee-do
fur	**la piel**	pee-el

further	**más lejos**	mas le-hos
furniture	**los muebles**	mwe-bles

G

gallery	**la galería**	ga-lair-**ee**-a
gamble (to)	**jugar**	hoo-gar
game	**el juego**	hwe-go
garage	**el garaje**	ga-ra-he
garbage	**la basura**	ba-soo-ra
garden	**el jardín**	har-**deen**
gas	**el gas**	gas
gate	**la entrada/la verja**	en-tra-da/bair-ha
gentleman	**el caballero/el señor**	ka-ba-llye-ro/sen-yor
genuine	**auténtico**	ow-**ten**-tee-ko
get (to)	**obtener**	ob-te-nair
get off (to)	**bajarse**	ba-har-se
get on (to)	**subirse**	soo-beer-se
gift	**el regalo**	re-ga-lo
gift wrap (to)	**envolver**	en-bol-bair
girl	**la muchacha**	moo-cha-cha
give (to)	**dar**	dar
glad	**contento**	kon-ten-to

glass	**el vaso**	ba-so
glasses	**las gafas**	ga-fas
gloomy	**triste**	trees-te
glorious	**magnífico**	mag-**nee**-fee-ko
gloves	**los guantes**	gwan-tes
go (to)	**ir**	eer
God	**Dios** *m*	dyos
gold	**el oro**	o-ro
gold plated	**chapado en oro**	cha-pa-do en o-ro
golf course	**el campo de golf**	kam-po de golf
good	**bueno**	bwe-no
government	**el gobierno**	go-byair-no
granddaughter	**la nieta**	nye-ta
grandfather	**el abuelo**	abwe-lo
grandmother	**la abuela**	abwe-la
grandson	**el nieto**	nye-to
grass	**la hierba**	yer-ba
grateful	**agradecido**	ag-ra-de-thee-do
gravel	**la grava**	gra-ba
great	**grande/fantástico**	gran-de/fan-**tas**-tee-ko
Great Britain	**Gran Bretaña** *f*	gran bre-ta-nya
groceries	**los comestibles**	ko-mes-tee-bles
ground	**el terreno**	ter-re-no

grow (to)	**crecer**	kre-thair
guarantee	**la garantía**	ga-ran-**tee**-a
guard	**el guardia**	gwar-dya
guest	**el huésped**	**wes**-ped
guest house	**la casa de huéspedes/la pensión**	ka-sa de **wes**-pe-des/pen-**syon**
guide	**el guía**	**gee**-a
guide book	**la guía**	**gee**-a
guided tour	**la excursión con guía**	es-koor-**syon** kon **gee**-a

hail	**el granizo**	gra-nee-tho
hair	**el pelo**	pe-lo
hairbrush	**el cepillo de pelo**	the-pee-llyo de pe-lo
hairdryer	**el secador**	se-ka-dor
hairgrips/hairpins	**las horquillas**	or-kee-llyas
hairspray	**la laca**	la-ka
half	**medio**	me-dyo
half board	**la media pensión**	me-dya pen-**syon**
hammer	**el martillo**	mar-tee-llyo
handbag	**el bolso**	bol-so
handkerchief	**el pañuelo**	pan-ywe-lo

handmade	**hecho a mano**	e-cho a ma-no
hang (to)	**colgar**	kol-gar
hanger	**la percha**	pair-cha
happen (to)	**suceder/ocurrir**	soo-the-der/o-koor-reer
happy	**feliz**	fe-leeth
happy birthday	**¡felicidades!**	fe-lee-thee-da-des
harbour	**el puerto**	pwer-to
hard	**duro**	doo-ro
harmful	**dañino**	da-nyee-no
harmless	**inofensivo**	ee-no-fen-see-bo
hat	**el sombrero**	som-brair-o
have (to)	**tener**	te-nair
have to (to)	**deber**	de-bair
he	**él**	el
headphones	**los auriculares**	aw-ree-koo-la-res
health	**la salud**	sa-lood
hear (to)	**oír**	o-**eer**
heart	**el corazón**	ko-ra-**thon**
heat	**el calor**	ka-lor
heating	**la calefacción**	ka-le-fak-**thyon**
heavy	**pesado**	pe-sa-do
hedge	**el seto**	se-to
heel *shoe*	**el tacón**	ta-**kon**
height	**la altura**	al-too-ra

helicopter	**el helicóptero**	e-lee-**kop**-te-ro
help	**la ayuda**	a-yoo-da
help (to)	**ayudar**	a-yoo-dar
her *adj.*	**su**	soo
here	**aquí**	a-**kee**
hers/his	**suyo/suya**	soo-yo/soo-ya
high	**alto**	al-to
hike (to)	**ir a andar/de caminata**	eer a an-dar/de ka-mee-na-ta
hill	**la colina**	ko-lee-na
hire (to)	**alquilar**	al-kee-lar
his	**su/suyo**	soo/soo-yo
history	**la historia**	ees-to-rya
hitch hike (to)	**hacer auto-stop**	a-thair ow-to-stop
hobby	**el hobby**	ho-bee
hold (to)	**tener**	te-nair
hole	**el agujero**	a-goo-hair-o
holiday	**el día de fiesta**	**dee**-a de fyes-ta
holidays	**las vacaciones**	ba-ka-thyo-nes
hollow	**hueco/vacío**	we-ko/ba-**thee**-o
(at) home	**en casa**	en ka-sa
honeymoon	**el viaje de novios**	bee-a-he de no-byos
hope	**la esperanza**	es-pair-an-tha
horse	**el caballo**	ka-ba-llyo

horse races	**las carreras de caballos**	kar-rair-as de ka-ba-llyos
horse riding (to go)	**montar a caballo**	mon-tar a ka-ba-llyo
hose	**la manguera**	man-ge-ra
hospital	**el hospital**	os-pee-tal
hostel	**el hostal/el albergue**	os-tal/al-bair-ge
hot	**caliente**	kal-yen-te
hot water bottle	**la bolsa (de agua caliente)**	bol-sa (de ag-wa kal-yen-te)
hour	**la hora**	o-ra
house	**la casa**	ka-sa
how?	**¿cómo?**	ko-mo
how much/many?	**¿cuánto?/¿cuántos?**	kwan-to/kwan-tos
hungry (to be)	**tener hambre**	te-nair am-bre
hunt (to)	**ir de caza**	eer de ka-tha
hurry (to)	**darse prisa**	dar-se pree-sa
hurt (to)	**doler**	do-lair
husband	**el marido**	ma-ree-do

I

I	**yo**	yo
ice	**el hielo**	ee-e-lo
ice cream	**el helado**	e-la-do
ice lolly	**el polo**	po-lo

identify (to)	**identificar a**	ee-den-tee-fee-kar a
if	**si**	see
ill	**enfermo**	en-fair-mo
imagine (to)	**imaginar a**	ee-ma-hee-nar a
immediately	**inmediatamente**	een-me-dya-ta-men-te
immersion heater	**el calentador**	ka-len-ta-dor
important	**importante**	eem-por-tan-te
in	**en**	en
include (to)	**incluir**	een-kloo-eer
included	**incluido**	een-kloo-ee-do
inconvenient	**inconveniente**	een-kon-be-nyen-te
incorrect	**incorrecto**	een-kor-rek-to
independent	**independiente**	een-de-pen-dyen-te
indoors	**dentro**	den-tro
industry	**la industria**	een-doos-trya
inexpensive	**barato**	ba-ra-to
inflammable	**inflamable**	een-fla-ma-ble
inflatable	**hinchable**	een-cha-ble
inflation	**la inflación**	een-fla-**thyon**
information (bureau)	**(la oficina de) información**	(o-fee-thee-na de) een-for-ma-**thyon**
ink	**la tinta**	teen-ta
inn	**la posada**	po-sa-da

insect	el insecto	een-sek-to
insect repellent	la loción anti-mosquitos	lo-**thyon** an-tee-mos-kee-tos
insect sting	la picadura de insecto	pee-ka-doo-ra de een-sek-to
inside	dentro (de)	den-tro
instead (of)	en lugar de	en loo-gar de
insurance	el seguro	se-goo-ro
insure (to)	asegurar	a-se-goo-rar
insured	asegurado	a-se-goo-ra-do
interest	el interés	een-te-**res**
interested	interesado	een-tair-es-a-do
interesting	interesante	een-tair-es-an-te
interpreter	el intérprete	een-**tair**-pre-te
into	en/dentro (de)	en/den-tro
introduce (to)	presentar	pre-sen-tar
invitation	la invitación	een-bee-ta-**thyon**
invite (to)	invitar	een-bee-tar
Ireland	Irlanda *f*	eer-lan-da
Irish	irlandés	eer-lan-**des**
iron (to)	planchar	plan-char
island	la isla	ees-la
it	lo/la	lo/la

J

jacket	**la chaqueta**	cha-ke-ta
jar	**el tarro**	tar-ro
jellyfish	**la medusa**	me-doo-sa
jewellery	**las joyas**	hoy-as
Jewish	**judío**	hoo-**dee**-o
job	**el trabajo**	tra-ba-ho
join (to)	**juntar**	hoon-tar
journey	**el viaje**	bya-he
jug	**la jarra**	har-ra
jump (to)	**saltar**	sal-tar
jumper	**el jersey**	hair-say

K

keep (to)	**guardar**	gwar-dar
key	**la llave**	llya-be
kick (to)	**dar una patada**	dar oon-a pa-ta-da
kind	**la clase**	kla-se
king	**el rey**	ray
kiss	**el beso**	be-so
kiss (to)	**besar**	be-sar
kitchen	**la cocina**	ko-thee-na

knife	el cuchillo	koo-chee-llyo
knock (to) *door*	llamar	llya-mar
know (to) *fact*	saber	sa-baír
know (to) *person*	conocer	ko-no-thair

L

label	la etiqueta	e-tee-ke-ta
lace	el encaje/la puntilla	en-ka-he/poon-tee-llya
lady	la señora	sen-yor-a
lake	el lago	la-go
lamp	la lámpara	lam-pa-ra
land	la tierra	tyer-ra
landlord/landlady	el casero/la casera	ka-se-ro/ka-se-ra
landmark	el lugar muy conocido	loo-gar mwee ko-no-thee-do
landscape	el paisaje	pa-ee-sa-he
lane	el camino	ka-mee-no
language	el idioma	ee-dyo-ma
large	grande	gran-de
last	último	ool-tee-mo
late	tarde	tar-de
laugh (to)	reír	re-eer
laundry	la lavandería	la-ban-dair-ee-a

lavatory	los servicios	sair-bee-thyos
lavatory paper	el papel higiénico	pa-pel ee-hee-e-nee-ko
law	la ley	lay
lawn	el césped	**thes**-ped
lawyer	el abogado	a-bo-ga-do
lead (to)	conducir	kon-doo-theer
leaf	la hoja	o-ha
learn (to)	aprender	a-pren-dair
leather	la piel/el cuero	pyel/kwair-o
leave (to) *abandon*	dejar	de-har
leave (to) *go out*	marcharse	mar-char-se
left *opp. right*	izquierdo	eeth-kyair-do
left luggage	la consigna	kon-seeg-na
lend (to)	prestar	pres-tar
length	la largura	lar-goo-ra
less	menos	me-nos
lesson	la lección	lek-**thyon**
let (to) *allow*	dejar	de-har
let (to) *rent*	alquilar	al-kee-lar
letter	la carta	kar-ta
library	la biblioteca	bee-blyo-te-ka
licence	el permiso	pair-mee-so
life	la vida	bee-da

lifebelt	el flotador/el salvavidas	flo-ta-dor/sal-ba-bee-das
lifeboat	el bote salvavidas	bo-te sal-ba-bee-das
lifeguard	el socorrista	so-kor-rees-ta
lifejacket	el chaleco salvavidas	cha-le-ko sal-ba-bee-das
lift	el ascensor	as-then-sor
light	la luz	looth
light *bulb*	la bombilla	bom-bee-llya
light *colour*	claro	kla-ro
lighter	el encendedor	en-then-de-dor
lighter fuel	la gasolina	ga-so-lee-na
lighthouse	el faro	fa-ro
lightning	el relámpago	re-**lam**-pa-go
like (to)	gustar	goos-tar
line	la línea	**lee**-ne-a
linen *material*	el lino	lee-no
linen *bed*	la ropa de cama	ro-pa de ka-ma
lingerie	la lencería	len-thair-**ee**-a
lipsalve	el cacao para los labios	ka-ka-o pa-ra los la-byos
lipstick	la barra de labios	bar-ra de la-byos
liquid *adj. and noun*	(el) líquido	**lee**-kee-do
listen	escuchar	es-koo-char
little	poco	po-ko

live (to)	**vivir**	bee-beer
local	**local**	lo-kal
lock (to)	**cerrar con llave**	ther-rar kon llya-be
long	**largo**	lar-go
look (to)	**mirar**	mee-rar
look (to) *seem*	**parecer**	pa-re-thair
look for (to)	**buscar**	boos-kar
loose	**suelto**	swel-to
lorry	**el camión**	ka-myon
lose (to)	**perder**	pair-dair
lost property office	**la oficina de objetos perdidos**	o-fee-thee-na dob-he-tos pair-dee-dos
(a) lot	**mucho**	moo-cho
loud	**ruidoso**	roo-ee-do-so
love (to)	**querer**	ke-rair
lovely	**hermoso**	air-mo-so
low	**bajo**	ba-ho
lucky	**afortunado**	a-for-too-na-do
lucky (to be)	**tener suerte**	te-nair swair-te
luggage	**el equipaje**	e-kee-pa-he
(piece of) luggage	**el bulto**	bool-to
lunch	**la comida/el almuerzo**	ko-mee-da/al-mwair-tho

M

mad	**loco**	lo-ko
magazine	**la revista**	re-bees-ta
maid	**la doncella**	don-the-llya
mail	**el correo**	kor-re-o
main street	**la calle principal**	ka-llye preen-thee-pal
make (to)	**hacer**	a-thair
make love (to)	**hacer el amor**	a-thair el a-mor
make-up	**el maquillaje**	ma-kee-llya-he
male *adj*	**masculino**	mas-koo-lee-no
man	**el hombre**	om-bre
man-made	**artificial**	ar-tee-fee-thyal
manage (to)	**arreglarse**	ar-reg-lar-se
manager	**el gerente**	he-ren-te
manicure	**la manicura**	ma-nee-koo-ra
many	**muchos**	moo-chos
map	**el mapa**	ma-pa
marble	**el mármol**	**mar**-mol
market	**el mercado**	maìr-ka-do
married	**casado**	ka-sa-do
marsh	**el pantano**	pan-ta-no
Mass	**la misa**	mee-sa
match	**la cerilla**	the-ree-llya

match *sport*	el partido	par-tee-do
material	la tela	te-la
mattress	el colchón	kol-**chon**
maybe	quizás	kee-**thas**
meal	la comida	ko-mee-da
mean (to)	significar	seeg-nee-fee-kar
measurements	las medidas	me-dee-das
meet (to)	encontrar/conocer	en-kon-trar/ko-no-thair
memory stick	el lápiz de memoria (USB)	la-peeth de me-mo-rya (oo-e-se-be)
mend (to)	reparar/arreglar	re-par-ar/ar-reg-lar
menstruation	el período	pair-**ee**-o-do
menu	el menú/la carta	me-**noo**/kar-ta
mess	el desorden	des-or-den
message	el recado	re-ka-do
messenger	el mensajero	men-sa-he-ro
metal	el metal	me-tal
midday	mediodía	me-dee-o-**dee**-a
middle	el medio	me-dyo
middle-aged	de mediana edad	de me-dya-na e-dad
middle-class	la clase media	cla-se me-dya
midnight	medianoche	me-dee-a-no-che
mild	suave	swa-be
mill	el molino	mo-lee-no

mine *pron.*	mío/mía	**mee**-o/**mee**-a
minute	el minuto	mee-noo-to
mirror	el espejo	es-pe-ho
Miss	la señorita	sen-yor-ee-ta
miss (to) *train etc.*	perder	pair-dair
mistake	la equivocación	e-kee-bo-ka-**thyon**
mix (to)	mezclar	meth-klar
mobile phone	el (teléfono) móvil	(te-**le**-fo-no) mo-beel
modern	moderno	mo-dair-no
moisturizer	la crema hidratante	kre-ma ee-dra-tan-te
moment	el momento	mo-men-to
monastery	el monasterio	mo-nas-te-ryo
money	el dinero	dee-nair-o
money order	el giro postal	hee-ro po-stal
monk	el monje	mon-he
month	el mes	mes
monument	el monumento	mo-noo-men-to
moon	la luna	loo-na
moorland	el páramo	**pa**-ra-mo
moped	el ciclomotor	thee-klo-mo-tor
more	más	mas
morning	la mañana	ma-nya-na

mortgage	**la hipoteca**	ee-po-te-ka
mosque	**la mezquita**	meth-kee-ta
mosquito	**el mosquito**	mos-kee-to
most	**la mayoría**	ma-yo-**ree**-a
mother	**la madre**	ma-dre
motor	**el motor**	mo-tor
motor bike	**la motocicleta**	mo-to-thee-kle-ta
motor boat	**la motora**	mo-tor-a
motor racing	**las carreras de coches**	kar-rair-as de ko-ches
motorway	**la autopista**	ow-to-pees-ta
mountain	**la montaña**	mon-tan-ya
mouse	**el ratón**	ra-**ton**
mouth	**la boca**	bo-ka
mouthwash	**el enjuague bucal**	en-hwa-ge boo-kal
move (to) *house*	**mudarse/cambiarse de casa**	moo-dar-se/kam-byar-se de ka-sa
Mr	**el señor**	sen-yor
Mrs	**la señora**	sen-yor-a
much	**mucho**	moo-cho
museum	**el museo**	moo-se-o
music	**la música**	**moo**-see-ka
muslim	**el musulmán**	moo-sool-**man**
must (to have to)	**deber**	de-bair
my	**mi**	mee

N

nail	**el clavo**	kla-bo
(finger) nail	**la uña**	oon-ya
nail polish	**la laca de uñas**	la-ka de oon-yas
nailbrush	**el cepillo de uñas**	the-pee-llyo de oon-yas
nailfile	**la lima**	lee-ma
name	**el nombre**	nom-bre
napkin	**la servilleta**	sair-bee-llye-ta
nappy	**el pañal**	pan-yal
narrow	**estrecho**	es-tre-cho
natural	**natural**	na-too-ral
near	**cerca**	thair-ka
nearly	**casi**	ka-see
necessary	**necesario**	ne-the-sa-ryo
necklace	**el collar**	ko-llyar
need (to)	**necesitar**	ne-the-see-tar
needle	**la aguja**	ag-oo-ha
nephew	**el sobrino**	so-bree-no
net	**la red**	red
never	**nunca**	noon-ka
new	**nuevo**	nwe-bo
news	**las noticias**	no-tee-thyas
newspaper	**el periódico**	pe-ree-o-dee-ko

New Zealand	**Nueva Zelanda** *f*	nwe-ba the-lan-da
New Zealander	**neozelandés**	ne-o-the-land-**es**
next	**próximo**	**pro**-see-mo
nice	**bonito**	bo-nee-to
niece	**la sobrina**	so-bree-na
night	**la noche**	no-che
nightclub	**la sala de fiestas**	sa-la de fyes-tas
nightdress	**el camisón**	ka-mee-**son**
no one	**ninguno**	neen-goo-no
nobody	**nadie**	na-dye
noisy	**ruidoso**	rwee-do-so
non-alcoholic	**sin alcohol**	seen al-ko-ol
none	**ninguno/nadie**	neen-goo-no/na-dye
normal	**normal**	nor-mal
north	**el norte**	nor-te
nosebleed	**la hemorragia nasal**	e-mo-rra-hya na-sal
not	**no**	no
notary	**el notario**	no-ta-ryo
note *money*	**el billete**	bee-llye-te
notebook	**el cuaderno de notas**	kwa-dair-no de no-tas
nothing	**nada**	na-da
notice	**el aviso**	a-bee-so
novel	**la novela**	no-be-la

now	**ahora**	a-or-a
number	**el número**	**noo**-mer-o
nylon	**el nylon**	nee-lon

O

obtain (to)	**obtener**	ob-te-nair
occasion	**la ocasión**	o-ka-**syon**
occupation	**el empleo**	em-ple-o
occupied	**ocupado**	o-koo-pa-do
odd *opp. even*	**desigual**	des-ee-gwal
odd *strange*	**raro**	ra-ro
of	**de**	de
of course	**desde luego**	des-de lwe-go
offer	**la oferta**	o-fair-ta
offer (to)	**ofrecer**	o-fre-thair
office	**la oficina**	o-fee-thee-na
official *adj.*	**oficial**	off-ee-thee-al
official *noun*	**el funcionario**	foon-thee-on-a-ryo
often	**a menudo**	a me-noo-do
oil	**el aceite**	a-thay-te
oily *food*	**aceitoso**	a-thay-to-so
oily *hair*	**graso**	gra-so
ointment	**la pomada/la crema**	po-ma-da/kre-ma

OK	¡vale!	ba-le
old	viejo	bye-ho
olive	la aceituna	a-thay-too-na
on	en/sobre	en/so-bre
on foot	a pie	a pee-ay
on time	a tiempo/a la hora	a tee-em-po/a la o-ra
once	una vez	oon-a beth
online	en internet	en in-ter-net
only	solamente	so-la-men-te
open	abierto	a-bee-air-to
open (to)	abrir	a-breer
open-air	al aire libre	al a-ee-re lee-bre
opening	la abertura	a-bair-too-ra
opera	la ópera	o-pair-a
opportunity	la oportunidad	op-or-too-nee-dad
opposite	enfrente (de)	en-fren-te
optician	el óptico	op-tee-ko
or	o	o
orchard	el huerto	wair-to
orchestra	la orquesta	or-kes-ta
order (to)	pedir	pe-deer
ordinary	ordinario	or-dee-na-ryo
other	otro	o-tro

our/ours	nuestro(s)	nwes-tro(s)
out/outside	fuera/afuera	fwe-ra/a-fwe-ra
out of order	no funciona	no foon-thyo-na
out of stock	se ha agotado	se a a-go-ta-do
over	sobre	so-bre
over there	por allí	por a-**llyee**
overcoat	el abrigo	ab-ree-go
overnight (to stay)	pasar la noche	pa-sar la no-che
owe (to)	deber	de-ber
owner	el propietario	pro-pye-ta-ryo

P

packet	el paquete	pa-ke-te
paddle (to)	chapotear	cha-po-te-ar
page	la página	**pa**-hee-na
paid	pagado	pa-ga-do
pain	el dolor	do-lor
painkiller	el analgésico	a-nal-**he**-see-ko
paint (to)	pintar	peen-tar
painting	la pintura	peen-too-ra
pair	el par	par
palace	el palacio	pa-la-thyo
pale	pálido	**pa**-lee-do

panties	**las bragas**	bra-gas
paper	**el papel**	pa-pel
parcel	**el paquete**	pa-ke-te
park	**el parque**	par-ke
park (to)	**aparcar**	a-par-kar
parking meter	**el parquímetro**	par-**kee**-me-tro
parking ticket	**la multa**	mool-ta
parliament	**el parlamento**	par-la-men-to
part	**la parte**	par-te
party	**la fiesta/el guateque**	fee-es-ta/gwa-te-ke
pass (to)	**pasar**	pa-sar
passenger	**el viajero**	bya-hair-o
passport	**el pasaporte**	pa-sa-por-te
past	**el pasado**	pa-sa-do
path	**la senda/el camino**	sen-da/ka-mee-no
patient	**el paciente**	pa-thyen-te
pavement	**la acera**	a-thair-a
pay (to)	**pagar**	pa-gar
payment	**el pago**	pa-go
peace	**la paz**	path
pearl	**la perla**	per-la
pebble	**la piedra**	pyed-ra
pedal	**el pedal**	pe-dal

pedestrian	el peatón	pe-a-**ton**
pedestrian crossing	el paso de peatones	pa-so de pe-a-to-nes
pen	el bolígrafo	bo-**lee**-gra-fo
pencil	el lápiz	la-peeth
penknife	la navaja	na-ba-ha
pensioner	el jubilado	hoo-bee-la-do
people	la gente	hen-te
per person	por persona	por pair-so-na
perfect	perfecto	per-fek-to
performance	la representación	re-pre-sen-ta-**thyon**
perfume	el perfume	pair-foo-me
perhaps	quizás	kee-**thas**
perishable	perecedero	pe-re-the-de-ro
permit	el permiso	pair-mee-so
permit (to)	permitir	pair-mee-teer
person	la persona	pair-so-na
personal	personal	pair-so-nal
petrol	la gasolina	ga-so-lee-na
petrol station	la gasolinera	ga-so-lee-nai-ra
photograph	la fotografía	fo-to-gra-**fee**-a
photographer	el fotógrafo	fo-**to**-gra-fo
piano	el piano	pya-no
pick (to)	escoger/elegir	es-ko-hair/el-e-heer

picnic	la merienda	me-ryen-da
picnic (to)	ir de merienda	eer de me-ryen-da
piece	la pieza/el pedazo	pye-tha/pe-da-tho
pier	el muelle	mwe-llye
pillow	la almohada	al-mo-ad-a
pin	el alfiler	al-fee-lair
(safety) pin	el imperdible	eem-pair-dee-ble
pipe	la pipa	pee-pa
place	el sitio	see-tyo
plan	el plano	pla-no
plant	la planta	plan-ta
plastic	el plástico	**plas**-tee-ko
plate	el plato	pla-to
platform	el andén	an-**den**
play	la obra de teatro	ob-ra de te-a-tro
play (to)	jugar	hoo-gar
player	el jugador	hoo-ga-dor
please	por favor	por fa-bor
pleased	encantado	en-kan-ta-do
plenty	de sobra	de so-bra
pliers	los alicates	a-lee-ka-tes
plug *bath*	el tapón	ta-**pon**
plug *electrical*	el enchufe	en-choo-fe

pocket	**el bolsillo**	bol-see-llyo
point	**el punto**	poon-to
poisonous	**venenoso**	be-ne-no-so
police station	**la comisaría**	ko-mee-sa-**ree**-a
policeman	**el agente de policía**	a-hen-te de po-lee-**thee**-a
political	**político**	po-**lee**-tee-ko
politician	**el político**	po-**lee**-tee-ko
politics	**la política**	po-**lee**-tee-ka
pollution	**la contaminación**	kon-ta-mee-na-**thyon**
pond	**el estanque**	es-tan-ke
poor	**pobre**	po-bre
popular	**popular**	po-poo-lar
porcelain	**la porcelana**	por-the-la-na
port	**el puerto**	pwer-to
possible	**posible**	po-see-ble
post (to)	**echar al correo**	e-char al kor-ray-o
post box	**el buzón**	boo-**thon**
post office	**(la oficina de) correos**	(o-fee-thee-na de) kor-ray-os
postcard	**la (tarjeta) postal**	(tar-he-ta) pos-tal
postman	**el cartero**	kar-tair-o
postpone (to)	**posponer**	pos-po-nair
pound	**la libra**	lee-bra
powder *cosmetic*	**los polvos**	pol-bos

prefer (to)	**preferir**	pre-fair-eer
pregnant	**embarazada**	em-ba-ra-tha-da
prepare (to)	**preparar**	pre-pa-rar
present *gift*	**el regalo**	re-ga-lo
president	**el presidente**	pre-see-den-te
press (to)	**planchar**	plan-char
pretty	**bonito**	bo-nee-to
price	**el precio**	pre-thyo
priest	**el cura/el sacerdote**	koo-ra/sa-thair-do-te
prime minister	**el primer ministro**	pree-mair mee-nees-tro
print (to)	**imprimir**	eem-pree-meer
private	**particular/privado**	par-tee-koo-lar/pree-ba-do
problem	**el problema**	pro-ble-ma
profession	**la profesión**	pro-fe-**syon**
programme	**el programa**	pro-gra-ma
promise	**la promesa**	pro-me-sa
promise (to)	**prometer**	pro-me-tair
prompt	**pronto**	pron-to
Protestant	**protestante**	pro-tes-tan-te
provide (to)	**proveer**	pro-bay-er
public	**público**	**poo**-blee-ko
public holiday	**el día de fiesta**	**dee**-a de fee-es-ta
pull (to)	**tirar**	tee-rar

pump	la bomba	bom-ba
pure	puro	poo-ro
purse	el monedero	mo-ne-dair-o
push (to)	empujar	em-poo-har
put (to)	poner	po-nair
pyjamas	el pijama	pee-ha-ma

Q

quality	la calidad	ka-lee-dad
quantity	la cantidad	kan-tee-dad
quarter	el cuarto	kwar-to
queen	la reina	re-ee-na
question	la pregunta	pre-goon-ta
queue	la cola	ko-la
queue (to)	ponerse a la cola	po-nair-se a la ko-la
quick	rápido	ra-pee-do
quiet	tranquilo	tran-kee-lo

R

race	la carrera	kar-re-ra
racecourse	el hipódromo	ee-po-dro-mo
radiator	el radiador	ra-dee-a-dor

radio	**la radio**	ra-dyo
railway	**el ferrocarril**	fer-ro-kar-ril
rain	**la lluvia**	llyoo-bya
rainbow	**arco iris**	ar-ko ee-rees
raincoat	**el impermeable**	eem-pair-me-a-ble
(it is) raining	**llueve**	llyoo-e-be
rare *unusual*	**raro**	ra-ro
rash	**la erupción**	e-roop-**thyon**
raw	**crudo**	kroo-do
razor	**la navaja de afeitar**	na-ba-ha de a-fay-tar
razor blades	**las cuchillas de afeitar**	koo-chee-llyas de a-fay-tar
reach (to)	**alcanzar**	al-kan-thar
read (to)	**leer**	lay-er
ready (to be)	**estar listo**	es-tar lees-to
real	**verdadero**	bair-da-dair-o
really	**verdaderamente**	bair-da-dair-a-men-te
reason	**la razón**	ra-**thon**
receipt	**el recibo/la factura**	re-thee-bo/fak-too-ra
receive (to)	**recibir**	re-thee-beer
recent	**reciente**	re-thyen-te
recipe	**la receta**	re-the-ta
recognize (to)	**reconocer**	re-kon-o-thair
recommend (to)	**recomendar**	re-ko-men-dar

record *sport*	el record	re-kord
refill	el repuesto/ el recambio	re-pwes-to/re-kam-byo
refrigerator	el refrigerador/la nevera	re-free-hair-a-dor/ ne-be-ra
refund (to)	devolver	de-bol-bair
register (to)	certificar	thair-tee-fee-kar
relatives	los parientes	pa-ree-en-tes
religion	la religión	re-lee-hee-on
remember (to)	acordarse de	a-kor-dar-se de
rent (to)	alquilar	al-kee-lar
repair (to)	arreglar	ar-reg-lar
repeat (to)	repetir	re-pe-teer
reply (to)	contestar	kon-tes-tar
reservation	la reserva	re-sair-ba
reserve (to)	reservar	re-sair-bar
reserved	reservado	re-sair-ba-do
restaurant	el restaurante	res-tow-ran-te
return (to) *go back*	volver	bol-bair
return (to) *give back*	devolver	de-bol-bair
reward	la recompensa	re-kom-pen-sa
ribbon	la cinta	theen-ta
rich	rico	ree-ko
ride	el paseo a caballo	pa-se-o a ka-ba-llyo

ride (to)	**montar a caballo**	mon-tar a ka-ba-llyo
right *opp. wrong*	**correcto**	kor-rek-to
right *opp. left*	**derecho**	de-re-cho
ring	**el anillo/la sortija**	a-nee-llyo/sor-tee-ha
ripe	**maduro**	ma-doo-ro
rise (to)	**levantar**	le-ban-tar
river	**el río**	**ree**-o
road	**la carretera**	kar-re-te-ra
road map	**el mapa/la guía**	ma-pa/**gee**-a
road sign	**las señales**	se-nya-les
road works	**los trabajos**	tra-ba-hos
rock	**la roca**	ro-ka
roll (to)	**rodar**	ro-dar
roof	**el tejado**	te-ha-do
room	**la habitación**	a-bee-ta-**thyon**
rope	**la soga/la cuerda**	so-ga/kwer-da
rotten	**podrido**	po-dree-do
rough *sea*	**revuelto**	re-bwel-to
rough *surface*	**áspero**	**as**-pair-o
round	**redondo**	re-don-do
rowing boat	**la barca/el bote de remos**	bar-ka/bo-te de re-mos
rubber	**la goma**	go-ma
rubbish	**la basura**	ba-soo-ra

ruin	la ruina	roo-ee-na
rule (to)	gobernar	go-bair-nar
run (to)	correr	kor-rair

S

sad	triste	trees-te
saddle	el sillín	see-llyeen
safe	seguro	se-goo-ro
sail	la vela	be-la
sailing boat	el barco de vela	bar-ko de be-la
sailor	el marinero	ma-ree-nair-o
sale *clearance*	las rebajas	re-ba-has
(for) sale	se vende	se ben-de
salesman	el vendedor	ben-de-dor
saleswoman	la vendedora	ben-de-do-ra
salt water	el agua salada *f*	a-gwa sa-la-da
same	mismo	mees-mo
sand	la arena	a-re-na
sandals	las sandalias	san-da-lyas
sanitary towels	las compresas (higiénicas)	kom-pre-sas (ee-hee-e-nee-kas)
satisfactory	aceptable	a-thep-ta-ble
saucer	el platito	pla-tee-to

save (to)	**salvar**	sal-bar
save (to) *money*	**ahorrar**	a-or-rar
say (to)	**decir**	de-theer
scald (to)	**quemarse**	ke-mar-se
scarf	**la bufanda**	boo-fan-da
scenery	**la vista/el paisaje**	bees-ta/pa-ee-sa-he
scent	**el perfume**	pair-foo-me
school	**la escuela/el colegio**	es-kwe-la/ko-le-hee-o
scissors	**las tijeras**	tee-hair-as
Scotland	**Escocia** *f*	es-ko-thya
Scottish	**escocés**	es-ko-**thes**
scratch (to)	**arañar**	a-ran-yar
screw	**el tornillo**	tor-nee-llyo
screwdriver	**el destornillador**	des-tor-nee-llya-dor
sculpture	**la escultura**	es-kool-too-ra
sea	**el mar**	mar
seasick	**mareado**	ma-re-a-do
season	**la temporada/la estación**	tem-po-ra-da/es-ta-**thyon**
seat	**el asiento**	a-see-en-to
seat belt	**el cinturón de seguridad**	theen-too-**ron** de se-goo-ree-dad
second	**segundo**	se-goon-do
second hand	**de segunda mano**	de se-goon-da ma-no

see (to)	**ver**	bair
seem (to)	**parecer**	pa-re-thair
self-catering hostel	**alojamiento con (derecho a) cocina**	a-lo-ha-mee-en-to kon (de-re-cho a) ko-thee-na
self-contained	**alojamiento con baño y cocina independiente**	a-lo-ha-mee-en-to kon ba-nyo ee ko-thee-na een-de-pen-dee-en-te
sell (to)	**vender**	ben-dair
send (to)	**enviar**	en-bee-ar
separate	**separado**	se-pa-ra-do
serious	**serio**	sair-ee-o
serve (to)	**servir**	sair-beer
service	**el servicio**	sair-bee-thyo
service *Catholic*	**la misa**	mee-sa
service *Protestant*	**el servicio**	sair-bee-thyo
several	**varios**	ba-ryos
sew (to)	**coser**	ko-sair
shade *colour*	**el matiz/el tono**	ma-teeth/to-no
shade *sun*	**la sombra**	som-bra
shallow	**poco profundo**	po-ko pro-foon-do
shampoo	**el champú**	cham-**poo**
shape	**la forma**	for-ma
share (to)	**repartir**	re-par-teer
sharp	**afilado/agudo**	a-fee-la-do/a-goo-do

shave (to)	**afeitar**	a-fay-tar
shaving brush	**la brocha de afeitar**	bro-cha de a-fay-tar
shaving cream	**la crema de afeitar**	kre-ma de a-fay-tar
she	**ella**	e-llya
sheet	**la sábana**	sa-ba-na
shelf	**el estante**	es-tan-te
shell	**la concha**	kon-cha
shine (to)	**brillar**	bree-llyar
shingle *beach*	**la playa de guijarros**	pla-ya de gee-har-ros
ship	**el barco**	bar-ko
shipping line	**la compañía marítima**	kom-pa-**nyee**-a ma-**ree**-tee-ma
shirt	**la camisa**	ka-mee-sa
shock	**la impresión**	eem-pre-**syon**
shoe polish	**el betún**	be-**toon**
shoelaces	**los cordones de zapatos**	kor-do-nes de tha-pa-tos
shoes	**los zapatos**	tha-pa-tos
shop	**la tienda**	tee-en-da
shopping centre	**el centro comercial**	then-tro ko-mair-thee-al
shore	**la orilla**	o-ree-llya
short	**corto**	kor-to
shorts	**los pantalones cortos**	pan-ta-lo-nes kor-tos
show	**el espectáculo**	es-pek-**ta**-koo-lo

show (to)	**mostrar/enseñar**	mos-trar/en-se-nyar
shower	**la ducha**	doo-cha
shut	**cerrado**	ther-ra-do
shut (to)	**cerrar**	ther-rar
sick	**enfermo**	en-fair-mo
side	**el lado**	la-do
sights	**los lugares interesantes**	loo-gar-es een-tair-es-an-tes
sign	**el letrero**	le-trair-o
sign (to)	**firmar**	feer-mar
signature	**la firma**	feer-ma
silver	**la plata**	pla-ta
simple	**sencillo**	sen-thee-llyo
since	**desde**	des-de
sing (to)	**cantar**	kan-tar
single *marital status*	**soltero**	sol-te-ro
single *ticket*	**de ida**	de ee-da
single room	**la habitación individual**	a-bee-ta-**thyon** een-dee-bee-dwal
sister	**la hermana**	air-ma-na
sit/sit down (to)	**sentarse**	sen-tar-se
size	**el tamaño**	ta-ma-nyo
size *clothes*	**la talla**	ta-llya
skid (to)	**resbalar**	res-ba-lar

skirt	la falda	fal-da
sky	el cielo	thee-e-lo
sleep (to)	dormir	dor-meer
sleeping bag	el saco de dormir	sa-ko de dor-meer
sleeve	la manga	man-ga
slice/piece	la porción/el trozo	por-**thyon**/tro-tho
slip/slide	el resbalón	res-ba-**lon**
slippers	las zapatillas	tha-pa-tee-llyas
slow	lento	len-to
small	pequeño	pe-ke-nyo
smart	elegante	e-le-gan-te
smell	el olor	o-lor
smell (to)	oler	o-lair
smile (to)	sonreír	son-re-**eer**
smoke (to)	fumar	foo-mar
(no) smoking	prohíbido fumar	pro-ee-bee-do foo-mar
snack	el snack/el bocadillo	es-nak/bo-ka-dee-llyo
snorkel	el tubo de bucear	too-bo de boo-the-ar
snow	la nieve	nye-be
(it is) snowing	nieva	nye-ba
so	así	a-**see**
soap	el jabón	ha-**bon**
soap powder	el detergente	de-tair-hen-te

sober	**sobrio**	so-bryo
socket *elec.*	**el enchufe**	en-choo-fe
socks	**los calcetines**	kal-the-tee-nes
soft	**suave/blando**	swa-be/bland-o
sold	**vendido**	ben-dee-do
sold out	**todo vendido**	to-do ben-dee-do
sole *shoe*	**la suela**	swe-la
solid	**sólido**	so-lee-do
some	**algunos**	al-goo-nos
somebody	**alguien**	alg-yen
somehow	**de alguna manera**	de al-goo-na ma-nair-a
something	**algo**	al-go
sometimes	**algunas veces**	al-goo-nas be-thes
somewhere	**en algún sitio**	en al-**goon** see-tyo
son	**el hijo**	ee-ho
song	**la canción**	kan-**thyon**
soon	**pronto**	pron-to
sort	**el tipo**	tee-po
sound	**el sonido**	so-nee-do
sound and light show	**el espectáculo de luz y sonido**	es-pek-**ta**-koo-lo de looth ee so-nee-do
sour	**agrio**	ag-ryo
south	**el sur**	soor

souvenir	el recuerdo	re-kwer-do
space	el espacio	es-pa-thyo
Spain	España f	es-pan-ya
Spanish	español	es-pan-yol
spanner	la llave inglesa	llya-be een-gle-sa
spare	sobrante	so-bran-te
speak (to)	hablar	ab-lar
speciality	la especialidad	es-pe-thya-lee-dad
spectacles	las gafas/los lentes	ga-fas/len-tes
speed	la velocidad	be-lo-thee-dad
speed limit	el límite de velocidad	lee-mee-te de be-lo-thee-dad
spend (to)	gastar	gas-tar
spice	la especia	es-pe-thya
spoon	la cuchara	koo-cha-ra
sports	los deportes	de-por-tes
spot *stain*	la mancha	man-cha
spring	la primavera	pree-ma-bai-ra
spring water	el agua de manantial f	a-gwa de man-ant-yal
square	la plaza	pla-tha
square *adj.*	cuadrado	kwad-ra-do
stage	el escenario	es-then-ar-ryo

stain	**la mancha**	man-cha
stained	**manchado**	man-cha-do
stairs	**la escalera**	es-ka-lair-a
stamp	**el sello**	se-llyo
stand (to)	**estar de pie**	es-tar de pee-ay
star	**la estrella**	es-tre-llya
start (to)	**empezar**	em-pe-thar
station	**la estación**	es-ta-**thyon**
statue	**la estatua**	es-ta-twa
stay (to)	**quedarse**	ke-dar-se
steward/stewardess	**el/la auxiliar de vuelo**	aw-see-lyar de bwe-lo
stick	**el bastón**	bas-**ton**
stiff	**rígido**	**ree**-hee-do
still *not moving*	**quieto**	kee-e-to
still *time*	**todavía**	to-da-**bee**-a
sting	**el aguijón/la picadura**	ag-ee-**hon**/pee-ka-doo-ra
stolen	**robado**	ro-ba-do
stone	**la piedra**	pee-e-dra
stool	**el taburete**	ta-boo-re-te
stop (to)	**parar**	pa-rar
store	**la tienda**	tee-en-da
storm	**la tormenta**	tor-men-ta

stove	**la cocina/el hornillo**	ko-thee-na/or-nee-llyo
straight	**recto**	rek-to
straight on	**todo seguido**	to-do se-gee-do
strange	**extraño**	es-tran-yo
strap	**la correa**	kor-ray-a
stream	**el arroyo**	ar-roy-o
street	**la calle**	ka-llye
street map	**el callejero**	ka-llye-hair-o
stretch (to)	**estirar**	es-tee-rar
string	**la cuerda**	kwer-da
strong	**fuerte**	fwer-te
student	**el estudiante**	es-too-dyan-te
style	**el estilo**	es-tee-lo
subject	**el tema**	te-ma
suburb	**las afueras**	a-fwe-ras
subway	**el paso subterráneo (UK)/el metro (US)**	pa-so soob-tair-**ran**-yo/me-tro
such	**tal**	tal
suddenly	**de repente**	de re-pen-te
suede	**el ante**	an-te
suggestion	**la sugerencia**	soo-hair-en-thya
suit	**el traje (de chaqueta)**	tra-hay (de cha-ke-ta)
suitcase	**la maleta**	ma-le-ta

summer	el verano	bai-ra-no
sun	el sol	sol
sunbathe (to)	tomar el sol	to-mar el sol
sunburn	la quemadura de sol	ke-ma-doo-ra de sol
sunglasses	las gafas de sol	ga-fas de sol
sunhat	el sombrero para el sol	som-brair-o pa-ra el sol
sunshade	la sombrilla/ el parasol	som-bree-llya/pa-ra-sol
sun cream	la crema protectora/ para el sol	kre-ma pro-tek-to-ra/ pa-ra el sol
supermarket	el supermercado	soo-per-mair-ka-do
supper	la cena	the-na
supplementary charge	el suplemento	soo-ple-men-to
sure	seguro	se-goo-ro
surfboard	la tabla de surf	ta-bla de soorf
surgery	el ambulatorio	am-boo-la-to-ryo
surgery hours	las horas de consulta	o-ras de kon-sool-ta
surprise	la sorpresa	sor-pre-sa
surroundings	los alrededores	al-re-de-do-res
sweat	el sudor	soo-dor
sweater	el jersey	hair-say
sweet	dulce	dool-the
sweets	los caramelos	ka-ra-me-los

swell (to)	**hincharse**	een-char-se
swim (to)	**nadar**	na-dar
swimming pool	**la piscina**	pees-thee-na
swing	**el columpio**	kol-oom-pyo
switch *light*	**la llave de la luz/ el interruptor**	llya-be de la looth/een-ter-roop-tor
swollen	**hinchado**	een-cha-do
synagogue	**la sinagoga**	see-na-go-ga

T

table	**la mesa**	me-sa
tablecloth	**el mantel**	man-tel
tablet	**la pastilla/la píldora**	pas-tee-llya/**peel**-do-ra
tailor	**el sastre**	sas-tre
take (to)	**tomar**	to-mar
talk (to)	**hablar**	ab-lar
tall	**alto**	al-to
tampon	**el tampón**	tam-**pon**
tank *reservoir*	**el tanque**	tan-ke
tanned	**bronceado**	bron-thee-a-do
tap	**el grifo**	gree-fo
tapestry	**la tapicería**	ta-pee-thair-**ree**-a
taste	**el gusto**	goos-to

taste (to)	**probar**	pro-bar
tax	**el impuesto (de lujo)**	eem-pwes-to (de loo-ho)
taxi	**el taxi**	tak-see
taxi rank	**la parada de taxis**	pa-ra-da de tak-see
teach (to)	**enseñar**	en-sen-yar
tear	**la rasgadura/el roto**	ras-ga-doo-ra/ro-to
tear (to)	**rasgar/romper**	ras-gar/rom-pair
telephone	**el teléfono**	te-**le**-fo-no
telephone (to)	**llamar por teléfono**	llya-mar por te-**le**-fo-no
telephone call	**la llamada telefónica**	llya-ma-da te-le-**fo**-nee-ka
telephone directory	**la guía telefónica**	**gee**-a te-le-**fo**-nee-ka
telephone number	**el número de teléfono**	**noo**-mair-o de te-**le**-fo-no
telephone operator	**la telefonista**	te-le-fo-nees-ta
television	**la televisión**	te-le-bee-**syon**
tell (to)	**decir**	de-theer
temperature	**la temperatura**	tem-pair-a-too-ra
temporary	**provisional**	pro-bee-syon-al
tennis	**el tenis**	te-nees
tent	**la tienda (de campaña)**	tee-en-da (de kam-pa-nya)
tent peg	**la piqueta**	pee-kay-ta
tent pole	**el palo de la tienda**	pa-lo de la tee-en-da
terrace	**la terraza**	ter-ra-tha

text message	**el texto**	tes-to
than	**que**	kay
that	**ese**	e-se
theatre	**el teatro**	te-a-tro
their	**su**	soo
then	**entonces**	en-ton-thes
there	**allí**	a-**llyee**
there is/are	**hay**	eye
thermometer	**el termómetro**	tair-**mo**-me-tro
these	**estos**	es-tos
they	**ellos**	e-llyos
thick	**grueso**	grwe-so
thief	**el ladrón**	la-**dron**
thin	**fino**	fee-no
thing	**la cosa**	ko-sa
think (to)	**pensar**	pen-sar
thirsty (to be)	**tener sed**	te-nair sed
this	**este**	es-te
those	**aquellos**	a-ke-llyos
thread	**el hilo**	ee-lo
through	**por**	por
throw (to)	**tirar**	tee-rar
thunder(storm)	**la tormenta**	tor-men-ta

ticket *theatre*	la entrada	en-tra-da
ticket *train*	el billete	bee-llye-te
ticket office	la taquilla	ta-kee-llya
tide	la marea	ma-re-a
tie	la corbata	kor-ba-ta
tight	ajustado/apretado	a-hoos-ta-do/a-pre-ta-do
tights (woollen)	los leotardos	le-o-tar-dos
(a pair of) tights	un par de medias	oon par de me-dyas
time	el tiempo/la hora	tee-em-po/o-ra
timetable	el horario	o-ra-ryo
tin	la lata	la-ta
tin opener	el abrelatas	a-bre-la-tas
tip	la propina	pro-pee-na
tip (to)	dar propina	dar pro-pee-na
tired (to be)	estar cansado	es-tar kan-sa-do
tissues	los pañuelos de papel	pan-ywe-los de pa-pel
to	a	a
tobacco (brown/virginia)	el tabaco (negro/rubio)	ta-ba-ko (ne-gro/roo-byo)
today	hoy	oy
together	juntos	hoon-tos
toilet	los servicios	sair-bee-thyos
toilet paper	el papel higiénico	pa-pel ee-hee-e-nee-ko
toll	el peaje	pe-a-he

tomorrow	**mañana**	ma-nya-na
tonight	**esta noche**	es-ta no-che
too *also*	**también**	tam-**byen**
too much/too many	**demasiado**	de-ma-see-a-do
toothbrush	**el cepillo de dientes**	the-pee-llyo de dyen-tes
toothpaste	**la pasta de dientes**	pas-ta de dyen-tes
toothpick	**el palillo**	pal-ee-llyo
top	**la cima**	thee-ma
torch	**la linterna**	leen-tair-na
torn	**roto**	ro-to
touch (to)	**tocar**	to-kar
tough	**duro**	doo-ro
tour	**la excursión**	es-koor-**syon**
tourist	**el turista**	too-rees-ta
tourist office	**la oficina de turismo**	o-fee-thee-na de too-rees-mo
towards	**hacia**	a-thya
towel	**la toalla**	to-a-llya
tower	**la torre**	tor-re
town	**la ciudad**	thee-oo-dad
town hall	**el ayuntamiento**	a-yoon-ta-myen-to
toy	**el juguete**	hoo-ge-te
traffic	**el tráfico**	**tra**-fee-ko
traffic jam	**el atasco**	a-tas-ko

traffic lights	el semáforo	se-**ma**-fo-ro
trailer	el remolque	re-mol-ke
train	el tren	tren
trainers	las zapatillas de deporte	tha-pa-tee-llyas de de-por-tay
tram	el tranvía	tran-**bee**-a
transfer money (to)	hacer una transferencia	a-ther oo-na trans-fair-en-thya
transit	tránsito	**tran**-see-to
translate (to)	traducir	tra-doo-theer
travel (to)	viajar	bee-a-har
travel agent	la agencia de viajes	a-hen-thya de bee-a-hes
traveller	el viajero	bee-a-hair-o
travellers' cheque	el cheque de viaje	che-ke de bee-a-he
treat (to)	invitar	een-bee-tar
treatment	el tratamiento	tra-ta-myen-to
tree	el árbol	**ar**-bol
trip	el viaje	bee-a-he
trouble	la dificultad	dee-fee-kool-tad
trousers	los pantalones	pan-ta-lo-nes
true	verdadero	bair-da-der-o
trunk *luggage*	el baúl	ba-**ool**
trunks *bathing*	el bañador	ban-ya-dor

truth	**la verdad**	bair-dad
try (to)	**intentar**	een-ten-tar
try on (to)	**probarse**	pro-bar-se
tunnel	**el túnel**	**too**-nel
turn (to)	**dar la vuelta/volver**	dar la bwel-ta/bol-bair
turning	**la vuelta**	bwel-ta
tweezers	**las pinzas**	pin-thas
twin bedded room	**la habitación de dos camas**	a-bee-ta-**thyon** de dos ka-mas
twisted	**torcido**	tor-thee-do

U

ugly	**feo**	fe-o
UK	**Reino Unido** *m*	ray-ee-no oo-nee-doh
umbrella	**el paraguas**	pa-ra-gwas
(beach) umbrella	**la sombrilla**	som-bree-llya
uncle	**el tío**	**tee**-o
uncomfortable	**incómodo**	een-**ko**-mo-do
unconscious	**inconsciente/ desmayado**	een-kons-thee-en-te/ des-ma-ya-do
underground	**el metro**	me-tro
under(neath)	**debajo (de)**	de-ba-ho
underpants	**los calzoncillos**	kal-thon-thee-llyos

understand	**entender**	en-ten-dair
underwater fishing	**la pesca submarina**	pes-ka soob-mar-ee-na
underwear	**la ropa interior**	ro-pa een-ter-yor
university	**la universidad**	oo-nee-bair-see-dad
unpack (to)	**deshacer las maletas**	des-a-thair las ma-le-tas
until	**hasta**	as-ta
unusual	**raro**	ra-ro
up/upstairs	**arriba**	ar-ree-ba
urgent	**urgente**	oor-hen-te
us	**nos**	nos
USA	**Estados Unidos** (de América) *m*	es-ta-dos oo-nee-dos (de a-**me**-ree-ka)
use (to)	**usar**	oo-sar
useful	**útil**	**oo**-teel
useless	**inútil**	een-**oo**-teel
usual	**habitual**	a-bee-twal
usually	**normalmente**	nor-mal-men-te

V

vacancies	**hay habitaciones**	eye a-bee-ta-thyo-nes
vacant	**libre**	lee-bre
vacation	**las vacaciones**	ba-ka-thyo-nes
valid	**válido**	**ba**-lee-do

valley	**el valle**	ba-llye
valuable	**valioso**	bal-lee-o-so
value	**el valor**	ba-lor
vase	**el florero**	flo-rair-o
VAT	**IVA** *m*	ee-ba
vegetables	**las verduras**	bair-doo-ras
vegetarian	**vegetariano**	be-he-ta-rya-no
vein	**la vena**	be-na
ventilation	**la ventilación**	ben-tee-la-**thyon**
very	**muy**	mwee
very little	**muy poco**	mwee po-ko
very much	**mucho**	moo-cho
vest	**la camiseta**	ka-mee-se-ta
view	**la vista panorámica**	bees-ta pa-no-**ra**-mee-ka
villa	**el chalet**	cha-lay
village	**el pueblo**	pwe-blo
vineyard	**la viña**	bee-nya
violin	**el violín**	bee-o-**leen**
visa	**el visado**	bee-sa-do
visibility	**la visibilidad**	bee-see-bee-lee-dad
visit	**la visita**	bee-see-ta
visit (to)	**visitar**	bee-see-tar
voice	**la voz**	both

voltage	**el voltaje**	bol-ta-he
voucher	**el bono**	bo-no
voyage	**el viaje**	bee-a-he

W

wait (to)	**esperar**	es-pair-ar
waiter	**el camarero**	ka-ma-rair-o
waiting room	**la sala de espera**	sa-la de es-pair-a
waitress	**la camarera**	ka-ma-rair-a
wake (to)	**despertar**	des-pair-tar
Wales	**Gales** *m*	ga-les
walk	**el paseo**	pa-se-o
walk (to)	**ir a pie/caminar**	eer a pee-ay/ka-meen-ar
wall	**la pared**	pa-red
wallet	**el billetero**	bee-llye-tair-o
want (to)	**querer**	ke-rair
wardrobe	**el armario**	ar-ma-ryo
warm *food, drink*	**caliente**	kal-yen-te
warm *weather*	**cálido**	**ka**-lee-do
washbasin	**el lavabo**	la-ba-bo
waste	**el desperdicio**	des-pair-dee-thyo
waste (to)	**desperdiciar**	des-pair-dee-thyar
watch	**el reloj**	re-loh

water (fresh/salt)	**el agua** (dulce/salada) *f*	a-gwa (dool-the/sa-la-da)
waterfall	**la cascada**	kas-ka-da
waterproof	**impermeable**	eem-pair-me-ab-le
waterskiing	**el esquí acuático**	es-**kee** a-**kwa**-tee-ko
wave	**la ola**	o-la
way	**el camino**	ka-mee-no
we	**nosotros**	no-so-tros
wear (to)	**llevar**	llye-bar
weather	**el tiempo**	tee-em-po
weather forecast	**el parte meteorológico**	par-te me-tai-o-ro-**lo**-hee-ko
wedding ring	**la alianza**	a-lee-an-tha
website	**la página web**	**pa**-hee-na web
week	**la semana**	se-ma-na
weekend	**el fin de semana**	feen de se-ma-na
weigh (to)	**pesar**	pe-sar
weight	**el peso**	pe-so
welcome	**¡bienvenido!**	byen-be-nee-do
well	**bien**	byen
well *water*	**el pozo**	po-tho
Welsh	**galés**	ga-**les**
west	**el oeste**	o-es-te
wet	**húmedo**	**oo**-me-do

what?	¿qué?	kay
wheel	la rueda	rwe-da
wheelchair	la silla de ruedas	see-llya de rwe-das
when?	¿cuándo?	kwan-do
where?	¿dónde?	don-de
which?	¿cuál?	kwal
while	mientras	myen-tras
who?	¿quién?	kyen
whole	todo entero	toh-do en-tair-o
whose?	¿de quién?	de kee-en
why?	¿por qué?	por kay
wide	ancho	an-cho
widow	la viuda	bee-oo-da
widower	el viudo	bee-oo-do
wife	la esposa	es-po-sa
wild	salvaje	sal-ba-he
win (to)	ganar	ga-nar
wind	el viento	bee-en-to
window	la ventana	ben-ta-na
wine merchant	el almacén de vinos	al-ma-**then** de bee-nos
wing	la ala	a-la
winter	el invierno	een-bee-air-no
winter sports	los deportes de invierno	de-por-tes de een-bee-air-no

wire	**el alambre**	al-am-bre
wish (to)	**desear**	de-se-ar
with	**con**	kon
without	**sin**	seen
woman	**la mujer**	moo-hair
wonderful	**maravilloso**	ma-ra-bee-llyo-so
wood	**el bosque**	bos-ke
wool	**la lana**	la-na
word	**la palabra**	pa-la-bra
work	**el trabajo**	tra-ba-ho
work (to)	**trabajar**	tra-ba-har
worry (to)	**preocuparse**	pre-o-koo-par-se
worse	**peor**	pe-or
worth (to be)	**valer**	ba-lair
wrap	**envolver**	en-bol-bair
write (to)	**escribir**	es-kree-beer
writing paper	**el papel de escribir**	pa-pel de es-kree-beer
wrong	**equivocado**	e-kee-bo-ka-do

yacht	**el yate**	ya-te
year	**el año**	an-yo
yesterday	**ayer**	a-yair

yet	**todavía**	to-da-**bee**-a
you	**usted/tú**	oos-te/too
young	**joven**	ho-ben
your	**su**	soo
youth hostel	**el albergue juvenil**	al-bair-ge hoo-be-neel

Z

| zip | **la cremallera** | kre-ma-llye-ra |
| zoo | **el (parque) zoológico/el zoo** | par-ke tho-o-**lo**-hee-ko/ tho-o |

INDEX